Lord Berners

By the same author

LORD DUNSANY

THE LETTERS OF EVELYN WAUGH (ED.)

THE LETTERS OF ANN FLEMING (ED.)

MARK AMORY

LORD BERNERS
The Last Eccentric

Chatto & Windus

LONDON

Published by Chatto & Windus 1998

2 4 6 8 10 9 7 5 3 1

First published in Great Britain in 1998 by
Chatto & Windus
Random House, 20 Vauxhall Bridge Road,
London SW1V 2SA

Random House Australia (Pty) Limited
20 Alfred Street, Milsons Point, Sydney,
New South Wales 2061, Australia

Random House New Zealand Limited
18 Poland Road, Glenfield,
Auckland 10, New Zealand

Random House South Africa (Pty) Limited
Endulini, 5A Jubilee Road, Parktown 2193, South Africa

Random House UK Limited Reg. No. 954009

A CIP catalogue record for this book
is available from the British Library

ISBN 1 85619 234 2

Papers used by Random House UK Limited are natural,
recyclable products made from wood grown in sustainable forests.
The manufacturing processes conform to the environmental
regulations of the country of origin.

Typeset by Deltatype Ltd, Birkenhead, Merseyside
Printed and bound in Great Britain by
Mackays of Chatham plc

For Charlotte

Contents

List of Illustrations

All pictures are by courtesy of The Berners Trust unless otherwise stated.

Section 2

Berners, Lee Miller and Gertrude Stein
Berners and *A Wedding Bouquet*
Berners, Frederick Ashton and Constant Lambert
Cecil Beaton
Margot Fonteyn
Elsa Schiaparelli, Berners, Moura Budberg, H. G. Wells, Robert Heber
    Percy and Tom Driberg
Berners, David and Rachel Cecil, and Frederick Ashton
Francis Rose
the frontispiece for *Count Omega*
the cover of *Red Roses and Red Noses*
scenery painted by Berners for *A Wedding Bouquet*
the cover of *Poisson d'Or*
the original score of *Poisson d'Or*
Temptation in the Wilderness by Briton Riviere
Nancy Mitford *(The Duchess of Devonshire)*
Princesse de Polignac, 1936 *(Mrs James Lees-Milne)*
Clarissa Churchill with Berners
Berners, Jennifer Heber Percy, unknown
Berners in 1943
Berners by Gregory Pieto
'Lord Berners uses Bromo lavatory paper'

Preface

Lord Berners died in 1950 and this book should have appeared long ago. In 1985 I stayed at Faringdon with Robert Heber Percy and was intrigued and charmed by stories about Berners, of whom I then knew nothing. With no idea that Heber Percy had lived with Berners for over fifteen years and inherited all the papers and copyrights, I suggested that he really should write about him. There seemed to be a hint of weariness as he shook his head and explained that he was not a writer, indeed that he had a lot of trouble getting over the page with a thank-you letter. The weariness was confirmed when I wrote asking whether, in that case, I could make an attempt and he replied, 'I am fed to the teeth with the idea of getting someone to write about Gerald, so unless you've got nothing better to do, I wouldn't try.'

Since then I have discovered the somewhat complicated history of that weariness. Immediately after Berners' death Heber Percy did not want a book of any sort. There was a moment when John Betjeman was going to try a memoir, but the moment passed. (He did write the entry in the *Dictionary of National Biography*.) After some years, Raymond Mortimer persuaded Heber Percy that something should be done, and when Philip Lane asked for access to papers for a university thesis he was encouraged. Lane completed what is in effect a brief life with, naturally, a heavy emphasis on the music. He has maintained his interest in Berners and supervised the recording of all Berners' works.

More years passed and Gavin Bryars made an approach. He was particularly interested in composers who also painted and published an article in which Berners was one example. As a result, Heber Percy asked him to write a full-scale biography and indeed he had such a contract with Oxford University Press in 1977. Although he did an impressive amount of research and came to know more about Berners than anyone else, his own career as a composer took off to such an extent that it became clear that he was never going to have time to write anything down. The idea of a partnership foundered. Many others, some distinguished, asked about the situation but, like me, they were discouraged.

Heber Percy died in 1987 and left the papers and copyrights to his widow, Lady Dorothy. She set up the Berners Trust and asked me to write the biography. With extraordinary generosity – and things are so lightly said that I must emphasise that their generosity really was extraordinary – Lane and Bryars gave me their work, as did Peter Dickinson, who had recorded several interviews and done some research when he was preparing the BBC programme which celebrated Berners' centenary. This book could scarcely exist without them – too many friends had died and other sources proved disappointing. There are some letters to Berners, but I have not traced many written by him, though fortunately (and curiously?) he made drafts, many of which have survived. There is an engagement book, but no diary. He appears in other people's books often, but briefly.

I confessed my total ignorance of music to Lady Dorothy, and her acceptance of this marked a shift in approach; my attempt was to be more about the man, less about the work. When musical comments are made the reader can be confident that they come from Lane, Bryars or Dickinson. But which? The scholarly has become tangled. I felt that I should do the research myself, and met those who were still alive. Bryars, Dickinson and I asked much the same questions and received much the same answers. I did not permit myself to read Lane until I had completed a draft, but then I found things I had missed and was allowed to incorporate them. It is fair to say, though, that Bryars' research has been the most extensive, underpins much of what I have written and seems to be faultless. Any mistakes are mine.

I had hoped to produce something in two or three years, but a job and a family stretched that to ten. All the papers have been shifted once and then split between town and country. That is the reason, though it does not rate as an excuse, for any omissions among those that helped me. I apologise to them. Also, I must insist, as I have elsewhere, how unfair such a list appears. One person might happen to remember a useful name, another search through papers, submit to repeated interrogation, save me from embarrassing error. Richard Brain has done all of these things and read the manuscript, as has Alan Bell. Eugenie Boyd has remained calm, friendly and efficient, not as easy as it sounds. Jonathan Burnham was first an important source and then my publisher and proved exemplary in both roles. I was fortunate to have the index compiled by Douglas Matthews, the kindest as well as most able of indexers. Lady Dorothy Heber Percy has been generous, helpful and never betrayed an impatience she must have felt. Among informants Lady Mosley was pre-eminent, as she had more to remember than anyone else and remembered it accurately. But I am grateful to all the following for their memories and, in some cases, for permission to quote copyright material:

The late Sir Harold Acton, Patricia Allsop, the Countess of Avon, Audrey Beecham, Betty Bennett, the late Sir Isaiah Berlin, Sarah Bradford, John Byrne, Lady Charteris, George Clive, Emile Coia, Artemis Cooper, Andrew Crowden, Meredith Daneman, Lady Alexandra Dacre, Caroline Dakers, Michael De-la-Noy, the Duke and Duchess of Devonshire, Lady Margaret Douglas-Home, Nigel Duck, Maureen, Marchioness of Dufferin and Ava, Lady Mary Dunn, Leslie Edwards, David Ekserdjian, Patrick Leigh Fermor, Daphne Fielding, the late Dame Margot Fonteyn, Alastair Forbes, Christopher France, Didier Gerard, Victoria Glendinning, Miron Grindea, Lady Harrod, Cynthia Hart-Davis, Lady Selina Hastings, Christopher Hawtree, Derek Hill, Bevis Hillier, Alan Hollinghurst, Richard Ingleby, Gerard Irvine, Susannah Johnston, Caroline Joll, Evelyn Joll, Julie Kavanagh, James Knox, Sharon Kusunoki, Archivist of the Edward James Foundation, Gerald Leach, James Lees-Milne and the late Avilde Lees-Milne, the Countess of Longford, John Lowe, Candida Lycett Green, Gladys McKenna, Noel Malcolm, Bill Mason, James Michie, Caroline Moorehead, Charlotte Mosley, Nigel Nicolson, Thomas O'Gorman, Sofka Papadimitriou, Alan Heber Percy, Diana Heber Percy, Kelvin Pollock, Michael Popkin, Anthony Powell, Alan Ross, Jennifer Ross, the late Dr A. L. Rowse, Richard Shepherd, Sir Reresby Sitwell, Francis Sitwell, D. J. Taylor, Hugo Vickers, Elizabeth Wansbrough, Sir Fred Warner, George Watson, Martin Webb, the Duke of Wellington, the late Oscar Wood, and Victoria Zinovieff.

For permission to quote from other copyright material, I must thank:

Alan Brodie Representation Ltd, 211 Piccadilly, London, W1V 9LD for permission to quote from Noël Coward © The Estate of Noël Coward, and for permission to quote from Terence Rattigan © The Terence Rattigan Trust; Colin Smythe Ltd on behalf of the George

Moore Estate for permission to quote from a letter from George Moore to Lord Berners; David Higham Associates for permission to quote from the work of Denton Welch; Mr Frank Magro and David Higham Associates for permission to quote from *Laughter in the Next Room* by the late Sir Osbert Sitwell, © The Estate of Sir Oswald Sitwell; Manches & Co. on behalf of The Worshipful Company of Musicians and Ms Annie Lambert for permission to quote from the work of Constant Lambert; The Society of Authors, on behalf of the Bernard Shaw Estate for permission to quote from a letter from George Bernard Shaw to Lord Berners; the Estate of Gertrude Stein for permission to quote from letters from Stein to Berners; William Heinemann for permission to quote from *To Keep the Ball Rolling* by Anthony Powell; Adrian Wright for permission to quote from *Letters to Friends* by K. B. McFarlane.

The author and publishers have made every effort to trace holders of copyright. They much regret if any inadvertent omissions have been made, but these can be rectified in future editions.

Chapter 1

Forebears

The ancient title of Berners has been traced back to the kings of Norway, Sweden and Denmark. A French connection, on what an Englishman might consider the wrong side, gave the order for the Normans to fire their arrows upwards and was thus directly responsible for shooting King Harold in the eye. A travelling Berners brought back a monkey from his Crusades with Richard I; a cuckolded Berners had his castle burned down, as well as his wife removed by King John; a charming Berners was a favourite of Richard II, in spite (or perhaps because) of which he was executed, his wife dying of grief. All this is recorded by a descendant in *The Spirit of the Berners Past*, which turns out, most suitably, to be a spoof. Gerald, fourteenth Lord Berners, though he was to paint moustaches on his ancestral portraits in much the same spirit, was not that descendant.

What is more reliably recorded is that Sir John Bourchier, son of a French count and the daughter of an English duke, great-grandson of Edward III and member of Parliament 1455–72, took his wife's maiden name for his barony. His grandson, who succeeded in 1474, was the most distinguished of the line. He translated the chronicles of Jean Froissart, our main source of knowledge about the Hundred Years War. It is said to be one of the noblest monuments of English prose, a rival to Malory. He also translated Marcus Aurelius and Huon of Bordeaux, which introduced King Oberon to the English and was used by Shakespeare when writing *A Midsummer Night's Dream*. Primarily a man of action, John Berners was a soldier, a diplomat and Chancellor of the Exchequer under Henry VIII. His less remarkable successors were mostly soldiers, sometimes clergymen, or, in Gerald's words, 'country squires or businessmen with recreations of an almost exclusively sporting nature'. Osbert Sitwell, in a fictional portrait, wrote that 'ever since the dawn of English History the [Berners] family had carried on a ceaseless but victorious feud against stags, otters, hares, badgers, rabbits and any other bigger non-domestic animals of which they were able to get within reach.'

The historian A. L. Rowse, in pointing out that Gerald Berners was often but wrongly thought to have Jewish blood, repeats Gerald's suggestion of a gypsy strain, but that is the only hint of the exotic. The title is an old one, its bearers conventional, although its descent is a wild zigzag of distant cousins. It passes to and through women and lay dormant for almost 200 years before 1720. Like a faithful but energetic dog on a walk, it always reappears, even if in an unexpected place.

The only interesting account of his grandparents comes from Gerald himself. His autobiography, *First Childhood*, takes 235 pages to get him to the age of thirteen, so it has space enough to dwell on them. It is his best book and a persuasive one, but it was published when he was fifty-one, by which time his image of himself and those surrounding him had long set into an acceptable form.

Some distortions are so marked as to seem deliberate. Lady Berners, his grandmother, who inherited the title rather than marrying it, was the least appealing character and is presented, under the ineffective disguise of 'Lady Bourchier' (Gerald liked to leave clues), as an ogre, 'not unlike Holbein's picture of Bloody Mary with just a touch of Charley's Aunt . . . one of the most forbidding awe-inspiring women I have ever known'. Dressed in black silk, like the Queen, she was ferociously religious, and Gerald claimed that she described herself in *Who's Who* as 'distinctly low', without any risk of being misunderstood (in fact she put 'distinctly Protestant'). Secular pictures were turned to the wall on Sundays. The twenty-two servants all went to church and, as they seated themselves, their 'satins' made a sound that was still remembered seventy years later. Daily prayers, normal enough, seemed to have the purpose of emphasising 'her own intimacy with God at the expense of her audience'. The only subjects permitted in her presence were 'the less sensational items of general news and those preferably of a theological nature . . . Without saying a single word she managed to radiate disapproval . . . the air seemed to grow heavy with it and the most garrulous talker would wilt and fall silent.'

She had been born Emma Wilson, an only child in a family well established in Leicestershire, as well as in Norfolk. She married Sir Henry Tyrwhitt when she was seventeen and he was twenty-nine. Sir Henry was a pleasant, easy-going man with a mild liking for politics, 'in which, however, he was never permitted to indulge'. Gerald's father, Hugh, was the third son of this ill-matched couple.

Lady Berners spent a good deal of her time paying minatory visits to the sick and the poor. She would set out on these charitable raids in a small pony-chaise, which she used to drive herself, armed with soup and propaganda. The rest of the day she passed in meditation in her grim little study at Stanley Hall in Shropshire, overlooking the 'rather smelly' moat. She constantly gave out bibles, which were a problem to dispose of, as the appropriate name was meticulously written in the front of each. Gerald recalls tossing one into that overlooked water and being appalled to discover that, far from sinking, it bobbed buoyantly on the surface.

This is a vivid image, but in fact there never was a moat at Stanley Hall, though there are a series of fish ponds on the far side of the drive and at some distance from the house; perhaps the bible bobbed in one of them. There was, however, a moat at Ashwellthorpe Hall in Norfolk, another family home, where Lady Berners lived following the death of her husband in 1894, and Gerald has clearly borrowed it. Similarly with the picture he paints of an Elizabethan house, 'deformed by later additions' and shut in on all sides by tall fir trees, 'so that even under a blue sky and when the sun shone its brightest, Stackwell [as he calls the house] looked as grim as an ogre's castle'. Much had been added during the nineteenth century (now once more removed), but old photographs and drawings show only one Wellingtonia and a Scots fir within fifty yards of even the enlarged building. Gerald created the wicked fairy's dark abode out of any available material.

Lady Berners had nine sons and three daughters but retained formidable energy, as well as will. Gerald's view of her is the highly prejudiced one of a child. She moved to Ashwellthorpe when he was just eleven and, though she survived for another twenty-three years, he scarcely saw her. Villagers there remembered her as a generous, or at least conscientious, old lady, giving parties at Christmas at which all the guests received presents with their names painstakingly attached. Gerald's view, however, is supported by his father, who, when asked if she was a baroness in her own right, replied, 'Yes, and everything else in her own wrong.' There is a story that she lined up six of her children and dealt the one on the end such a blow that the whole row fell over. Nor did hardship bring them together. They were not a fond family, certainly in later years. All of them grew up to be worldly and irreligious, except one who became a vicar, but – possibly a more subtle revenge – extremely High Church.

Though the parents were rich, the children, apart from the eldest son, were not, because they were too many. Gerald's father, Hugh, went into the navy at thirteen and was reasonably successful. As a boy, however, he had been brought up with ideas above his income, so at twenty-six he conveniently married the daughter of an immensely rich neighbour.

William Foster, that neighbour, was an ironmaster and employed 5,000 people in south Staffordshire alone, becoming the Liberal member of Parliament there for eleven years. His fortune was based on the expansion of the railways. Much money went on building churches, vicarages and schools, but without denting the surface of his riches. In 1843 he married Isabelle Grazebrook, and Gerald was to remember this grandmother as having 'the air of an elderly Madonna, placid and matriarchal . . . she had never been known to utter an unkind word or a hasty judgement'. The only criticism Gerald would allow was 'limited'. William and Isabelle had six children, of which Julia was the third, and in 1867 moved to Apley Park in Shropshire, 'a huge neo-Gothic building of grey stone built towards the end of the eighteenth century. It was a little like Strawberry Hill in appearance and if not quite so airy and fantastic in its architecture, was quite as turreted and castellated'.

'Arley', as Gerald calls it, is enhanced by its castellation, where Stanley was deformed. It is said to overlook the river, which is in fact a mile or so away. The stone is indeed grey, which could be seen as depressing, but Gerald is painting a contrast; he remembers being happy here and the park, not entirely unlike the land just across the river, was 'an earthly paradise for children'. Gerald viewed his mother's family as conventional mid-Victorians, well behaved, devoid of any excess of imagination, perhaps of imagination at all, fond of each other, happy to hunt and shoot at Apley, less delighted to be transported to Belgrave Square in the summer. Once they went to Europe, a great adventure but not exactly enjoyable. Gerald thought that Julia had been romantic when young but, with 'a nice well-trimmed landscape-gardener's kind of romanticism', preferring Scott to Byron; although when she got married, she hurried off to buy *Don Juan*, which had previously been forbidden her.

Sir Henry Tyrwhitt's Stanley Hall was only three miles away from Apley Park, with a convenient bridge across the Severn, so Gerald's parents must have known each other when Julia was sixteen and Hugh was eleven. By 1882, Hugh Tyrwhitt had seen the world. He could be exceptionally charming when there was something in it for him, and his attentions must have seemed exciting to Julia, while her long acquaintance with him was reassuring. They married in 1882 when she was thirty-one and their only child, Gerald Hugh, was born thirteen months later, on 18 September 1883.

When he married, Lieutenant Tyrwhitt's allowance was just enough to pay for his cigars, but his wife's family was as rich as his own was grand. Gerald not only thought but put into print that his father had married for money: 'It is difficult to believe that he could ever have been seriously in love with my mother. But it is only fair to add that he does not seem to have been the kind of man who could ever have been seriously in love with anyone.' On her wedding, Julia received £30,000 – no more than her share, though the equivalent today of about £1¾ million. (Gerald describes this as being enough for his father to pay off his debts, after that, she had only a modest income.)

At much the same time Julia's father, who had had a stroke, went almost literally barking mad. Gerald remembered him sitting alone in a darkened room, groaning and cursing continually. 'He could be heard all over the house . . . I never saw him smile or take an interest in anything.' He came to meals and went to church, though on at least one occasion a string of expletives caused the service to be curtailed. Gerald was not frightened; on the contrary, he used to listen with interest and do imitations for his younger cousins, aware that this was a dreadful lapse of taste which would be severely punished if overheard. Foster did not die until 1899, when he was eighty-five and Gerald was fifteen. He left £2½ million, a gigantic fortune.

Gerald saw his father as 'worldly, cynical, intolerant of any kind of inferiority, reserved and self-possessed' and again 'curious, moody, rather brilliant'. He became a naval captain at forty-three, going on to command the *Renown* when it took the Prince of Wales to India in 1905. The son admired the father's elegance: 'He took a great deal of trouble about his clothes. He was a small well-built man. He wore a neat, pointed beard and he walked with an imposing swagger. He had that easy superiority of manner which enables people to command respectful attention whether on a battleship or in a restaurant. Anyone meeting him for the first time might have taken him for minor royalty.' Gerald also admired his wit. He recounts with admiration how a boring neighbour told his father that someone had kicked his wife, adding,

'And in public too! It's not cricket, is it?' '"No," said my father, stifling a yawn, "It sounds more like football."'

Gerald admitted that his father was strict and critical, but the most important thing about the way Gerald saw his father was that it was not often. This was not only because of Hugh's career, which he took seriously (two years after his wedding he was away for months, failing to relieve Gordon at Khartoum), but because he found that his wife bored and irritated him. Even when his father was present, Gerald sensed that he was not trying, that what was presented to the family was not nearly as impressive as what was presented to the world. His only child was of peripheral importance. When it was suggested that he should beat Gerald for some wickedness, Hugh said he could not be bothered. 'I suppose I ought to have been grateful but I remember being offended by his lack of interest.' Noting that a child's view of God may be based on that of his father, Gerald quotes himself as replying defiantly to a threat of divine vengeance made by a nanny, 'Nonsense. God doesn't care what we do.' Years later he still seemed to admire his father greatly, but still from a distance.

Although Gerald talks of visiting Apley, the family seems in fact to have lived there during his early years. That it was not gloomier depended on the kindly disposition of his maternal grandmother. Unmarried Uncle James and crippled Aunt Constance lived there too, and someone he calls Cousin Emily, 'a very disagreeable young woman . . . of small stature, lean and cross-eyed', used to come and stay for lengthy periods; but there were no other children. Younger cousins and neighbours are mentioned, but Gerald looked back on a little boy very much alone, not only in age but in character. However, nobody's portrait of his own childhood can be accepted as objective. Gerald's considered opinion was that he fought his way single-handed out of totally philistine surroundings in which there was no sympathy for his deepest feelings and that, though it was a bore to complain and he did not indulge in it, nobody knew the trouble he'd seen, nobody knew his struggle. The little evidence there is, however, suggests that, though broadly true, this is not the whole truth. The most complicated reactions, the heart of any contradictions, unsurprisingly concern his mother.

The blandest version, endorsed by many of his friends of later years, is that Gerald adored her, surprising though that might seem (Harold Nicolson thought that she had the face of Mr Gladstone and the brain of a peahen), and always behaved well towards her. Certainly he wrote many letters, gave her a house when he could, visited her frequently. There is no known instance of his speaking against her. His own version never contradicts this directly – he is too loyal – but it does undermine it. He begins with the assertion that 'Fox-hunting was the dominant interest in my mother's life, the one thing she was good at.' Even that has a sting, from someone who never cared for hunting; but no one who knew Julia could disagree. More or less deserted by an unloving husband, she turned not to her son but to her horses. He in turn devotes as many pages to the housekeeper as to his mother, drawing a purposeful distinction: the housekeeper (who does not sound particularly warm or lovable) taught Gerald to believe in fairies; his mother opposed all imagination.

His beliefs got him into trouble: bad Cousin Emily saw him in the mirror when he was trying to turn her into a toad; he attempted to cure his mad grandfather by placing a wreath of snowdrops ('self-righteous little flowers') on his head. Nevertheless to Gerald this lack of interest in fantasy or imagination was a crucial failing of his mother, representing a large part of what he had to overcome and a lifelong complaint. In notes jotted down only a few years before his death he recorded, 'Play I wrote at the age of seventeen – under the influence of Ibsen . . . my mother pronounced it morbid and said "Why couldn't I write a play like Charley's Aunt?"' Elsewhere he wrote that at eighteen he 'was determined to brave parental displeasure and devote my life to music', but then, honestly, changed it to the weaker 'almost made up my mind to . . .' Again: 'How many mothers, I wonder, out of maternal solicitude, have ruined the chances of their sons.' But at least the blighting mothers are allowed solicitude as a motive.

He recognised the closeness that the two of them shared when he was young, but it was not what he would have chosen: 'My discrimination was acute enough to let me realise that, of my two parents, [my father] was by far the more interesting. But association with and dependence on my mother led me to give her all my affection and to take her side rather than his.' So she does receive all his affection, but only because she is there and in power. With that power she tried to thwart Gerald's deepest wishes: 'The thought of any son of hers becoming a professional artist filled her with horror.' She had got him off to a crippling start because of her own taste, 'which with the cocksureness of her Victorian mentality she believed to be the last word in artistic refinement . . . for many years she continued to quote the opinions of her governesses on aesthetic matters'. This comment was written when he was middle-aged and Julia was dead, but the irritation lingered on.

Gerald's letters to his mother have survived, as few of his papers have, and would seem certain to throw light on his daily life, or at least to contain examples of his writing at its most relaxed and personal; these hopes are for the most part disappointed. It seems almost as if he was being dull to keep her at a distance, but his own explanation is slightly different:

> it was necessary to exercise the utmost caution to avoid telling her anything that she might seize upon as a motive for alarms and excursions. The slightest provocation would elicit expressions of maternal anxiety. 'I hope you are not getting into a foreign way of thinking.' 'I hope you are taking plenty of exercise and not sitting about all the time talking. Foreigners lead such unhealthy lives.' 'I hope you are not falling in love with the niece.'

Solicitude indeed. By this time, Gerald had gone abroad, while still in his teens, and parted from her with 'intense relief'.

One or two friends thought Gerald felt guilty about not seeing more of his mother when he was grown up, but that he could not bring himself to prolong visits because of the tedium, the undisguisable fact that they had nothing in common. He himself gracefully offers a milder version of the belief widespread among children that they are foundlings, that they must have sprung from something different from, and better than, their parents: 'I am unable to trace any single one of my distinctive traits to my grandparents and still less to my parents ... there were certain disadvantages to being a sport (in the biological sense) in an exclusively sporting environment.'

In the biological sense only. Inevitably his mother made it clear that to ride well was the main aim in life, and started Gerald riding as soon as he could walk; inevitably it was a disaster. He fell off, was laughed at and humiliated, accepted her view that he was uniquely inept. (In fact he became perfectly competent.) Shooting was no more successful:

> One day, after luncheon, I went for a walk with Albert [a neighbouring child] in the woods. He was carrying a gun. As we approached a clearing we saw a large rabbit sitting a few yards away. Albert handed me his gun. I took a shot at the rabbit and missed it, and I shall always remember the manner in which Albert took back the gun from me as one of the most

contemptuously eloquent pieces of mime I have ever experienced. I
know it depressed me for several days afterwards.

His interest in, even enthusiasm for, canoeing impressed nobody.

No sooner has a less amiable portrait of Mrs Tyrwhitt been
assembled from Gerald's later writings than it has to be modified again,
partly by other things he said, partly by her own diary, partly by
comments from others. The diary is extremely dull, but there are many
fond references and constant reports that Gerald is looking well. No one
remark is proof that she loved him, but the sum of them is: 'Drove to
the station to meet G. Train $1\frac{1}{2}$ hours late. Arrived looking very well
with six wax-bills and a tame mouse.' 'Meyrick and I worked nearly all
day decorating G.'s bicycle.' 'Gerald took Remove at Eton!!!' His own
earliest letters are full of humour and high spirits – 'I'm so frisky today I
am drawing you a picture . . . A wonderful new American drink called
ice-cream soda . . . it's rot that you can't come to the concert.'

Gerald admits that there were signs that Julia was rather proud of his
artistic side. She played the piano to him and allowed him to look at her
own efficient watercolours, took him to the National Gallery and the
Royal Academy, allowed him to read *Trilby* after a schoolmaster had
confiscated it. When, at the age of ten, he wrote a funeral dirge for her,
she was amused and used to ask him to play it at parties. So there must
have been parties, occasionally. Christabel Aberconway recorded a
much later scene:

> He was devoted to his old mother, but couldn't resist training his parrot
> to walk across the room in front of her chair with his bowler hat covering
> the parrot, with the brim almost sweeping the floor. Nevertheless this
> strange sight of a self-moving hat didn't seem to surprise Gerald's
> mother, which did surprise Gerald; perhaps Gerald wasn't aware how
> well, even in old age, Gerald's mother understood her son.

There are no fundamental contradictions in Gerald's feelings for his
mother. His image – of two great houses, run by his grandmothers (a
good fairy, and a bad fairy), in which men are of little consequence –
stands. His mother, unworldly but unchallenged, changeable but always
returning to convention, loved him when he was small, and worried
about his enthusiasm for the arts, which were outside her range, only
when it threatened his career or threatened to become his career. 'My
mother used to think literature and painting were less dangerous to me
than music', and she was right. Gerald recorded 'the lack of affection

that held between my two parents. I thought at first that it was the
normal relationship between husbands and wives.' This was the more
insidious legacy, though he does not himself connect it with the
emotional timidity that was to turn to a crippling shyness and spread
across his whole life.

Chapter II

First Childhood

When Gerald was six, his mother moved to Althrey, a small house near Wrexham in Clwyd, close to the border with Shropshire. He did not care for it, thinking two storeys too few, and longed for the spaciousness of Apley. He also came to think that times were changing for the worse. 'The nineties in a distant provincial neighbourhood such as ours were a tawdry and unprepossessing period, a certain solid grandeur had given way to gimcrack.' All around there was nothing but 'a welter of cane and bamboo furniture, draped easels, standard lamps with flounces, mirrors with roses . . .' Surprisingly he allows that his mother's jumble of the excellent and the trashy, Chippendale and Sheraton amid crude late-Victorian pieces, things bought or kept because she had become fond of them or liked the giver, combined to produce 'so delightful an atmosphere of peace and content that people would exclaim upon entering it for the first time "What a charming room"'. It was the formula he would himself follow years later at Faringdon, but with more striking effect. His mother's taste was less catholic, her mind less lively and her humour non-existent. Her room reflected 'an inner harmony of the soul'.

The position of the house was good. Meadows sloped down before it to the River Dee, 'a winding picturesque stream, not unlike the Severn which made an almost complete circle leaving in the same direction as that it entered, as though it had met with some geological opposition and was not going to insist'. If the river managed to be reminiscent of Apley, the woods surpassed it by containing a greater variety of birds. Gerald's enthusiasm for birds had already reached the point where he felt that he had been one in a previous incarnation and 'in my earliest childhood I used to like pretending to be a bird. In default of being able to fly I used to enjoy making nests for myself in a haybarn and I had a passion for ornithology.' He deprecates this interest – 'at an early age I became a bird bore' – but is not really apologetic.

In later years Gerald seemed uncertain whether he was happy or lonely, or both, at this time. 'I liked being in the country. I had a Wordsworthian enjoyment of nature, and in my childhood, when I could spend my time rambling in the woods, boating on the river or riding about the countryside without having to join in collective sport, I had been blissfully happy.' In this mood he remembers his resentment at being forced to spend time with boring neighbours. On other occasions, however, he remembers being dull by himself, but reconciles the two by claiming that it was the solitary routine of getting up, eating, resting and going to bed without friends that was lowering.

Sometimes he was too much for his mother. She had four dogs: a collie, a fox-terrier, a spaniel and a bloodhound. It was the spaniel that he threw out of a first-floor window. This was done in a spirit of scientific enquiry. He had heard it remarked that if you threw a dog into water it instinctively swam. Would it, if thrown into the air, instinctively fly? 'It was a fat dog and I had some difficulty in lifting it up onto the window-sill. After giving it an encouraging pat, I pushed it off. I watched the unfortunate animal gyrating in the air, its long ringletted ears and tail spread out by centrifugal force.' In retrospect, the face reminded him of George Eliot. The animal was unhurt; not so Gerald. His father refusing to beat him, his mother felt that she must do it herself. At the first blow with a bedroom slipper he became enraged, seized it and hit her about the bosom and face until she ran from the room. This was the most dramatic example of a formidable temper. As is natural, he remembered victories: how, when he was put out of a pony-cart and made to run along behind, his rage was so sustained that he had, eventually, to be allowed back in without repentance; how, after he had been shut in a dark cupboard, he locked all the lavatories and threw the keys in a pond – *and* there were visitors in the house. Yet, in later life, he was almost never known to get angry, rarely even to show irritation.

Gerald's lack of enthusiasm for his local contemporaries has already been mentioned. For one particular bossy girl it was something closer to hatred. His account of Nesta is mixed up with his failure to achieve Manliness, indeed his failure to discover exactly what Manliness was. She could ride and climb and told him that he should have been born a girl. She persuaded him to exchange a toy horse for a doll, to the mortification of his mother. 'Nesta of course was delighted – it was just the effect she had hoped to produce.' There was a violent suggestive climax to the feud. With two other boys, who rather liked Nesta, she and Gerald climbed a haystack. She taunted him, he pushed her off and she cut her leg on a cart below. 'She broke out into a torrent of abuse, at the same time pulling down her stocking to examine the wound. Then a very odd thing happened. For a moment the air seemed full of electricity. We were beset by the primaeval panic that brings about mass hysteria, pogroms or stampedes. I jumped down from the haystack, followed by the two boys. We all three fell upon Nesta simultaneously and, tearing away her clothes, each of us gave her a resounding smack on her bare bottom.' The outrage, the nearest that seven-year-olds could get to gang-rape, was over in a flash. Nesta ran sobbing to the house and was gone before they followed, never to return. The boys were sheepish. A little later, indoors, Gerald – who in his own eyes was entirely responsible – hating her now for making him behave like a cad, broke into shrill laughter, which could not be quieted, and finally turned to hysterical howling. Whatever his mother was told on her return, she was strangely complacent, commenting, 'Well, I hope it will be a lesson to her not to be so bumptious.' Again this is an aggression that Gerald would seem incapable of showing in later years.

Grown-up neighbours proved more attractive. A faintly ridiculous pair of women, who used to make trips to Europe, showed Gerald their sketches of Italy and Switzerland and kindled a burning desire for 'abroad'. Later, he was allowed to visit someone whom he had heard described as 'a woman of fashion', 'a beauty', 'very *fin de siècle*'. She had two daughters. He was entranced by their style, perhaps in a tiny way falling in love with the family. His mother was impressed too. When she explained a bruise on her neck and received the comment 'How disappointing, my dear, that it should only be a hunting accident, I had hoped you had a passionate lover,' Gerald thought her secretly pleased. This went against all Julia's firmest instincts, including her mistrust of cleverness. As her husband consistently bested her in rational argument, she had been forced to abandon it in favour of prejudice. When Gerald tried to speak in the manner of these sophisticates, his aphorisms were condemned, fairly but unkindly, as 'trying to be clever'. No one ever accused her of that fault.

Neighbours might offer glimpses of other worlds; they could not alter the reality of his. Gerald was found wanting in areas in which he had no wish to compete. Nor, as yet, did he have much idea of what he did want. Nature in general, and birds in particular, had turned out to be acceptable outlets for his enthusiasm and sensitivity. He tried watercolours, in the manner of Turner, and produced a sunset that outdid his hero's 'most lurid efforts in almost every respect'. His father commented that, although he was sure it was very nicely painted, he was not sufficiently fond of either poached eggs or tomato soup for the picture to have any very great appeal to him. 'This chilling appreciation rather put me off sunsets.' At Apley, Gerald had fastened on the house itself, and its furnishings. There had been a screen in the drawing-room covered with pictures cut from magazines. It glowed in his memory: 'A gigantic green and crimson parakeet appeared to have alighted on the spire of Cologne cathedral, whilst a company of mediaeval knights on richly caparisoned horses caracoled in front of the sphinx and the pyramids.' Later he found that though these things were indeed there, they formed but a small part of the whole, which comprised also political cartoons and sporting prints. He had selected what he was yearning for, the startling juxtapositions that fed his imagination, and had rejected what was never to appeal to him.

Music, which was to be his escape from his uncongenial surroundings, first appeared in his life visually. He had had no interest in it; indeed, as loathsome Cousin Emily sang, he was against it. Then, in the library at Apley, with its classical busts and leather armchairs, he came upon an ancient volume of 'Pieces for the Harp'. 'My imagination was strangely moved by the sight of these black waves of notes undulating across the page, and, having collected all the blank sheets of paper I could find, I set to work to cover them with imitation cadenzas.' He drew music he had never heard and could not read. 'After a while, helped no doubt by the romantic character of the titles, they came to suggest surging waves of melody and rhythm.'

When a visitor sat down to play the piano, Gerald was sent out, as it was assumed, reasonably enough, that he would be bored. Through the half-open door the little boy heard the Fantaisie Impromptu by Chopin. He stood entranced. Afterwards she played it for him over and over again, and other pieces too. She even taught him to play the first few bars. When this artistic missionary had departed, Gerald found that no one minded or indeed noticed if he played in the billiard-room – vast, gloomy and smelling of tobacco smoke, as billiard-rooms do. He says that his mother was a little ashamed but reassured by the family that music was harmless. An aunt gave him 'a thick volume bound in scarlet cloth', which contained a mazurka by Chopin. The piano tuner helped with lessons. Soon Gerald was asked to play in the drawing-room and delighted in doing so – usually the mazurka. He said that Cousin Emily also played the piece, did not care for a rival and had it banned. Even so, music had been successfully enlisted in the struggle of Little Gerald against the Philistines.

Gerald's formal education began without undue upset when he was seven. He walked a few hundred yards to a mild, bearded tutor who filled him with enthusiasm for Greek and Latin mythology. He could not, however, be persuaded to like arithmetic: 'When I read in one of my bird-books that crows experienced difficulty in counting up to more than six I sympathised with them heartily, and having previously rather disliked crows, I began to regard them with an almost sentimental interest.' After two years, a Swiss governess, Bertha Fasnacht, was thought desirable. This move was less successful; indeed, his volcanic temper not yet extinguished, Gerald soon reached open warfare, pointing to an atlas and crying derisively, 'Switzerland is only a third-rate country. It has no coastline', before tearing it to pieces. His ears were boxed. The end to which the governess came was elaborate. With the help of the gardener's boy, a water-closet in the shrubbery was booby-trapped so that it dealt a terrific blow to a descending bottom – more alarming than painful, Gerald claimed. In any case, it was enough.

   The way was now cleared for the far more formidable alternative of boarding school. Gerald allows that Cheam was perhaps a good school; 'certainly it was expensive'. His father and uncles had been there, and now it had about a hundred boys. Though he felt small and did not much care for his new bowler hat, he was not at first too apprehensive, even when the headmaster told his mother, 'We shall make a man of him.' The first advice he received was sound: do not under any circumstances let it be known what your sisters are called. Having none, Gerald was in no danger, but later turned this knowledge against an enemy who, from that moment on, could not so much as pick up a pen without cries of 'Writing to Tabitha and Jane?' He was not a completely defenceless innocent. Soon, however, he pictured himself as just as unhappy as most boys in such circumstances seem to have been (though his letters home remain jaunty). The food was foul, the beating and the bullying were savage, and the threat of them made him walk in constant fear; he was hopeless at games, at best bored, often humiliated. The list is a familiar one. Gerald's own account is so vividly written that it convinces, and clearly he thought then and always that his headmaster was quite exceptionally sadistic. He may have been right, but standards in these things are high.

One traditional figure, often the only benevolent one, is glimpsed but snatched away – the inspiring teacher. 'In his hands the *Iliad*, the *Odyssey*, the *Aeneid*, the odes of Horace became something more than mere exercises in syntax. Alas! I was only in his class for a single term and the enthusiasm he had succeeded in arousing for the Latin and Greek authors was speedily dispelled by his successor.' Other masters tended to seem dim or odd, or both. One very, very old one, always interested in agriculture, managed only with the greatest difficulty to mount the pulpit for his farewell address. 'My good cows,' he began and burst into tears. Gerald had one hero whom he calls Longworth and describes as a suitable figure for the role, Captain of the Second Eleven, a tall athletic youth with regular features and an engaging smile, but hopelessly out of reach. Gerald wrote to his mother to see if she could in some way engineer an introduction. In vain.

Holidays flew past, terms dragged. If Gerald's misery was conventional, it was misery nonetheless. His homesickness was so acute at one moment that matron gave him a dose of castor-oil. Then music came to the rescue. Sammy, the music master, was not talented. He referred to Bach, Beethoven and Mozart as 'those boring old boys' and insisted on mid-Victorian drawing-room pieces. At the end of the winter term there was a school concert. Gerald despised what he had been allotted, 'The Lover and the Bird', but its riot of trills and arpeggios sounded difficult, he played it with great dash and scored a considerable success. Both his parents were present and they were pleased. Gerald was delighted that others should see his father's elegance and his glamorous personality. More important than all this, Longworth Major said '"Well played", as if I had hit a boundary or scored a goal.'

Even more wonderful, the Easter term seemed to carry on as happily as the winter one had ended. Athletics were much more acceptable than team games, and briefer; the headmaster was mysteriously benign; and Longworth smiled and asked if Gerald had enjoyed the holidays. A friendship blossomed, turning to – for want of a better word – love. Gerald, denying all consciousness of sex, otherwise holds back nothing: 'His image haunted my waking thoughts and dreams. Anything in the least way related to him, however commonplace, however trivial, was imbued with an almost celestial radiance . . . but of what Longworth was really like I have no longer the vaguest idea. I imagine he must have been a very ordinary sort of boy.'

Summer came, and though Longworth tried to coach him, cricket remained a tedious business. Meetings were difficult, the tension perhaps slackened. Longworth used to go onto the roof at night to smoke. Gerald was greatly excited to have been entrusted with this dangerous secret; then one evening Longworth invited him to come too. Terrified, thrilled, Gerald could not refuse and crept up the ladder with fumbling hands under a full moon. He feared he might not be able to light a cigarette – he never had done – and indeed, several matches sputtered out before this was achieved. He puffed vigorously, happiness stole over him. Then it grew cold:

> My nightgown flapped in the wind and my teeth began to chatter . . . The light of the moon fell full on his [Longworth's] face and made it glow like alabaster against the shadowy background. Never before in my life had I seen such disturbing beauty in a human face. For a moment I forgot my acute discomfort and stared at him in wonder. He had perhaps some telepathic inkling of the wave of awe-struck admiration that swept over me, for he suddenly threw his arm round my neck and drew me closer to him. Then a dreadful thing occurred. Almost before I knew what was happening I was violently sick.

When he had recovered sufficiently to descend, they parted and Longworth 'gave me a look in which fury was mingled with contempt'.

That summer Gerald was not quite eleven and he spent three more years at Cheam, an undistinguished scholar, generally in the lower half of the form. He does not record those years, saying only that 'the Longworth episode and the change at Apley cast a benumbing spell on the closing years of my childhood' and that it was not until Eton that his adolescence began. He was not too numbed, though, to enjoy Stanley J. Weyman and H. Rider Haggard, and he had further successes in the school concert – 'I was encored, only I didn't play it again.' A composition of his was performed, and he wrote a bright, even cheeky limerick to his mother:

> There was a young lady called Julia
> Whose manners were very peculiar.
> She went in with a look
> That frightened the cook.
> That awful young lady called Julia.

The whole of *First Childhood* is written with a clarity and detail that persuade. The drama with Longworth adds an open emotional intensity that Gerald never attempts elsewhere. It is impossible now to discover any alternative account, corroborative or not.

Straight after the disaster with Longworth, Gerald records changes at Apley, entirely for the worse. There is a hymn of hate to the detestable Cousin Emily, who, at thirty, 'had developed into a prematurely aged wizened little creature. Her beady eyes had just a little more expression than those of a frog and slightly less than those of a parrot.' She gradually took control and 'her increasing domination was like some strange insidious mildew'. No one else noticed.

His account is overdone, almost hysterical, and unconvincing. The bad fairy has entered his childhood paradise in a new guise and ruined everything. Perhaps, as he grew up, Apley lost its magic and he needed, in retrospect, an explanation as to why he no longer fitted in, or felt at one with it. Emily may have been a nasty person, but she is loaded with all the particular faults that Gerald came to feel he had been at war with – lack of imagination, hatred of the new, conventional authority. He also gets in a muddle about his grandfathers' funerals, seeming to confuse one with another, although they were five years apart. Whatever the facts, the emotional bleakness of these years remained important to him.

Chapter III

Eton

In the spring of 1897 Gerald was thirteen and a half (not fourteen and a half, as he himself states) and, with his Eton entrance examinations upon him, he was given extra coaching. His tutor, whom he calls 'Mr Prout', was a dangerous radical who referred casually to 'the idle rich'. '"Oh, but Mr Prout," said Mrs Tyrwhitt, "all the rich people I know are very busy. They always have a lot to do." "I don't count hunting and shooting," said Mr Prout, "or going to parties." "Why not?" my mother asked,' and the subject was dropped.

Gerald objected not to his politics, not to being patted on the head and having his hair stroked suspiciously often, but to his smugness and flatulence. Nevertheless, he worked hard and took 'remove', the best place available to a boy not sitting for a scholarship. It seems odd, perhaps the result of a lack of parental confidence, to make him cram, only for him to sail through. (This was the last exam, Gerald later noted, he was ever to pass.) His favourite writers at this time were Dickens, Thackeray, Kipling, Rider Haggard, Anthony Hope and Marie Corelli; and painters: Raphael, Greuze, Turner and Lord Leighton – dated but creditable enough lists for a boy not yet at his public school (and, in the case of Turner, showing Gerald to be rather ahead of fashion).

Gerald was uncharacteristically confident when he first arrived at Eton. Friends had spoken well of it and he liked the look of the place: the river, the castle, the gay and friendly High Street, the neat eighteenth-century houses. No tourists (a contemporary saw just three in his years there) and very little traffic: just a few tradesmen's vans and four-wheeled cabs.

His house, called Coleridge House and now destroyed, was on the right of Keate's Lane as it heads away from the High Street towards open, if bleak, country. His mother saw his room as something into which she would be reluctant to place a pantry boy, but, thinking along the same lines, Gerald was pleasantly reminded of the servants' quarters at Apley and thought it 'a snug little den'. The light filtering through the leaves of a plane tree gave it the rustic air of a potting-shed.

This had been a good house but was sinking, and A. A. Somerville was not the man to buck a trend. As Sir Annesley, he became Conservative MP for Windsor in 1922 and he was not a brute, indeed he was popular, but totally ineffectual. Gerald was rather relieved to find standards less than demanding; he would not have found a group bound together by the pursuit of success at games naturally congenial. A Scot and an Irish boy asked him to have tea with them each day and he wrote home that he had already made two delightful friends.

He conscientiously learned all the things that new boys were supposed to do or, more often, not do – eat in the street, sit on a certain wall, furl one's umbrella. The work was boring and remained so. Classics dominated, and 'Homer became tedious, Horace commonplace and Greek tragedy a grammatical inferno.' The author A. C. Benson taught him and was an exception. Languages were skimpy but, surprisingly, there was occasional astronomy. Games were tedious – soccer existed, but rugger had failed and tennis had yet to appear – and Gerald was allowed to avoid them all. He was always to claim that Eton had not merely taught him nothing, but had set him back several years, by blunting a natural enthusiasm for learning. A few surviving reports seem to agree.

The word he used to sum up his life at Eton was 'leisurely'. 'I passed a good deal of my time sauntering in the streets or in the playing fields, bathing or going to the river, frequenting the sock [food] shops when I had money to spend. Later when I had acquired a little more self-confidence I used to go out sketching.' An artist in a sporting world, he was at best tolerated. Perhaps he was also hungry, as his five shillings a week pocket money (though worth over £15 today) was quickly gone and the food was neither good nor plentiful.

Nevertheless, tea was an event and you were likely to become friendly with those with whom you shared it; but not Gerald. His relationship with the Scot and the Irish boy turned to something approaching mutual loathing. Nor did he find anyone else that he liked more. Nor did anyone else like him. By the end of his second term there were, by his own account, very few boys who would speak to him at all. He sat silent throughout the conversations at meals and 'long hours of enforced solitude, spent in my room within earshot of the noisy companionship from which I was debarred, brought with them an intolerable sense of inferiority and loneliness.' He was acutely aware of being odd-looking; known as 'newt', he would sign letters with a drawing of one, mocking himself in order to pre-empt the mockery of others.

In an echo of the drama with Longworth, music brought him to the attention of an older boy and then left him worse off than before. Though he had promised his mother that he would not allow music to interfere with his studies, a piano in the dining-room proved too great a temptation. He crept down one evening with a volume of Chopin nocturnes – 'the mere touch of the keys after so long an abstinence was joy to me' – but soon he was interrupted. The older boy, whom he calls Ainslie, merely asked for some tunes from the musical of the moment, *The Geisha*. Gerald had seen it and obliged. Further performances were demanded and were a success; he even introduced a little Chopin without giving offence. But if there was a moment of hubris, nemesis was on its way. The senior boys acknowledged that their relationship with Gerald was slightly altered – that he was now an entertainer as well as a junior – by nodding to him or even smiling in public. Gerald's contemporaries, ignorant of the truth, assumed that the favour he had found was in some form sexual, and disapproved. The horrid Irishman would no longer have tea with him. Gerald, innocent in every sense, was baffled and eventually vindicated but, unfairly, he was not entirely forgiven.

Finally, his first great friend appears. He calls him 'Marston', an ugly, clever, impertinent contemporary with a long face and unruly hair. His father was rumoured to have been a grocer from Wolverhampton, but he admitted only that he was 'in the fortunate position of being an orphan'. For the first time Gerald's hero worship was intellectual. Marston recommended books, and Gerald began to spend happy hours in the school library. Marston was the centre of a group, 'a sort of schoolboy version of the Souls', which was exactly what Gerald needed: like-minds bolstering each other's confidence in elegance, wit and the arts, while the uncomprehending and potentially hostile philistines prowled around outside the magic circle.

After they had been friends for nearly a year, however, Gerald made a disastrous social blunder: he asked Marston to stay. This was not being bold or loyal or defiant, it was being naive. Things went wrong immediately. 'Marston appeared almost to glory in his ignorance of country pursuits and was unsympathetic about dogs and horses.' On Sunday he criticised the vicar. Soon he moved on to Queen Victoria, 'A tiresome old woman who had only acquired importance through having lived so long', and continued with his fear that the politicians might 'take it into their heads to try and achieve popularity by living a long time and resembling old ladies'. By instinct, presumably, rather than intent, the grocer's boy was attacking what Julia Tyrwhitt held most dear. Nor did she care for his style. As we know, she disliked all cleverness, and that of a schoolboy was cleverness at its most naked.

That night she came to Gerald's room. She launched her attack immediately and Gerald tried to defend Marston. Dirty? Well, weren't many of the saints dirty? But Marston was not a saint; not even, perhaps, quite a gentleman. Perhaps not, but he was a genius. Not the sort of genius of whom Mrs Tyrwhitt could approve, like Edison, Cecil Rhodes. Anyway, Gerald liked him. 'That, my dear, is just what I'm complaining about.'

Marston cut short his visit. Gerald felt badly about not having put up a better defence of his friend, but he also felt that Marston's personality, which among the books of the school library had seemed so brilliant, had produced in rural surroundings an effect that was a little meretricious. It had struck a jarring note, like one of the new-fangled motor-cars in a country lane. The friendship foundered. Another round had been won by his mother and all she stood for.

Gerald decided to reform, which turned out to mean taking rowing seriously. It was not a success, and soon a new hero arrived. Deniston, at sixteen, was a few months older and, if not exactly stupid, certainly not clever; but he was elegant and 'an object of a good deal of scandalous gossip'. Gerald, who would not have dared approach him, was simply picked up on the way out of chapel: 'Care for a walk?' The motive soon appeared. 'I hope you are going to be amusing,' Deniston said, 'I've heard that you are.' Reassuringly, he agreed that the boys in Somerville's were indeed a ghastly lot, except 'one fellow there I liked quite a lot. He was sacked.'

Gerald was in a fever of nervous excitement, but he must have been sufficiently amusing, for soon they did everything together, even went sketching, though Deniston did not actually attempt it himself: 'Why on earth should I? I'm good at cricket. I'm better looking and better dressed than most people, and that's quite enough, I should have thought.' Gerald secretly wondered if he did not agree.

Deniston's mother was a friend, even 'a friend', of the Prince of Wales, and Gerald later saw this new relationship as an example of his lifelong oscillation between the world of scholarship and the world of fashion. This is fair enough, if art is substituted for scholarship and it is allowed that fashion was represented in these early days by handsome youths; Gerald had in fact fallen for what sounds like the school tart. That certainly is how the puritanical boys of Somerville's house looked upon it. An anonymous letter in the hand of the Irish boy threatened that, if the two continued to meet, their housemaster would be told. A photograph of Deniston was taken from Gerald's mantelpiece, torn up and thrown into his grate. The elegant new hero was up to this, however. Deniston knocked off the Irish top-hat in the High Street, humiliating its owner before the world.

Simultaneously with fashion, music had reappeared. The junior Souls did not care for Wagner, but Deniston had a kind word for him and by coincidence Gerald came across a book called *A Synopsis of Wagner's Nibelungen Ring*. Without having heard a note of the music, he was enchanted in an entirely literary way by this new realm of gnomes and gods. Then he saw a vocal score of *Das Rheingold* in a shop window. He frightened the shopkeeper by the violence with which he burst in, but he was allowed to handle it, and his excitement and longing, recalled in *First Childhood*, were vivid:

> I turned the pages feverishly. There they were, the Rhinemaidens swimming about in semi-quavers, Alberich climbing up from the depths of the Rhine to the accompaniment of syncopated quavers and rising arpeggios, the theft of the gold followed by a scurry of descending scales out of which emerged the majestic strains of the Valhalla motif.

Alas, the score cost twelve shillings, beyond his means. There was a consolation, however, in the form of a libretto for only one shilling. The translation was hopeless, but Gerald soared past the style, read it again and again and 'accompanied it on the dining-room piano with an improvisation based on the memory of my brief glimpse of the score'. He thought of writing an opera himself but could not find a sufficiently inspiring subject. In a letter to his mother he does mention a musical play 'in more than one act', and this is probably *An Egyptian Princess*, which was found among his papers and deals with characters called Abanazar, Iris, Boubastes and Serapis. In its two short acts are thirteen numbers, seven solos, four choruses, a duet and a trio. There are interludes of dance. The obvious influence is not Wagner at all, but Gilbert and Sullivan ('A dear little maid am I,' sings Iris) and musical comedy, so this light work, impressive for a schoolboy with scarcely any training, probably dates from a little earlier. There are already anticipations of his musical sense of humour; for instance, in a chorus of owls that repeat 'Tyrwhitt, Tyrwhitt'.

Still he returned to gaze longingly into the shop window at *Rheingold*. This exciting impasse was broken by the appearance of his father, who, having nothing better to do in London, had popped down to see Gerald. Disloyalty to his mother was immediate. His father belonged to the world of fashion, as his mother did not. 'It was perhaps the first time in my life that I had seen my father away from home. Devoted as I was to my mother . . . it was far more exciting to be in his company than in hers.' As before, he wished to exhibit his father's social style and, with unprecedented social adroitness, when he saw Deniston, not yet a close friend, across School Yard, he managed to engineer a meeting. It was a brilliant success. His father was acquainted with the glamorous mother, and Gerald felt glory reflecting upon him from every side. To crown it all, his father asked if he wanted anything. A book, rather an expensive book? Yes, he could just about manage twelve shillings and he slipped Gerald two sovereigns. All was well, it was still there and his life was transformed: 'As I sat unspoken to at meals, my thoughts wandered happily in a maze of Wagnerian legend. My ears, deaf to the chatter of my neighbours, were charmed by Wagnerian harmony, Mr Somerville was dispossessed by Alberich and the clinking of the cutlery by the anvils of the Nibelungen.' At home he staged Wagner productions in a doll's house.

The above account is, as usual, Gerald's own and, as usual, the scant documentary evidence does not support the detail. His few surviving letters of the time to his mother are consistently cheerful, even high-spirited, and conventional, decorated with drawings and talking freely of the sketching of which she was supposed to disapprove. The tone is almost flippant, one beginning, 'Dearest Ma, I am so sorry for not 'avin' wrote before but – (excuse left out)'; another complains in turn, 'You're getting very casual in your letters.' There is no suggestion of unpopularity or of feuds with particular boys; indeed, 'can't I be photographed? . . . lots of chaps want my photograph', and when he is: 'I think they are very good and very flattering.' He thanks her for a chocolate cake, refers to a visit to meet his father and does have music lessons, as well as German, £3 10 shillings extra. Another letter includes:

I have got the Rheingold by Wagner. It is lovely. I should like to go to Beaurheit [*sic*] to see the Wagner festival. Is there a chance of us going to the Wagner festival next holidays? I am sketching a great deal . . . I am rowing in a race on Tuesday. It is very hot again today. Where is father now? Is he in London? He has never been down to Eton as he said he would.

If 'never' means what it says and not 'never again', then the whole scene of his father's almost magical appearance and promotion of Gerald's love of music and friendship with Deniston must be a wish-fulfilling conflation of the facts. He has his music; his father has not yet come. Possibly his father gave him the money in London; or perhaps it was indeed his mother who paid, despite Gerald adding in his own version, 'If it had been my mother I should have felt obliged to tell her it was a musical score, and it would probably have been denied to me.' She certainly bought him the score of *Die Walküre* later on.

In any case, just when everything was going better, Gerald was definitely and suddenly struck down by rheumatic fever – 'extraordinary pains in all my joints'. After more than a week, he was deemed well enough to move to Windsor. Julia Tyrwhitt came and stayed there for two weeks before taking him home.

The next term, probably the summer of 1899, Gerald tells us, Deniston and he are friends (the illness never mentioned). The boys in his house like him better as a recovering invalid and he is able to continue not being intimate with any of them, in the confident knowledge that this is now his choice. A new friend popped up with 'a small narrow face and a prominent beaklike nose that was surmounted by enormous goggles'. Certainly not fashionable, he turned out to be artistic – an expressionist dancer in need of an accompanist. Gerald was given by him such titles as 'The Soul of Man in Conflict with the Universe' and 'Ideal Beauty emerging from a Chrysalis of Materialism', and was told that Beethoven and Brahms would be suitable. Not sufficiently familiar with them, he instead composed something himself, and what might be seen as his first ballet score was a surprising success: 'He advanced to the centre of the room and began to revolve rapidly, launching out defiant gestures in every direction. After this had gone on for some time, he returned to his crouching position.' And so on.

When told to imagine the beaky nose and goggles as a beautiful woman, Gerald was surprised to find that he could: 'My sense of humour had been completely knocked out and I was able to disregard the absurdity of his physique and see only the beauty of the idea.' His friend grudgingly allowed that 'You seem to have a real talent for Pantomime music.' It was the collision of Gerald's two worlds that brought this partnership to an end. Deniston was allowed to watch, but he interrupted facetiously and commented afterwards, 'Your little friend is quite ridiculous.' Gerald replied with spirit that Deniston would never have thought so if he were better-looking. Nevertheless Gerald was shaken, recognising that what Deniston said was true, if not the whole truth. Again a friendship foundered under criticism, this time from Fashion rather than Convention.

Suddenly, when it all seemed most promising, and after only two-and-a-half years, Eton was over. Gerald was less than well once more, perhaps exaggerating his condition in his letters, and his mother, terrified by the illness of the summer, whisked him away, saying that it was an unhealthy spot. It was now December, and he was a little over sixteen. An appeal to his father did no good. Husband and wife were now far apart and growing still more distant. (Old William Foster, the mad grandfather, died that autumn. He had taken particular trouble to exclude Hugh Tyrwhitt from his will, though Julia received another £20,000.) Gerald expected at least a dramatic farewell from Deniston, but the sophisticate refused to oblige, leaving Gerald with the reflection that he had been the fonder of the two and that this had been the pattern of his life so far. Still, any such melancholy was blown away by the promise of the future – France. Abroad meant colour, romance, adventure and the unknown and he was to be there by himself. Already he felt 'an ecstasy of longing'.

Chapter IV

Europe

Few of Gerald's array of sixteen uncles and aunts seemed to him to do anything much in the way of work, and Gerald himself was rather put out when it was made clear to him that he was expected if not exactly to earn his living, then to find some occupation. In time, his mother would leave a solid sum, his father nothing at all. Otherwise he had an unmarried uncle of forty-five, Sir Raymond Tyrwhitt, from whom he might inherit the baronetcy, and who would himself inherit the Berners peerage from Gerald's grandmother and pass that on, too. There were houses and land that were entailed, but no compelling reason why money should accompany either title, which might not be his for forty or fifty years, always assuming in any case that Sir Raymond did not marry and have a child.

So there must be a career, but not many careers were deemed suitable. The idea of going to university, which might have transformed Gerald's life, does not seem to have occurred to anyone. Gerald himself thought of the Church for a moment – but only for a moment. Mrs Tyrwhitt was against the army and even more firmly against the navy, in which his father was still doing creditably.

It was Captain Tyrwhitt who pushed diplomacy as an acceptable last resort, when in fact it was ideal, though not in the sense that Gerald would ever be a successful ambassador or, indeed, achieve anything of note in this line. It was the immediate effect on his life that was so satisfactory – being wafted out of England in 1900 and away from his mother to learn the necessary languages. First, French: the widowed daughter of an impoverished aristocrat, who had a château in Normandy in which she received young Englishmen as paying guests for this very purpose, was recommended. A ready linguist, Gerald had scarcely added, while at Cheam and Eton, to the meagre foundation laid by the Swiss governess; indeed, he had forgotten what he once knew.

Away from her home and the hunting field, Julia Tyrwhitt became tentative and her lack of experience led to inefficiency. She looked at the map and chose the shortest rather than the most convenient route, via Newhaven and Caen. Almost fifty years later Gerald remembered his first visual impressions of a foreign land with astonishing clarity:

> on both sides of the canal there were long lines of poplars whose reflections on the surface of the water looked like sleepers on a liquid track . . . there was a frosty nip in the air and the scent of charcoal roasting coffee. Overhead the sky lightened to a pale transparent blue and the light mists that lay on the fields began to dissolve into a sort of golden glow.

His first French omelette and croissant 'with rich Normandy butter' delighted him just as much, though he had been brought up to conceal such delight. Where he had found, while sketching, that the English countryside had to be rearranged, France seemed to 'compose' itself naturally; the trees were more graceful, the buildings more harmonious. All this was observed by his mother with, he suspected, disapproval. 'The cows,' remarked her maid, 'do not seem as nice as those in England.' His rapture was genuine but also satisfyingly rebellious.

Mother and maid stayed only one night to deliver him and were seen off with intense relief. Gerald's past disappeared with them and he promptly fell in love with the present. His hostess should, in his opinion, have presided over some salon in Paris, not because she was in the least chic – on the contrary, she was rather scruffy – but because of her formidable personality, tempered by wit and charm. She had a daughter, Henriette. Soon 'her voice, her laughter, her movements, her changes of expression filled me with exquisite delight. I was thrilled anew each time she came into the room . . . However my love was innocent and chaste, unsullied by physical lust, rather a muffish affair in fact.' (His closest approach so far to lust with a woman had been his approach to 'a flamboyant-looking blonde lady' in Windsor. They had spoken of the weather – 'it was conversation that might have taken place on any rectory lawn' – and, though most exciting, that was as far as it had gone.)

As for the other inhabitants of the house at Résenlieu, outside Gacé, it has to be admitted that as Gerald's facility in French returned, so the glamorous mystery that he had discerned in one old woman came to reside entirely in her oriental jewellery, and the worldly son of the house turned out to be half-witted once you got beyond his sophisticated little beard. Still, he did have a married mistress, whom he insisted Gerald meet. She was a dumpy, respectable creature and Gerald was filled with depression and claustrophobia as he struggled to make conversation in her drawing-room, fiddling with a foul glass of grenadine. Three other schoolboys arrived after some weeks and they too were dreadful.

But nothing, in the end, could dent his happiness. Whether sketching 'with the most daring greens and yellows that I could find to do justice to the grass and foliage', bathing naked in the river, or in the library playing the piano, which was a little dilapidated but had a pleasant mellow tone, he was in a trance of delight. This almost, but not quite, rendered him impervious to criticism. A neighbour, generally accepted as a composer but one who conveniently believed that music was a private art that should not be shared, told Gerald that his technique at the piano was fundamentally wrong and that if he wanted to play seriously he would have to forget everything and begin again. Gerald does not dispute the verdict: 'As piano lessons had been denied me [what about his great success at the Cheam school concert and what then were those 'music' lessons at Eton?] I had been obliged to evolve a method of my own. My performance had more temperament than accuracy. However I had a good musical sense that enabled me to "get away with it" and impress people who didn't know much about music.' The mother and daughter were among those thus impressed and were gratifyingly annoyed to hear his talent being belittled.

Gerald appreciated that from the outside his routine might look dull:

Life at Résenlieu continued to flow on calmly and delightfully. Nothing very exciting ever happened but there was in the air a perpetual simmering of pleasant activity. The days that passed were like the pages of a diary of trivial events kept by someone with an intense joie de vivre.

It was during this halcyon period that I became aware of curious moods of exaltation that would sometimes come upon me, attacks of ecstasy almost orgiastic in their violence.

I can remember the first time this experience occurred. I was standing one night at my bedroom window looking out at the nocturnal landscape as I had often done before. All at once my tranquil enjoyment seemed to swell to a greater intenseness, my senses to be endowed with a magical receptive capacity. It was as if the scene before me, the silver radiance of the sky, the deep velvety shadows of the woods, the gleaming surface of the lake, were about to reveal some rapturous significance, some glorious reality hitherto concealed from my normal vision. If I had been religious

I should no doubt have believed it to be some form of divine revelation,
of which faith would have supplied the meaning. As it was, although it
passed away and seemed to leave everything as it had been before, there
remained a feeling of encouragement as if from a premonition of some
eternal and wonderful reality lying behind the appearance of things.

This was recorded very much later, when he was ill and indeed had not
long to live. Some of the concerns and reactions are more those of a
dying man, a lifelong atheist who did not wish to reconsider, than of an
adolescent who did not know what he thought; many people who had
glimpsed an 'eternal and wonderful reality behind the appearance of
things' would simply call it God, without needing a meaning supplied
by faith. There is also an uncharacteristic trace of self-consciousness and
a general feeling of artifice in the writing. Whether in 1900 he actually
felt everything he describes or whether time and the act of writing
worked on his memories, it is certain that he never wrote as vividly
when he was not emotionally involved.

Gerald said repeatedly throughout his grown-up years some version
of 'Decidedly I have no talent for religion. To be religious it is as
necessary to have talent as it is to be a musician, a painter or a writer. I
am fairly intelligent – but theology is as impossible to understand as
would be a treaty of counterpoint to an un-musical journalist.' Yet he
never ceased to pick away at this incomprehensible subject, rather than
dismissing it from his mind. Among his last notes is: 'Sometimes in
moments of joie de vivre, I like to think that there is somebody there
whom I can thank.'

One thing he learned immediately is how hard it is to share such
feelings. A similar feeling took hold of him in a quarry 'teeming with
animal life', but when he forced the sympathetic Henriette to come and
look at it, she was indignant: 'Well really,' she exclaimed, 'to drag me all
this way to look at this stone-pit', and indeed so it seemed to him by
then. It was over, and so were his eight months in France.

On his way back he spent a night in Paris with an ancient relation of
his hostess. The old woman surprised him after dinner by giving him a
latch-key and, he thought, a wink and telling him to go out and amuse
himself. He felt inadequate to the situation but obediently started on an
unplanned stroll. Soon:

my licentious imagination was roused to the highest pitch. Couples
sitting on the benches, solitary figures wandering in the semi-obscurity,
even groups of respectable bourgeois, discussing no doubt politics or

domestic affairs, were for me the most intriguing representations of evil. I longed for adventure. At the same time I knew that if anything of the kind had occurred I should have been terrified. My yearnings were frustrated by the sense of my own inexperience. I continued to walk on in a sense of almost feverish agitation until at last fatigue overcame and compelled me to return, unsatisfied and feeling a little foolish, to the Rue du Bac.

This is perhaps the typical experience of an English boy of his type alone in Paris when seventeen. What is not clear from his account, again written long afterwards and planned for publication (though not in fact published), is what form his licentious imaginings took. He had just left a house where he 'loved' a girl but with a love 'free of lust'. One of the boys at Résenlieu had had effeminate looks and an affected manner, referring for instance to his father as 'just a teeny bit vulgar'. The others put this down to his not having been at Eton or Harrow, but he shocked them when he casually revealed that his mother had met Oscar Wilde. Later, in 1905, when Gerald told his own mother that Strauss's *Salomé* was based on a play of Wilde's, she exclaimed, 'Oh, hush, dear'; it was not a name to be mentioned. He adds that, though he knew about homosexuality, 'for a long time I imagined that it was a form of vice that was confined to public schools and only very rarely practised by adults and then only by foreigners'. No longer at school, not a foreigner, almost an adult, Gerald was probably struggling to conform, to do whatever it was that others did, but in a peculiarly uninformed and unfocused way. A stifling blanket of silence had fallen over the topic, though it is unclear who might have enlightened him had this not been so.

The reader of his autobiography is given no hint that Gerald himself is to be exclusively homosexual. Indeed, in his account of meeting the dumpy mistress only months before, he writes, 'it had been a terrible experience and one that might well have had a serious effect on my sexual life'. The implication of 'might well' is that it did not, and so that he was in time to be attracted to women in the normal manner. All this suggests only that Gerald, who was to live openly with a man for almost twenty years, was capable of being mildly disingenuous to the end. The timid, ignorant boy in Paris remains a convincing picture.

After Christmas at home, he was off again (alone this time – it was the middle of the hunting season) to learn German in Dresden. Berlin was then thought to be old-fashioned and dull, Vienna glamorous but

wicked. Gerald knew only of the china, and expected Dresden to be a
city of ornate architecture and to contain people who, though somewhat
pastoral, possessed an airy eighteenth-century elegance. Again the detail
of his account is impressive. The bell at his *pension* in the Lindenau
Strasse sounded 'like an angry hornet' and when the door opened of its
own accord, a device new to him, 'I felt like a traveller in a fairy tale
about to be lured into the ogre's castle and for a moment I hesitated to
enter the dark inner court.' Some such forebodings were justified. He
did not like the place – he was in the modern quarter – his hosts, his
companions or his teacher. His considered summing up was that 'The
Saxons appeared to me to be an unattractive race, unprepossessing,
unfriendly, gross in appearance and manners ... The place was
pervaded by an atmosphere of heaviness, drabness, an absence of
vitality. Mr Perry's establishment accentuated the gloom.'

A fellow pupil, perhaps trying to alleviate this atmosphere, drew on
the blackboard a caricature of Perry: bald head, bushy moustache, large
beaky nose. Retribution was swift. The boys had gone to the theatre and
were amazed and rather impressed (how had he known they were
there?) to be confronted by an enraged Perry in the interval. It was
assumed that Gerald was the artist and he did not deny it. A letter
complaining that Gerald had been very rude was sent to Julia Tyrwhitt,
who came out and stayed for a month, surely longer than was necessary.
She seems to have enjoyed herself, though her diary records events, and
rarely reactions. Only when she sees a copy in needlework of Raphael's
Madonna does she allow herself a 'Wonderful', and soon she has
arranged to take needlework lessons. This time she seems to have been
effective, calming Perry, arranging riding lessons and a summer in the
country for Gerald. One opera was enough for her (*Nausikaa*): 'long
and boring', thought Gerald; 'lovely scenery, but did not care for the
music', his mother recorded. Betraying something of his loneliness
before her arrival, Gerald says that her visit was his happiest time in
Dresden.

Music at first failed him. There was a stuffy English circle with
which he became acquainted, and a musical circle that was just as bad,
and so even more disappointing:

All these ladies took music very seriously, as seriously as in England
people took sport. Unfortunately there was in most cases more
earnestness than talent ... I was dismayed by the drabness, the squalor
of the place [the music academy], the grubby unattractive appearance of

the music students, the peculiarly dreary sound of the instruments being practised . . .

If these externals were dismaying, surely *The Ring* itself would rekindle his enthusiasm. On the contrary, Gerald found what many others have complained of, and nothing more: the singers were too old, too fat and too ugly, the evening too long, the auditorium too hot, and it was hard not to fall asleep. He did not complete the cycle. At this vulnerable moment Wagner was by chance further attacked and ridiculed. Gerald came upon *Der Fall Wagner* by Nietzsche and revelled in it. 'What appealed to me most in the book was the treatment of certain absurdities of which I was already half aware', absurdities of plot and dialogue. He also acquired a leather-bound copy of Nietzsche's *Also Sprach Zarathustra*, of which he read all and understood some. Again, the idea that God was dead was familiar and welcome. He also remembered afterwards that he used to enjoy leaving the book on his table or looking at it in cafés so that people might think, 'What a very cultivated young Englishman'. As he had first been drawn to the appearance of music, so he enjoyed the cover of the book, 'the lettering and the quasi-Biblical lay-out'. He liked objects that stood for art.

Undaunted by Wagner, Gerald went to the opera every week for five shillings. *Fidelio* was Beethoven's one and only opera, he explained to his mother; *Carmen* was 'awfully exciting'. What bowled him over, however, was a concert that included Richard Strauss's *Till Eulenspiegel*, which had been written seven years before:

> These early musical experiences of mine were something akin to falling in love. When first Richard Strauss swam into my ken I could think of little else. The sight of a Richard Strauss score in a shop window was like meeting a beloved one at a street corner. Although I could hardly read an orchestral score I got hold of the score of 'Don Juan' and would pore over it in a state of wild excitement. The mere printed notes seemed to radiate a mystical rapture even greater than the actual sounds when I heard them in a concert hall.

Now he wanted to write a symphonic poem. So he must study orchestration. He tells his mother both that Miss Sproston, whom she knows and who had taken Gerald to the depressing music academy, approves and that a violinist, Hans Neumann (perhaps thrown in to impress her), is the go-between. He asks also if she will send the five shillings a week that lessons cost. He pleads that his teacher, Professor

Kretschmer, is a very distinguished composer and that his opera *Die Folkunger* is excellent, somehow conveying the strong impression that he had never heard of him the week before. Soon Gerald is in his presence:

> His longish gray hair was brushed back from his forehead and he had a drooping moustache. In the house he always wore a black velvet coat edged with braid. His study where I had my lessons was a most inspiring room with faded laurel wreaths tied up with scarlet ribands on the walls: there was a huge grand piano, a mask of Beethoven and book-cases filled with scores and books on music.

Edmund Kretschmer's laurels have all faded now. He is best remembered, if at all, for the opera *The Fair Melusine*. For Gerald, however, he was the real thing at last, his first close contact with a creator. His appearance, his surroundings deserved respectful, even reverent attention; but how long did this relationship last? Gerald says flatly that he had three lessons only, but that is nonsense unless he is embezzling; he asks for money – more than fifteen shillings – more than once, and acknowledges it. Equally hard to establish is the timing, as his letters are undated. Certainly he was seeing Kretschmer in December 1901.

Before that he had been whisked away for a drab summer with a drab family in the country. The wooded valley itself near Bad Harzburg, a little over fifty miles south-east of Hanover, was pretty enough, but the Mullers were not his sort. In a dreadful reminder of past humiliations he failed physically, first by missing a falcon (could this be a mistranslation? But Gerald knew about birds) with a gun and then, much worse, by driving into a ditch: 'the German horses didn't seem to respond to the reins in the same way that English horses did.' Happily, mad Uncle Peter put in an appearance, which livened things up. A vast bachelor of fifty, when he teased his hosts it was like 'the onslaught of a huge butterfly on a small cabbage'. They went for walks together, Uncle Peter mopping his great brow with a purple handkerchief and puffing a lot, while they discussed Nietzsche and Heine with enthusiasm. Gerald was relieved to hear that he could regard Nietzsche as a wit and poet and ignore the philosophy. Uncle Peter really was a bit mad. One morning he sat on the porch for an hour watching the rain and repeating:

Peter, Peter, Peterlein.
Peterlein, es regnet.

Nevertheless, after his departure it was Gerald who grew despondent:

> That I now entered a period of the blackest depression cannot wholly be
> attributed to the fact that I was left alone with the Mullers. My daily
> lessons continued at the same dead level of dreariness ... I was
> compelled to fall back on nature. I took my solitary walks in the woods
> where I had formerly been with Onkel Peter and I passed sadly by the
> now deserted inn. At night I looked out on the moonlit garden trying in
> vain to feel poetical in the manner of Heine. I became a prey to morbid
> introspection in which there revolved a pessimistic review of my
> character and panic about the examination which I was sure I should
> never succeed in passing.

He considered that he would never be 'a useful member of society' and
even went back to brooding on what the headmaster of his private
school had had to say about his lack of talent for games. This gloom:

> although it is often started by some adverse experience, some mental
> shock, persists when the original cause has disappeared. It is impossible
> to be convinced that one is being unreasonable. A sort of negative reason
> establishes itself and reigns supreme. Having suffered from long spells of
> accidie during my life I have found that the simplest and most effective
> cure for it is a complete change of scene.

Years later, Diana Mosley, trying to cheer Gerald up, pointed out that
the black mood must pass, for it always did. 'No, it doesn't,' he replied.
'My mother died in the middle of one.' His grandfather too had sighed
and groaned right up to his death.

Gerald made a conscious decision not to allow himself to become 'a
prey to morbid introspection'. He resolved to look to the sunlight, to
ignore the shadows and the depths. He stuck to this decision for almost
forty years and it moulded both his life and his art. While never quite
acknowledging that this might be a mistake, he was sometimes
muddled, sometimes defensive, about this approach. It was assailed, as
the twentieth century continued, at every level, in scholarly articles,
trashy films, artless conversation. It became a truth universally
acknowledged that difficulties repressed or avoided festered and grew
rank. Gerald was not a child of the twentieth century; he was born a
Victorian – but a late Victorian, one open to doubts.

When someone said that he had known from an early age that he was
to be a great man, Gerald replied that he had always determined,
'whatever size I might achieve', to be as happy as possible. The other
pooh-poohed happiness, suggesting that too much might hinder
greatness, and Gerald, after running through a few great men and
checking on how they scored (Goethe happy, Beethoven unhappy, etc.),
fell back on their having been happy when they were working: 'I don't
believe any work of art is achieved in sadness . . . you don't write a
tragedy any better for being tragic.' He does not discuss whether it
helps to have been tragic in the past. His own work deliberately avoids
profundity, steers towards jokes, liveliness, wishing to please, but in the
knowledge that those unexamined depths exist. Gerald might have said,
with Oscar Wilde, 'I shunned sorrow and suffering of every kind. I
hated both.'

Yet despite this deliberate attempt to polish the surface and live on it,
when Gerald read *The Science of Life* by H. G. Wells he unswervingly
placed himself as an introvert, seeing this as a fate he might struggle
against but could not alter: 'From a misguided sense of duty I have
sometimes endeavoured to cultivate a more extrovert point of view. But
this has never proved a success. Once an introvert always an introvert.'
Cyril Connolly's *The Unquiet Grave* filled him with 'the greatest
excitement and pleasure', but he writes as a fellow melancholic of an
opposite type:

> My temperament, my Weltanschauung, seems to be so different from
> yours that I find it in places a little difficult to understand. This is no
> doubt to your credit for I am essentially a lepidopterous character [he
> alters this to 'my character is essentially superficial, lepidopterous and
> polichinelle'] beneath an impassive exterior, lacking in profundity, my
> motto being 'Why worry?' which perhaps gives me what Rebecca West
> calls 'my inner strength' . . . Also I have always been favoured by fortune
> and circumstances and this has given me 'courage in another's troubles,
> kindness in my own' which one can do if one is in good health and has
> the means to erect a barrier between oneself and the follies and
> wickedness of humanity . . . Also the painstaking elimination of regret,
> remorse and the sense of guilt.

He was not in fact as selfish as he makes himself sound; indeed, with
friends he was exceptionally thoughtful and generous. Less so to the
great world, which he put down to shyness and a fear of being
meddlesome, which, between them, impeded 'my love for the human

race', as did an aesthetic distaste for 'the rather repulsive character and appearance of many of its members'.

So Gerald saw himself as permanently threatened by depression and doomed to be an introvert, though this was not to be encouraged. The best chance of happiness lay in work. One should attempt the almost impossible task of loving everybody, but it was very convenient to have the money and circumstances that allowed one to pick and choose.

Many of these reflections came much later, but Gerald was already erecting the defences he saw as essential. Of these German days, and even earlier, he was to write that he was never able to establish 'anything but rather a superficial relationship with my friends, even with Deniston whom I had so passionately adored', though he blames this on his having been an only child and thus 'forming at an early age the habit of solitude'. He adds, however, 'Being always a little doubtful about my character, I instinctively surrounded it with a protective barrier, again to prevent people prying into it too closely and discovering its deficiencies.' In certain contemporary novels he says that he read of 'young men who discuss in the most profound manner their souls, their religion and their plans for bettering the world'. He adds, with world-weary nonchalance, 'I was rather glad I did not know any such young men,' but it does not ring true. He had in fact tried to discuss such things and found that it was not easy for him and that he was not good at it; he had no talent for intimacy. More generally, Gerald was never to love Germany as he loved Italy and France. At the end of his stay he once again felt lonely and bewildered, but now also apprehensive of failure.

For the next seven years Gerald zig-zagged about Europe, rarely staying in the same place for more than three or four months. There is only one further, brief, piece of autobiographical writing. Mrs Tyrwhitt's diary gives a detailed and reliable account of his movements from Germany to France, occasionally to Italy, with constant returns to England. As a clue to what was going on in his mind, or how he was reacting, we have only the stream of letters to his mother, not the most revealing source for a reserved young man in his twenties who resents and guards against her interference. He is entirely dependent on her for money, though she does not seem to refuse his frequent requests. He suggests where he might go next and she acquiesces. Once he moves without consulting her, is ticked off and replies that prompt action was necessary (mosquitoes).

Frequently he stresses what excellent teachers he has found and how hard he is working, never less than six hours a day (though there is mention of the afternoon being too hot to concentrate) and he even resolves to increase his burden to ten. Languages dominate, but history, geography and arithmetic are studied too: 'The history paper is fearfully hard', but later, 'I seem to be getting better at history.' There is little mention of sketching, but Julia has already told him once to leave his equipment behind, and still fears cultural distractions, so it would be tactless to go on about it. When he is seized with enthusiasm for some cushions he has designed and wants her to execute – 'background of pale yellow silk or satin. Bird, white silk with dark gray outlines and no shading ... I've done another screen design which I enclose – you might call one night and the other morning' – he immediately adds, 'Don't write and say I am wasting my time drawing these things. They don't take a minute and I can't work the whole day long.' Skating is an acceptable recreation, though, and he is proud of his progress: 'I was getting quite respectable on skates and had just mastered the outside edge – one must have practice.'

No girl is ever mentioned. There is, however, a network of young Old Etonians leaping from admired tutor to recommended boarding-house, criss-crossing the continent, all preparing for the same Foreign Office examination. They are referred to only by surname, but identification is confident: 'Palairet' must be Charles Palairet, who, a year older than Gerald, became an attaché in 1905 and was ambassador to the Greek government in 1942. 'I am really getting frightfully depressed about my work,' Gerald wrote from Weimar, 'Palairet is much cleverer than I am, and I am slowly beginning to realise how very ignorant I am. I don't think I shall ever know anything about history and geography.' 'Kennard' is Coleridge Kennard, two years younger, safely in the Foreign Office by 1908, though out again by 1918. (His son has written, 'He courted my mother with such persistence and indiscretion that the Ambassador, whilst fully appreciating Sir Coleridge's elegant hand, concise reports and impeccable dress style, sent him packing ... beneath the foppish exterior an uncertain artistic temperament struggled, not always in vain. It flickered occasionally into a few slim and elegant volumes.') 'Robartes' is Gerald Agar-Robartes, who succeeded as Viscount Clifden in 1930.

These are the friends with whom Gerald lamented that he was incapable of being intimate, and only Robartes remained in his life even for a time. They were not quite from the world of art or the world of fashion, though they might have had a nodding acquaintance with either. He never made friends of his own age and had few friends at all. Robartes must have come closest. He was a connoisseur with a preference for the eighteenth century, though his own enormous house in Cornwall, Lanhydrock, was originally Jacobean. He and Gerald shared a house in London for some time. A little later, Henry Moore, who succeeded as Earl of Drogheda in 1908, saw most of Gerald, though he got off to a tepid start ('seems quite nice'). Moore passed top into the Foreign Office in 1907 and, perhaps the more remarkable feat, persuaded Gerald to have golf lessons and actually appear on a golf course. Gerald was not rebelling against his class, and never did.

A return to Résenlieu in 1902 was followed by a stint at Scoones's, the London tutors. Gerald lived in lodgings but naturally saw his mother often and she records hunting (several times), canoeing (once) and going to the theatre (*'The Water Babies*. Very stupid') with him. Next year he returned to Germany, to Weimar, not Dresden – a change greatly for the better. When he was lying ill in 1947:

> through the open window came the smell of the garden after rain. That peculiar delicious smell carried me back some forty years to Weimar, to one occasion when I was walking across some allotment gardens in the middle of that delightful, countrified, provincial town ... I was transported back quite naturally and in a flash to a time when I was a young man unsuspecting and incurious of the future.

There was a theatre in Weimar to which he went two or three times a week, delicious cakes and ice-cream, a good bookshop. Everything was saturated by the memory of Goethe, and Gerald found in Johann Eckermann's *Conversations with Goethe* a work of unconscious humour that he reread all his life. The acolyte humbly misunderstanding the master was just the sort of joke that he enjoyed, though he liked more knockabout jokes too. He and Palairet, for instance, would gum down one of the halma pieces so that, sooner or later, one of the maiden ladies in their *pension* would upset the whole board; or would play cards with the family photographs, the ugliest face winning the trick (and, most hilarious of all, were caught doing so, upon which Palairet resourcefully dropped them all on the floor).

The final fragment of autobiography tells also of his discovery of Ibsen. He went to an amateur production of *Ghosts* in a hall on the outskirts of the town and was bowled over. This drama of venereal disease had shaken London fifteen years before and one of the ladies at the *pension* said it gave her the collywobbles. Gerald perhaps surprisingly was as smitten as he would have been by a new composer. He read *Rosmersholm*, *Hedda Gabler*, *The Lady from the Sea* and *John Gabriel Borkman*, revelled in their profound Norwegian gloom and could talk of nothing else. He wrote a play himself about a married woman who falls in love with another man. Her husband goes mad, her lover leaves her. Palairet was 'very kind about it' but said that he thought some people were creative, others just receptive. (Though Palairet had specifically referred to himself, Gerald worried about being 'just receptive' for weeks.) He wrote another play about a married man who fell in love but, unfortunately, with a young lady who – for reasons left to the reader's imagination – was debarred from sexual intercourse. He showed it to his mother, who was not appreciative. This places her in the role he prefers – the philistine who cannot understand new art – but at least he could show her such a work and she read it.

His days in Weimar end with a lyrical account of Christmas. Snow fell, tinsel appeared. 'On Christmas day we all went to an afternoon service in the Stadt Kirche which filled me with Christmas emotion.' There was a marvellous tree and presents for all, arranged in a little bower of cotton-wool ornamented with silver stars, stucco angels and glittering glass balls. There was *gluhwein*, punch, they got a little drunk and they sang. 'That Christmas in Weimar was one of the passages of my youth that remained imprinted in glowing colours on my memory and often during the periods during which we were at war with Germany it used to come back to me, arousing most inappropriately a revival of affection and a feeling of nostalgic regret.' Gerald's sincerity is not in doubt, but his killjoy mother states in her diary, '21 December, 1903: G arrived at 9.30 very well but thin.' There is no getting round it. He either made Christmas in Weimar up, or remembered it incorrectly, or muddled separate events.

In 1904 Gerald went to Italy for the first time and sent back ecstatic letters. Lugano was the most beautiful place he had ever seen; Florence was enchanting, surrounded by olive trees that 'glittered in the sun in the most elegant way'; Sorrento inspired him to verse:

> I shall never forget when I went to
> The beautiful town of Sorrento.
> So prettily perched on a cliff
> And looks as if

> The tiniest whiff
> Of wind from the lea
> Would cause it to fall
> Hotel – guests and all
> Down into the azure sea.
> One may say that its principal charm
> Lies in its unique situation
> So sheltered and warm
> And so peaceful and calm
> And possessing no railway station.
> I have said rather more than I meant to
> Of the beautiful town of Sorrento.

It is only fair to mention that this is an unpolished draft and has the comment 'One could go on for hours like this' before the last couplet.

There was then a return to Weimar, a holiday with his mother in Norway, then he was moving back and forth between Hanover (pretty surroundings, hideous town) and Paris, with excursions to a quiet village named Pérusson near Tours. From Pérusson he claimed to have tricked his mother with references to the Church: 'No, I'm not thinking of becoming a Roman Catholic just at present. I put in those effusions about the RC religion on purpose and you rose beautifully.' He continued to tease on this subject: 'You will be glad to hear that I went to church this morning but derived no benefit from it whatever. I'm afraid I have no sympathy with a religion that is based on adultery.' In Paris he visited the Louvre every day and finally reckoned that he had seen it all. In general his spirits remained high.

If, in his letters, he does not emphasise sketching, how much more should he be wary of mentioning music. Yet he does not seem to be being cagey. From Dresden he had written, 'He [Kretschmer] likes my march very much and may have it performed in time', which is the first we hear of a composition actually achieved. Nothing more is said of that. He hired a piano to keep in his room in Weimar and began work on a symphonic poem inspired by Dante's *Inferno*, so boring in Italy a few months before, but 'beyond inventing an opening theme with which I was not particularly pleased I did not progress very far'.

An important part of his musical education was his attendance at performances and his buying of scores. He bought the work of many contemporaries and reports on what he has seen: *The Magic Flute* is 'like a pantomime', *Martha* is 'so quaint and early Victorian', Wagner is still out of favour, *Lohengrin* being 'boring in places', but Strauss

continues to elicit a stronger response: 'I have just bought *Salomé* by
Richard Strauss, his latest opera has just come out in Dresden where it
has enjoyed a triumph. It is perfectly hideous. I'm afraid Strauss is
really going mad. I have got some lovely things by Claude Debussy.'
Perhaps two months later:

> You will be astonished to hear that we went to Dresden the other day to
> hear *Salomé* by Richard Strauss. It was probably the only chance I would
> ever get of hearing it – and it was well worth waiting for. It is a
> wonderful opera, quite the most wonderful I have ever seen – a perfectly
> immense orchestra but not at all noisy. He gets the most marvellous
> effects and the orchestration surpasses any of his other works.

This is the reverse of his preference for 'the mere printed note that
seemed to radiate a mystical rapture even greater than the actual sounds
when I heard them in the concert hall'.

These years form the basis of his ease in Europe, but they produced
no success in either his official career or his real one. It seems that he
composed, but nothing survives; and, a terrible blow, he failed his
exams, not once but twice. In December 1905 he wrote to his mother
that he was not ready to take them again and, though he might scrape
through and was anxious to get them over with, 'it's not worth risking
another defeat'. He sounds distraught, but confident that he should pass
if he handles the timing correctly. However, on 4 June 1907 his mother
recorded, 'G failed history and terribly upset'. Harold Nicolson says,
'he was impeded by a strange nervous malady and failed to pass'.
Clearly Gerald was clever enough and had worked hard enough; later he
blamed Eton for having let him get away with bright remarks but never
teaching him to concentrate or construct a sentence. His confidence,
which had been growing, diminished once more. There is a fragment of
a letter from Germany that reads, 'At 6.30 Dr Martin comes to psycho-
analyse me', which may date from this time.

Another blow, though one that it is hard to measure, came with the
death of his father. Julia Tyrwhitt's laconic diary gives away nothing but
dates and places: in December 1906 Hugh Tyrwhitt had been suddenly
taken ill and had gone into a nursing-home. Almost a year later the
Tyrwhitts were together on a boat, the *Caledonia*, making its way to
Port Said, when he died suddenly and was buried at sea. Gerald and his
father had met often enough in recent years, but a single innocuous
letter to Gerald is all that survives of their relationship. Gerald brings

up his name without restraint in his letters home, sees him as a support, a potential helper, and says – as someone mentioning something ridiculous – that it was doubted whether a letter addressed to his mother would reach his father: 'they must think you are divorced'. When he hears that his father too is taking French lessons, Gerald looks forward to their chatting in that language. Nevertheless Hugh had withdrawn, faded to the edge of Gerald's life; possibly had a mistress. Whatever his exact status, there was unfinished business between them. Gerald felt a failure in his father's eyes; he had not yet redeemed himself, and now he never would.

Nor did his death end the worries of Gerald as a son. His mother wrote asking whether she ought to marry again within a year. (The almost interminable mourning of Queen Victoria had set high standards.) One of her letters began, 'Knowing, as you do, how much I disliked your father . . .' Gerald said that if her happiness lay that way, then she should do it, but that it was no good asking for his advice. He was, however, sure that one manoeuvre would be a mistake: 'I think the idea of posting letters to them [her family] the day before the wedding is not a good one: it savours too much of a practical joke.'

Presumably this was meant to avoid criticism, or even some attempt at interference, for almost the moment the year had elapsed, Julia Tyrwhitt married Colonel Ward Bennitt, 'a mature companion of her fox-hunting days'. Gerald never really got on with his step-father and nor did his chauffeur William Crack: 'He was a funny old chap. Never used to think we did enough work. That sort of thing.' But Julia was very happy with him and they died within weeks of each other twenty years later. Gerald visited them conscientiously when he was in England.

This was no more often now than it had been. Gerald had said before his exams that if he failed, he would join the Salvation Army or apply for the situation of private secretary to Miss Pankhurst. In the event he did neither, but battled on. In 1908 and 1909 he was in Vienna, learning how an embassy is run but also reading Edward Gibbon's *Decline and Fall* and watching Sarah Bernhardt. He also battled on with his music. In 1908 he took lessons from Mr Tovey of Englefield Green, later Sir Donald Tovey. Sometimes he stayed as late as eight o'clock, sometimes he stayed the night. Later it is quoted and requoted that he 'studied music in England with one of the more orthodox professors, as a result of which he entered the diplomatic service'. Clearly the suggestion of cause and effect is unfair to Tovey. Indeed, Gerald made a habit of studying with those who were academic, rather than creative at the highest level, such as Kretschmer and, later, Thomas Armstrong, the organist at Christ Church, Oxford. It was his official career, however, that took the next step forward when, in 1910, he finally achieved a post as honorary attaché to the embassy in Constantinople.

Chapter v

A Diplomat at Last

An honorary attaché was not an important person. There were then no clerical staff of any sort abroad and Gerald's duties consisted of typing, filing, deciphering and registering. For this he was not paid. The job was given to a suitable young man with some influence, and part of being suitable was having private means. If, however, he was a very small cog, it was in a very large machine. The British Empire was at the height of its prestige; the Ottoman Empire, to which he was posted, was, after five centuries, finally crumbling. The year before, the Young Turks had shown their strength in the army and the Sultan of Constantinople, acknowledged from India to central Russia, was not to remain in office for many weeks.

This historic moment, which he was so well placed to observe, did not take up much space in Gerald's letters to his mother, perhaps for fear of alarming her, perhaps for fear of boring her, most likely because he was not much interested in it himself. He wrote immediately and reassuringly of the comfortable, if slow, trip on the *Oriental Express*, of the snow and mud in the streets and of his instant purchase of galoshes. He admired the view across the Bosphorus in conventional terms but, on his first and almost last glance outside Europe, remained uninterested in foreign politics or local customs. His time was diverted by composing nonsense rhymes – some smutty, this one clean:

> A thing that Uncle George detests
> Is finding mouse shit in his vests
> But what he even more abhors
> Is seeing Auntie in her drawers.

He covered the embassy registers with facetious drawings. In a more ambitious version of the halma joke, Gerald attached the spectacles of a pompous senior member of Chancery with hidden threads to all the paraphernalia on his desk, so that when he snatched them up, as was his

habit, 'ink, blotter and paper cascaded to the floor'. Cultural events were
so rare that when an Oscar Wilde comedy was put on, merely its title –
Lady Windermere's Fly-Whisk – kept them happy.

To be fair, when the uprising occurred towards the end of April
1909, Gerald did write an account:

> It was all very exciting. We were awoken at five o'clock in the morning
> by a violent fusillade which continued till eleven o'clock. The invading
> army from Salonika had at last entered the capital and the mutinous
> troops in the Taxim barracks set up a valiant resistance. All the embassy
> collected on the roof in pyjamas and all kinds of queer costumes.

Gerald was the first Christian to enter the Old Seraglio of the now
dethroned sultan: 'It is a real Arabian Nights palace with tiled
courtyards, roof gardens, marble baths and fountains, dark murderous-
looking corridors with latticed windows, secret stairways and so forth.'
He also enjoyed an outing to Broussa, the old capital and port of Mount
Olympus, 'like a great forest garden, mulberry trees and pomegranate
trees and gigantic cypresses dotted with red-tiled wooden houses and
occasional mosques'.

In August his handwriting is shaky because he has just swum the
Hellespont; it took about an hour and the water was deliciously warm.
This self-proclaimed athletic failure also kept ponies on the far side of
the Bosphorus and rode among ancient ruins. For news from home he
depended largely on letters from his mother and the copies of the *Tatler*
that she sent. Others wrote, too; his relationship with Lady Berners had
improved but he notes with exasperation, 'Had a letter from Grandmother, commenting on the fearful catastrophes that were happening in
the various corners of the globe, she remarked that "it is a comfort to
think that the Lord reigneth over all". It is hard to see where the
comfort comes in. She should really give up writing like Voltaire.' Most
people would have been lonely, but Gerald did not mind his own
company. There was a shop in Constantinople where he could buy
musical scores. Later he was to describe his diplomatic years as the
happiest of his life and that included this quiet, distant beginning.

In the new year he asked for ten weeks' leave and seems to have got
rather more. In February 1910 he was back in the embassy in Vienna,
where he had been asked to help with the scenery and the music for
some tableaux vivants, and built a 'most enchanting fairy palace out of
cardboard with minarets and illuminated windows'. This detained him,

though he was eager to see Faringdon, the house his mother had taken near Oxford, with which she declared herself delighted. When he arrived in March, he too was 'pleased with the place'.

From Paris in May, on his way back to Constantinople, he is grateful for a pair of trousers ('I had another pair so I wasn't inconvenienced') and reassuring about the colonel's lapses of memory ('they happen to everybody'). On arrival he finds it surprisingly cold. There is an expedition to an island in the Sea of Marmora, where all the dogs that have been cleared off the streets by the new regime are being dumped: 'They look miserable and I suppose the poor things will die in time of that and madness.' Gerald despises the Turks and has no hope that things will improve. That his new servant is Greek means that he will be less honest but more intelligent. There is talk of war with Greece, which he frivolously favours, 'It would do them both good.'

Regardless of the extent to which they are justified, these are not the thoughts of someone who is deeply and enthusiastically involved with the country. Plans for dinner parties are 'rather amusing', and somewhat in Gerald's own later style: 'one for all the bores in the place, the second for all the people with red noses and the third for all the ladies who are going to have babies. I expect they may cause some indignation if any suspicion dawns on the guests.' The reality of the great formal dinners to mark the accession of George V at the end of August is less appealing. Gerald is, however, conventional, even stuffy, when his ambassador is criticised in the *Daily Mail*, 'I don't think people should be allowed to criticise government officials in that way.' Winston Churchill comes to stay and is rude to everyone; he too is admonished with a patronising, 'I fancy he can't help it.'

Gerald sounds in need of a new friend or a new posting; he received both. He notes without comment that Nicolson is coming out to work with him, but it was to be a great boon. Harold Nicolson, three years younger, had been at Balliol, had experienced similar European crammers and passed his examinations in 1909. 'Without being strictly handsome, he was cherubic and very lively', and he was engaged to Vita Sackville-West. He was also homosexual, but confident that he would grow out of it. What Gerald felt about sex remains unknown, but it is likely that he was less sure of himself and less active. They overlapped only for a few weeks, but Nicolson became one of his rare, close friends and came to Faringdon whenever they were both in England.

Meanwhile there was a ridiculous incident. Worldly Nicolson complained that there were no aesthetes in Constantinople, but then

found that Ronald Firbank, whom he had already met and not much
liked but who was most definitely an aesthete, was there on his way back
from Egypt. He arranged to take the shy novelist sailing on the
Bosphorus with a picnic. A note arrived from Firbank at the last
moment: 'Today is too wonderful. It is the most wonderful day that
ever happened; it would be too much for me: let us keep today as
something marvellous that did not occur.' Nicolson left his card with
'Silly ass' written on it and stormed off in a sulk. On his return he found
his room filled with madonna-lilies. He was unappeased.

Firbank too was to be, in his own manner, a friend, but not until after
the war and in Rome, to which Gerald was now sent. The move may
have been a calculation by his superiors that he would prove more
useful there, for he was appointed in September just before war between
Turkey and Italy was declared, though he did not arrive until
December. The declaration was particularly brusque. Italy issued an
ultimatum that the Turks should accept military occupation of their
territory in North Africa, an Italian gunboat arriving before it expired.
It was an unprovoked and cynical calculation to which the Turks were
not in a position to respond. British opinion was hostile and that
hostility was in turn resented by the Italians. War, even a small war that
the British were not actually fighting, meant work. British ships were
detained, naval law had to be looked up.
    So Gerald arrived at a busy time but this is not apparent in his letters
– only in their absence, if the silence of his early months is ascribed to
overwork (there is a note that he has rooms in the embassy, 'most
palatial apartments with walls hung in brocade and old Venetian
chairs'). He was attached to Chancery, where there were two secretaries
and another honorary attaché, and altogether they cost less than £500 a
year. It is more likely, however, that he was kept from his letters by
pleasant personal engagements. In a novel written years later he recalls
that:

> Rome in those days . . . was an easy place to live in. Social life had an
> agreeable amateurish quality and had not yet been hustled into English
> and American standards of efficiency. The entertainments were magnifi-
> cent and simple. There were moonlit nights and nightingales but no
> night-clubs and in many quarters the grandeurs and curiosities of Papal
> Rome continued to prevail.

His ambassador, Sir Rennell Rodd, allowed that 'social life was little affected by a war which was carefully localised and which exacted relatively few sacrifices'. Gerald, familiar with Italy but not with Roman society, was captivated. He was to love the city for the rest of his life.

By April 1912 he is lunching with the Borgheses in their exquisite villa by the sea, regretting that he is overdrawn – 'it is rather tiresome and it is the first time that it has happened to me' – and observing that 'the ordinary standard of morality does not appear to exist in Rome'. Sir Rennell, who had been in command since 1908, was possessed of many virtues, a dignified appearance, great politeness and experience, a remarkable grasp of languages; he translated the classics, painted in watercolour, and had written verse ('Hail, ancient people of the Northern Sea . . .').

Lady Rodd was rather different; she was plain-speaking, not to say bossy, and had earned the names of Lady Rude and Tiger Lil. Though not interested in her own appearance (her one hat was sent back to London every year to be retrimmed), she lived for Beauty. She painted, she thought about her garden. Gerald always maintained that the attachés held a competition to design the most hideous building with the greatest number of architectural oddities. Lady Rodd saw it, exclaimed, 'My dream house,' and built it on land given to her husband by a grateful Italian government. Gerald seems to have preferred her. The fourth of her five children, Peter, then eight, later married Nancy Mitford, and Gerald and she were to exchange stories about the family, Lady Rodd in particular.

The dream house was built at Posilipo, on the Bay of Naples, where Lord Rosebery had just given his villa to be used as a summer embassy. He had left it completely furnished, and there were ilex groves and orange orchards, bathing every day at twelve o'clock, then perhaps a cruise in the yacht and sketching from the deck, with the Rodds in the evening, in a little harbour off Pozzuoli, though 'somehow it is rather hard to leave the garden'. Gerald had found an entirely congenial niche; flurries of work are hard to imagine, and are certainly never mentioned, even as a nuisance. In the same novel Gerald writes, 'the days passed in a nirvana of delight and some of the happiest moments of my life were spent in lazy amphibian existence . . . The Bosphorus seemed very far away.' Sir Rennell conducted 'interminable negotiations . . . which were typical of the Turkish genius for protracting discussion and deferring an obviously inevitable settlement'; but Gerald's role in these discussions was not too demanding.

On his return to Rome, Gerald resumed his social life. He told his
mother of meeting George Eliot's husband: 'He is said to have
attempted suicide three times during the honeymoon. I expect she was a
trying woman to live with.' Johnny Cross, twenty years younger than
Eliot, did indeed go mad and threw himself into the Grand Canal
shortly after they were married in 1880.

Gerald already knew many Italians. He stayed with the Pansa family
and was to do so again the next Christmas. He also mentions that he
dined with the Marchesa Casati, makes no comment, yet must have
been bubbling with excitement. The marchioness was perhaps the
ultimate example of the high style of the fashionable world that had
always attracted Gerald, but was also for much of the time a recluse. A
self-created exotic, she had a dead-white face, eyes not only black
themselves but heavily accentuated by black make-up, and hair of vivid
orange. She was surrounded by animals: there were monkeys in her
drawing-room, snakes in her hall, a leopard on a lead, albino blackbirds
in the air. She had a tiger-skin hat and was accompanied by a half-naked
black servant.

Her parties were, of course, extraordinary. She used lighting in then
unknown ways so that, for instance, a huge alabaster vase filled with
roses glowed from within. The parties could also be dangerous: the
leopard ripped a few guests at one, and attendant Nubians barely
survived being dipped in gold paint. Her entire existence was devoted to
visual extravagance and effect, and she was in touch with the artistic
avant-garde. She spent several fortunes carelessly and ended up
penniless in London, where she showed uncomplaining courage; Gerald
never deserted her.

In the new year, Tiger Lil also decided to give a party. Her parties
too were famous and spectacular, but this one was to crown them all.
Then King George of Greece was assassinated and it had to be
postponed – but not cancelled. Then the Pope was ill, but preparations
went ahead. It was a fancy-dress ball, 'a pageant of the ages'. Would it
be undignified for the ambassador himself to dress up? No, it would
not, and he despised 'the diffident' who 'adjusted their scruples by
putting on dominoes'. He appeared as an Elizabethan ambassador in a
home-made copy of the white silk suit of Sir Walter Raleigh. The list of
illustrious names, often impersonating their own ancestors – Sforza,
d'Este, Sermoneta, Lichtenstein, Orsini – rolls on impressively. The
Marchesa Casati was a sun-goddess as conceived by Leon Bakst. Each
group would make an entrance, then there might be a tableau or a few

steps. Lady Rodd came first, in a classic dress of blue and gold and a crown of turquoise, as Juno. She was accompanied by Greek gods and Amazons, Mrs George Keppel a statuesque Minerva, Princess Potenziani an ideal Venus, her son Francis a graceful Mercury. Children scattered rose petals. A bevy of Greek maidens performed a classic and dignified dance until, in a *coup de théâtre*, they were suddenly terrified, reports Sir Rennell, by 'the inrush of Tyrwhitt amazingly disguised as Pan' (the *Tatler* thought him a satyr and so did the Duchesa Sermoneta, who called him 'a prancing satyr complete with horns and tail and grey fur').

It is a great loss that no photograph exists. For much of Gerald is present in that moment: the glittering European assembly, brought together by the British, with every eye momentarily on the wild figure who revels in their attention, as long as he is allowed to remain in disguise, still young (not yet thirty) and unassured beneath the paint. As he became part of the international fashionable world, it became part of him; yet his chosen role remained ambiguous, privileged but mocking.

If Gerald's letters to his mother do not give a vivid account of his social life, they are almost completely silent about his artistic activities. He admits to going to the theatre and sketching: 'The country is very difficult, there are no foregrounds – one has to invent them – and the scenery consists entirely of distant mountains.' He reports sight-seeing: Raphael and Michelangelo are approved at the Vatican, but the gardens are not properly kept up. Otherwise he sticks to the weather ('how delightful Lyme Regis must be') and sending his compliments to the colonel.

In January 1913, however, he does admit to having founded a quartet society:

> About thirty people each subscribe £1 a month ... The concerts take place once a week at Mrs Parr's house [the residence of the American ambassador]. They generally give Mozart, Beethoven, and a lot of early (sixteenth- and seventeenth-century) Italian music. It is a delightful way of having music. One sits in comfortable arm-chairs in a private house with none of that chilling, gloomy atmosphere of a public concert room, and above all we choose our own programme.

Could she find and send some volumes of quartets? 'They are small and fattish, bound with purply red leather backs.'

In Dresden, Gerald had written a march and set a love poem to music. Nothing has survived that is known to have been written in Constantinople. In Rome, he had rooms overlooking the Spanish Steps and discovered that when street musicians were too insistent he could drive them away by playing something discordant on his own piano; possibly of his own composition? Again, he was buying musical scores. A colleague at the embassy remembered him at this time as 'not fervent about anything but music'; and he had already in 1911 introduced himself to Stravinsky, through Klukovsky, who had known him in St Petersburg.

It was a momentous meeting. Gerald was to pronounce as his considered opinion that Stravinsky was the only genius he had ever known, and there was distinguished competition. Stravinsky returned the compliment by saying more than once that Gerald was the most interesting British composer of the twentieth century. Allowing for friendship, for they became and remained friends, and allowing for enmity – for Stravinsky may have wanted to convey something of his opinion of Walton, Britten or whoever – it is still a judgement that carries weight. Stravinsky was only one year older than Gerald but his first symphony in 1907 had caught the attention of Diaghilev and he had already written the music for *Firebird* and *Petrushka*, with *The Rite of Spring* to follow soon. During the war he lived in Switzerland but occasionally visited Rome. It may have been this meeting itself that nudged Gerald back into composing. It does appear that Stravinsky was first impressed by his musical intelligence, rather than by seeing anything that he had already written.

Certainly Gerald's first mature compositions were started as early as 1913. *Three Songs in the German Manner* are settings of poems by Heine.[*] The first, *Du bist wie eine Blume*, had been accepted as expressing tender emotion about a lily-white maiden met by the poet on a country walk, until (Gerald says) a biography revealed that in fact the poem had been to a lily-white pig. No such biographer has been identified. Gerald mixed snatches of Teutonic sentimentality with simulated grunts, and uses some of the musical techniques that appear in his first published piano pieces. The second song sticks to the farmyard and tells of King Wiswamitra yearning for a particular cow, Gerald adding a touching imitation of the naïve spirit of German folk

---

[*] Gerald referred to them as a 'Lieder Album', borrowing the term from a set of songs by Max Reger, which he had bought in Constantinople.

song. The last (written first) tells of the journey of the Magi to the manger. When they were published Gerald, who helped with the cost, designed the cover himself, 'very plain and unpretentious and not at all German,' as he reported to Stravinsky.

It was not until the following year that Alfredo Casella, much of whose life was dedicated to championing contemporary music, returned to Rome after studying with Fauré in Paris. He was a pianist, lecturer and organiser, as well as a prolific avant-garde composer. The same age as Gerald, he too knew the Marchesa Casati and soon they became friends, though Gerald later allowed himself to smile at his self-promotion. Casella and Stravinsky both saw Gerald's early work and were genuinely impressed by its talent, advanced technique and originality, which was enormously encouraging.

Another new acquaintance was Giacomo Balla, also championed by the marchesa. He had signed the Futurist Manifesto in 1910 and painted some fine and idiosyncratic pictures, with titles such as *Speeding Car* and *Light*. The Futurists, who rejected the past and advocated the destruction of museums, celebrated movement and the machine. The writers used industrial imagery and dislocated grammar in the interest of onomatopoeia. The painters tried to convey movement, as in Balla's most famous picture, *Dog on a Leash*, painted in 1912, in which the legs of the dog proliferate, as in a multiple-exposure photograph. He was older than the others, indeed a couple of years older than Gerald, and became an uncle to the movement. Gerald was to own at least one of his pictures.

Balla had created the first 'happening' with Diaghilev, and Diaghilev always became the centre of any group he joined; he dominated this one whenever he was there. Eleven years older than Gerald, this extravagant, flamboyant figure had already contrived to place ballet at the centre of the artistic world, drawing in the most talented composers and painters. His creation, the Ballets Russes, was the sensation of Europe. The seasons before the war saw perhaps its greatest achievements. In 1911, Karsavina and Nijinsky had conquered London. Each new production was a fresh triumph. The conquest, however, in London, as opposed to Paris, was of society; the intellectuals were not to succumb for another ten years. Frivolous magazines chattered of the costumes, the jewels, who sat in which box and which royalty were present; the more solemn weeklies remained silent or mocked. It was the opera-goers, worshippers of Puccini, who were ecstatic: 'Diaghilev's public

resembled nothing so much as an exclusive club where the British
ruling class displayed its brilliant plumage.'

It is frustratingly unrecorded that Gerald had seen the Ballets Russes,
but inconceivable that he had not. All that most attracted him was here
drawn together. He had had the opportunity in London. When in
November 1911 his mother records 'G went away' and two weeks later
'G returns from London', he could, for instance, have seen Pavlova in
Giselle, among her last performances with the company. Now, in Rome,
he was on the edge of this dazzling creative circle.

In 1914 Gerald wrote *Le Poisson d'Or*. It was dedicated to Stravinsky,
who particularly liked it. A poem by Gerald, a pastiche of Jules Renard,
appears at the head of the score:

> Morne et solitaire, le poisson d'or
> Tournoie dans son bol de cristal.
>   Il rêve une petite compagne, belle et brillante,
> Comme une pièce de vingt francs . . .
> Mais, hélas! Quelque imbécile malavisé lui jette
> Une miette de pain.
>   L'image disparait dans l'eau troublée.
>   Le poisson d'or avale sans joie la miette de pain
> Et continue à tournoyer, morne et solitaire,
> Dans son bol de cristal.

The sad goldfish, longing for a shining mate, receives only a crumb,
which it swallows. This can be listened to as a story or as a tightly
constructed design. The music follows the implied narrative of the
poem in a quite literal way. The opening, for example, meanders with a
group of somewhat inconsequential repeated phrases depicting the
solitary fish. The appearance of the breadcrumb, dropped into the bowl,
is illustrated with a rapid and very loud downward glissando. At the
end, the pathos of the opening is resumed. Another, even shorter piano
piece, *Dispute entre le papillon et le crapaud*, probably dates from the
same time.

The war came as a surprise to Gerald. It was as late as 31 July 1914 that
he wrote, 'We are all considerably perturbed here. Things look very
black . . . We were all so peaceful up to a few days ago . . . I will write
again later. We are rather busy with telegrams etc. just now.' Busy he
remained – not leaving Rome during the hot summer, not going home
for four years, writing about once a month to his mother. The policy

was for diplomats to remain diplomats, though a few managed to struggle free and fight. Of Charlie Lister, Asquith's nephew, who had been an attaché in Rome and was killed in 1915, Sir Rennell wrote, 'I never quite understood how he succeeded on the outbreak of war in cutting himself free from the reins of public service when the spirit of the crusade moved him.' Lady Gerald Wellesley went quite a bit further: 'He has brought odium on the whole diplomatic corps.' Her husband, who was to succeed his own nephew to become Duke of Wellington in 1943, had also been in Constantinople, where 'fireflies perched on the rim of the champagne glasses', and was already a friend. When he was posted to the embassy in Rome, the friendship flourished. Gerald made no attempt to cut himself free of diplomatic life, but there was no disgrace in that; even in the age of white feathers, no one thought that he should.

Britain declared war on Germany on 4 August. Italy was neutral for over nine months, and although Sir Rennell insisted that he was always confident that the people were with the Allies, several louder voices were not so sure. It was clearly a relief when on 15 May 1915 Italy came in on the Allies' side. Lady Gerald Wellesley mentions eating endless pasta and Sir Rennell is grateful for Virginia hams from the American ambassador, but in Rome there was no danger and not much discomfort, just work and apprehension.

Lady Rodd gave musical entertainments to raise money for the wounded. All of this must have impinged on a now hard-working Gerald. The only major military event was the disastrous defeat at Caporetto in 1917, a gloomy time in any case. The Germans broke through the Italian line and almost reached Venice. The Italian 2nd Army fled, but then stood firm at Piave (where Hemingway was wounded in the legs). When this was announced, Sir Rennell reports, 'Orlando, President of the Council, in an access of enthusiasm threw his arms round my neck.' It was the turning point, victory now only a matter of time.

In a dramatic story ('It was in the Ibsen Room that the tragedy occurred . . .') Gerald later wrote of how, the Villa Rosebery no longer in use owing to pressure of work, he sometimes escaped to Sorrento: 'At the back of the hotel there was a little garden shaded with ilexes and orange trees, in which if one tired of gazing on the vast expanse of sea and sky from the terrace one could sit and look up through the foliage at the towering heights that overhung the town.' His story concerns an unfaithful wife throwing herself into the ravine when surprised with a lover by her obnoxious children. Perhaps it was here also, far from the madding war, that Gerald wrote music. *Fragments Psychologiques* comprises three pieces that are indeed fragmentary and named *Hate*, *Laughter* and *A Sigh*. *Hate* employs bitonal chords to produce what has been called 'an oil and vinegar mixture'. From the outset, dissonance constitutes the rule, rather than the exception, but harmonic coherence is maintained. Some find *Laughter* imitates the sound of its title. *A Sigh* is not, as might be expected, a downward phrase but a succession of rising semitones, falling a tone so that the effect is wistful rather than regretful.

The most important of his early works was *Trois Petites Marches Funèbres*, written in 1916. The first march is intended to portray the dreary pomp of an official funeral on a rainy day – for it usually does rain on such occasions – the procession of ministers and ambassadors, the idle and indifferent onlookers and the general conglomeration of frock-coats, top-hats and umbrellas, musty uniforms dug up from the depths of cupboards – in fact, the kind of mourning that reeks of mothballs. The predominant feature of this march is repetitive figuration. The first phrase is an obvious poke at the opening of Beethoven's Fifth, the arrival of the cortège at the place of rite or rest heralded by a series of modal chords, courtesy of Vaughan Williams. The lack of resolve at the end may suggest the eternal uncertainty of what comes after death, with the feeling that Gerald is not very hopeful for this particular statesman.

The second march is simple and direct – a child mourns a pet canary with real emotion. There is a slow tune and above it the little bird's tweets; on the page someone who could not read music might grasp the shape of it visually, perhaps even be intrigued as to how it would sound, as Gerald himself had been when he was a boy. The third march, *Pour une tante à héritage*, is taken at a jaunty speed, financial hope clearly outstripping family feeling.

The next year Gerald wrote what was to become his first orchestral work. It is actually called *Three Pieces* (*Trois Morceaux*) and it was thought that they were written as piano solos, then orchestrated, then arranged for piano duet at the suggestion of the publishers for better distribution – common practice at the time. Again, the three pieces have a theme in common, but also marked contrasts. Gerald offers representations of a Chinese screen, the delicate tints of an old Viennese porcelain and the crude, barbaric colours of Russian peasant art. Beneath the audaciously brilliant impressions, however, lurks half-concealed mockery somewhere just short of parody, for each piece is deliberately cast in the vein of a stereotyped form of folklore or genre music. The composer often leaves his audience in doubt as to where he wishes their sympathies to lie. Gerald's music was immediately interesting, original, witty, with an obvious jokiness often signalled by the titles; beyond that there is a melancholy. It did not develop or deepen, or become more complex. He arrived, like Athene, fully formed, and at intervals produced new examples of what was essentially the same talent adapted to the circumstances. At this early stage he does not seem interested in courting the public, so much as in defining a position that will be fully understood only by musicians.

Of course in the middle of the greatest war the world had ever seen, this went unnoticed, but not by the handful whose attention Gerald craved. A certain respect was due to Stravinsky, but at first Gerald stops only just short of an uncharacteristic, if understandable, sycophancy. A letter to Stravinsky in May 1916 says that he is:

> overjoyed to learn, through Madame Khvoshinsky [the wife of a Russian diplomat] that you will consent to see me and give me some guidance if I come to Switzerland for a few days. I fear that I will be a nuisance to you; nevertheless I do hope to accept your kind offer, for a half-hour conversation with you will undoubtedly mean more to me than a century of lessons with academics.

Their letters were in French, but some of Gerald's drafts (he made drafts for quite unimportant correspondence), which are in English, survive. Already he allows himself a modern, almost a Futurist, joke: 'Balla asked me to send you his best regards. I also relay to you his cry: "Viva l'Italia" but you must take care in unwrapping this exclamation, because it is deafeningly loud.'

All went well, though we know no details of the visit, for in August he recalls 'with joy our charming strolls together'. He also mentions running into the influential Count Enrico San Martino di Valperga, president of the Academia di Santa Cecilia, and pointing out that Stravinsky is owed some money. San Martino says this is Toscanini's business and he must take it up with Casella. Gerald became useful as Stravinsky's man in Rome and in October passed on San Martino's offer to him to conduct a concert of his own work; this was accepted in principle, the details to be haggled over.

From then on Gerald addresses Stravinsky as 'Cher ami', and ends

'Your devoted Gerald Tyrwhitt'. He is less successful in an approach to Diaghilev in March 1917:

> In accordance with your request, I told Diaghilev to send you the money and to inform you of his plans. 'Yes, yes', he replied with a benevolent smile and I can't imagine why he does not capitulate . . . Near my house I have discovered a tiny, dirty little theatre/music hall, which I want you to see when you come. They have a variety programme and an orchestra *à tout crever*. I took Picasso and Cocteau there the other night, and they were thrilled . . .

Gerald helped to paint some of the sets.

When Stravinsky did come later that month he had dinner (he recalled later) with 'Ansermet, Bakst, Picasso, whom I then met for the first time, Cocteau, Balla, Lord Berners [*sic*], Massine and many others . . . round Diaghilev's lavishly hospitable table'. On his return to Switzerland he took a portrait that Picasso had made of him. The military authorities, not up with the latest developments in painting, said that it was not a portrait but a plan. 'Yes,' said the composer, 'the plan of my face but of nothing else.' It was no good, and the portrait had to be sent in Gerald's name to Sir Rennell, who later sent it on to Diaghilev in Paris in the diplomatic bag.

It was at about this time that young Harold Acton, who had just started at Eton, was brought by his father to Gerald's rooms:

> I remember tin goldfish that used to stir in big bellied bowls, some of which were filled with blue and green water like those in chemists' windows, and transparent Javanese puppets like those on strings. He was anxious to surprise one. He created the atmosphere of a toyshop where the toys might spring to life and dance tarantellas or something pop out of a cushion.

Acton saw Gerald as part of the Futurist set and by now it was true.

On 30 March 1917 Alfredo Casella played *Trois Petites Marches Funèbres* at the Academia di Santa Cecilia, the first professional performance of any work by Gerald. In April, Diaghilev presented a Russian programme that would normally have begun with 'God Save the Tsar'. Unfortunately the Tsar had abdicated a few weeks earlier, so something else was needed. Diaghilev decided on the 'Song of the Volga Boatman' and asked Stravinsky to orchestrate it. Casella recalls, 'Helped by Lord Berners [*sic*] and Ansermet, who copied off the parts,

Stravinsky worked all night arranging the melody for an orchestra of wind instruments.' This shows the measure of Stravinsky's trust in Gerald's musicianship.

He remained, however, a naïve negotiator. In September, Diaghilev promised Stravinsky 5,000 francs, explaining that he too had terrible financial difficulties because of the costumes that had caught fire on a train in Brazil. Gerald was 'really shocked that Diaghilev after his proclamation has sent you nothing. He promised emphatically . . .'

In 1917, Gerald wrote another set of three, this time the *Valses Bourgeoises*. He always loved waltzes and remained faithful to them when he came to write ballet scores. All the now familiar Berners trademarks are here, not least the unchanging bass accompaniment for the first forty bars of *Valse brillante*. The piece is brilliant and decorative, thereby producing a welcome contrast to the inevitable, yet harmonically hardly predictable, oom-pah-pahs. Stravinsky called bars 41 to 44 'one of the most impudent passages in modern music'.

In January 1918, Gerald asked permission to use Stravinsky's *Five Easy Pieces* to accompany *L'Uomo dai Baffi*, a marionette show being presented by Gilbert Clavel and the Futurist Fortunato Depero, who made the puppets, thus eliminating human performers. There were four separate plays. Perhaps permission was refused, for Gerald himself provided the music; it was now that Casella arranged *Trois Petites Marches Funèbres*, one of the *Fragments* (*Laughter*) and the unpublished *Portsmouth Point* for a group of ten instruments (effectively his only piece of chamber music). The evening went well and was much praised by Casella himself; Gerald reported to his mother, in restrained terms, that his own music 'sounds very well on the orchestra and had a great success with the public'. In February he reports to Stravinsky that 'Life here is very peaceful, not to say monotonous. The Countess San Martino is still very beautiful, and Casella continues to be very pleased with Casella. The Marchesa Casati presented a Futurist show, with works by Balla, Depero, Boccioni.' When the war is mentioned at all, it is flippantly: 'International incidents and other minutiae aside, I am well and hope that you are too.'

And he was. Gerald's generation of upper-class Englishmen was not simply shaken by the war, it was tested, transformed, and, when not killed in action, in many cases broken. Almost alone, it seems, Gerald swam against the terrible tide. His fits of gloom had come before. He had fewer friends than most and many of them were diplomats, who survived; he had practically no relations of an age to be sacrificed.

Having blossomed in Italy, he continued to do so, having found rather belatedly what some discover at university – congenial friends, a beautiful background, exciting ideas, stimulating work – not with undergraduates but with the most talented creators of his time. Of course they were the happiest days of his life.

Chapter VI

The Composer Inherits

Gerald used to tell different stories about how he inherited, and how unexpectedly. To some a whole row of uncles fell off a bridge; to others a bus mowed down a column of mourning Tyrwhitts on their way to a family funeral. In fact, his uncle died aged sixty-three, childless and unmarried. Gerald was the only son of the next brother – the natural heir. His grandfather had died in 1894, so his uncle had then become Sir Raymond, fourth baronet. His grandmother had died in 1917, so Sir Raymond had also been for one year the thirteenth Lord Berners. On Sir Raymond's death, both titles passed ineluctably to Gerald. Furthermore, there was an entail that property had to accompany them.

Gerald could not help having foreseen his inheritance, though his first comment was 'it is possible that Uncle Raymond may have a wife and child hidden away somewhere'. Indeed, he had already been consulted about Berners heirlooms, and had written, 'I should regret, if ever I succeed, having to let the pictures go.' That he was not quite prepared is backed up by a complicated little tradition of name-taking. Lady Berners' heirs had each taken her maiden name of Wilson before they inherited – her eldest son when he was twenty-two, Sir Raymond when his brother died. Gerald had not anticipated his succession in the same way and only became Tyrwhitt-Wilson by royal licence in 1919, by which time his surname was cloaked by his title.

The money was another matter. Berners (as he had now become) had no idea how much to expect, and at one time feared debts. In his first, prompt letter he adds, 'of course the two death duties following so quickly will cut an enormous slice out of the income'. He is not at all grasping: when told that the contents of the main house, Stanley Hall, are to be divided, like Sir Raymond's money, between the brothers and sisters, he comments, 'This is rather a relief . . . if I live at Stanley I should prefer to have my own things . . . in any case I shall have to live very modestly for a few years I imagine.' His portion was land and houses, his good luck that the law of entail was altered so that it was possible to sell them.

As befitted a Futurist, he had no interest in the past, no feeling for possessions handed down over the generations. Already his grandmother's estate was on the market. This was fine – 'it seems to be a very favourable moment for selling land' – but was not his decision. It went for over £38,500. The silver went as well, also fine by Gerald, as it was 'of no artistic value whatever and of an uninteresting period'. Keythorpe Grange in Leicestershire, which Sir Raymond had kept for hunting and shooting, was offered to the family before it too was put up for sale with the land. The tenants bought most of it for more than £150,000. Family portraits were put in the stables for years, until these were needed for horses. Some of the trappings of the past, however, he liked: 'I never fully realised before how nice the Berners arms are. A Greyhound and an Eagle, symbolical of the two most admirable qualities – swiftness and clarity of vision; but I should like to change "Le bon temps viendra" to "Le bon temps est venu".'

Osbert Sitwell bases the hero of his story *The Love-Bird* closely on Berners:

> [He was] pleased at having created the false impression of brutal lack of sentiment. Actually and in fact he had been thoughtful and practical, had adapted his situation to his time. It was pointless and hopeless he felt in these days to own vast, draughty machicolated mansions, ugly in their conglomerated selves, even if full of beautiful objects.

Any impression of brutality was not resented. Frequent lunches with uncles seem to have been entirely amiable. Fields and houses disappeared to be replaced by money, but in November 1918 Gerald wrote, 'I fear I shall always be torn between Faringdon and Stanley.' Almost a year later when he has, after much negotiation, managed to turn the nine-year lease into ownership, he still writes, 'It is awful about the taxes going up so much. Just when I have bought Faringdon. I shall certainly be obliged to sell Stanley now I fear.'

He was not really torn between Stanley and Faringdon, as he did not live at either. Stanley was indeed sold and Faringdon given to his mother for the rest of her life. The family portraits were put in the stables she did not require. Berners had a bachelor flat in it, two rooms and a bathroom, discreet almost to the point of invisibility. An obscure flight of stairs led down into the semi-basement, and a business room, which had once contained a billiard-table, now had a piano, as well as some books with good bindings; there he could compose without disturbing anyone. The main rooms retained his mother's style. When the Berners Estate Company was set up in 1922 there were properties worth £60,000 (now well over £1½ million) and investments worth £190,000 (£5½ million). From 1924–5 to 1935–6 the average income from the estate, without enormous fluctuation, was over £7,000 a year (£234,000).

The war ended, as it had begun, more quickly than Berners expected. He had been abroad for so much of his youth that he would have to be 'discovered' by London society. What would be found? He was single; possessed of an old if not particularly distinguished title; definitely rich (in spite of rising taxes); if not quite young at thirty-five, then not quite middle-aged either; talented, though not yet proved; charming if not handsome.

His friends have not tried to conceal the latter omission. Osbert Sitwell: 'Strongly drawn, rather Habsburg cast of his features ... his natural air of quiet, ugly distinction.' Lady Diana Cooper: 'more like a figure in a tailor's shop than a composer.' Harold Acton: 'He always seemed middle-aged ... Not remarkable in appearance, by no means.' Lord Sackville, when Harold Nicolson took him to Knole, thought he looked like an oyster. And, most outspoken, Beverley Nichols: 'He was remarkably ugly – short, swarthy, bald, dumpy and simian. There is a legend that nobody who has ever seen Gerald in his bath is ever quite the same again.'

Berners had indeed gone bald young, continued to grow balder and did not care for it. His monocle was to cause young Reresby Sitwell, son of Osbert, to call him 'window-face'. Edward James remembered his laugh as a combination of a chuckle and clearing his throat, Lady Mosley as a delighted sneeze. His voice was dull and toneless and he did not use it often in company. Far from holding the table with anecdotes and imitations, he would listen quietly and then interject a phrase or two. This was enough. Berners was acclaimed as both witty and charming. His remarks were rarely unkind, though he has been described as 'a dormouse with a bite'. The brilliant description of T. E. Lawrence – 'always backing into the limelight' – is attributed to him. Above all, he was terrified of being boring: 'I don't think personally that I am a bore but then nobody does ... I am luckily sensitive to other

people's reactions and if I notice the slightest tendency to yawn or
otherwise indicate tedium, I fade away as rapidly as the man did when
the Snark turned out to be a boojum.'

Just as powerful was his aversion to being bored. He drew a
distinction between being bored by things (never) and being bored by
people (often and quickly, though he does not say so). Indeed, his
epitaph for himself was:

> Here lies Lord Berners
> One of the learners,
> His great love of learning
> May earn him a burning,
> But, praise to the Lord,
> He seldom was bored.

There is no mention of creativity and it is not clear why learning should
lead to burning. The nearest Berners got to wickedness was in his liking
for flamboyance, for people who behaved wildly, perhaps badly, in a
way that he himself never could. The 1920s were to become famous for
just this sort of sparkle and excess.

Naturally, his life continued in its previous pattern but soon there
were a few acquisitions. He continued as acting private secretary to the
Ambassador in Rome until June 1919, almost a year, so had to return
there. On his way back he ran into old friends in Paris. He dined with
Harold Nicolson, lunched with Mrs Parr, saw Gerald Robartes and the
Marchesa Casati. When he arrived, he wrote, 'I am thinking of buying a
new motor . . . it is probably cheaper than trains . . . Lady Rodd is as
usual very busy getting up all sorts of charity entertainments.' The car
was a Fiat, to be followed by a Lancia. Soon he has a new apartment
and, undaunted by there being no food in the shops, no newspapers, 'all
sorts of tumults and the streets full of soldiers', he 'has been writing a
lot of music and am now orchestrating a Spanish thing that I began
when I was at Faringdon'. This was *Fantaisie Espagnole*, written, like
Three Pieces, first as a piano solo, then scored for orchestra, then for
piano duet. The orchestra was the largest Berners ever used, with
almost quadruple woodwind and two harps. Also, like *Three Pieces*, it
displayed a real awareness of orchestral colour and subtlety, and there
were moments when he showed his debt not only to Stravinsky but also
to Nikolai Rimsky-Korsakov and Emmanuel Chabrier. Something
between an imitation, a parody and a caricature of the conventional

musical representation of Spain, it was also a conscious reply to those who said that he could not write a tune; by his own reckoning he included no fewer than seventy. Constant Lambert was to write:

> It would be an exaggeration to say that the Spanish National style was invented by a Russian, Glinka, and destroyed by an Englishman, Lord Berners; for after the latter's amazingly brilliant parody of Spanish mannerisms, it is impossible to hear most Spanish music without a certain satiric feeling breaking through.

More immediately important was Stravinsky's continuing approval: 'He is very pleased with my latest composition and says I have made great progress.' Meanwhile *Le Poisson d'Or* was published with unusual care and elegance. The front cover, frontispiece and vignette on the back were specially painted by Natalia Goncharova, who was already known in England for her designs for Diaghilev's *Le Coq d'Or*. She was a friend and made two unrecognisable drawings of Berners. *Three Pieces*, in the piano duet version, became *Trois Morceaux* and the *couverture*, *illustrations et ornament* were by Goncharova's partner, Mikhail Larionov, also known for his ballet designs. Larionov wrote with great enthusiasm, suggesting, before he had actually heard the music, that a ballet could be made and that he would be willing to provide the costume and sets.

When not in Paris, Berners kept in touch, writing to Stravinsky that he had been to the ballet and seen Diaghilev several times, indeed had seen the new year of 1919 in with him. Berners seems to have had an operation in February, for he received a letter saying, 'I hope you are well again and the anaesthetist's finger is too.'

Certainly he had by then acquired London rooms in Half Moon Street: 'delightful, I am lucky to have got them . . . I am dining tonight with Sitwell and Wyndham Lewis.' He bought a beautiful saloon carriage, a very nice Persian carpet, quite cheap, and 'everyone admires my pictures very much. I have been very lucky in the two I bought – one doesn't often get a Wouwerman for £4' (though the last is now thought not to be genuine). Anthony Powell was taken by Osbert Sitwell to have tea with Nellie Burton, who let those Half Moon Street rooms to single gentlemen. He remembered her as 'respectful, chatty, infinitely understanding . . . [with] the air of a ladysmaid retired after long service in a very "good" family but also a suggestion that something a shade louche was taking place in the background of her premises.' She once confided to Berners, 'Them two Sitwells have got into a groove', which amused Osbert.

Gradually, new names appear and old ones move closer. Titles so fill Berners' letters that it seems he is trying to impress his mother, who has to have some of these grand acquaintances explained: 'Last night I had a little dinner-party here. The Grand Duke Dimitri, Lady Cunard, Lady Islington, and Lady Lavery, the wife of the artist – a very beautiful woman. We went to the opera which was packed. It is being a great success. I met the Duchess of Westminster again.'

Lady Lavery enhanced her acknowledged beauty with such imaginative make-up that Berners is said to have spread the rumour that the First Lord of the Admiralty, after lunching with her, entirely revised his plans for camouflaging the Mediterranean Fleet. By 1921, however, they were friendly enough to go carol singing in black masks with Lady Diana Cooper and raise £100 for charity. Some of these names came to Faringdon. His mother found Norah Lindsay, who took photographs and created gardens as well as being a neighbour at Sutton Courtenay, 'very amusing', but Osbert Sitwell less so. At work on a crossword puzzle, she asked those in the room, 'What do you do when you are dealing the cards at bridge?'

'Put the ace up my sleeve.'

'Quite a wit, Mr Sitwell.'

She made no comment on the Marchesa Casati, who brought a boa-constrictor with her in a glass case. Mrs Tyrwhitt asked, 'Wouldn't it like something to eat?'

'No, it had a goat this morning.'

'It does seem so inhospitable.'

Others did comment. Her fellow guest, the Duchess of Sermoneta, thought:

> Luisa looked even stranger in appearance . . . She had added lashes two inches long to her enormous eyes and her hair was more flame-like than ever. She came down to supper in tight white satin trousers and announced her intention of visiting Oxford with us next day . . . At dinner I could not understand why the others were so hilarious, until I found that Gerald Berners was wearing a false nose which I, being extremely short-sighted, had not spotted, and therefore persisted in talking to him quite seriously.

Siegfried Sassoon came for a quieter weekend and recorded, 'During dinner chatted about fox-hunting to B[erners]'s step-father, a most engaging colonel about eighty years old.' After dinner Berners perused something by Scriabin and the colonel nodded over a battalion war history. 'B's mother is a vague agreeable lady beautifully draped in old lace; probably a keen gardener; the drawing-room is full of freesias, and they are thinking of getting a new troupe of goldfish for the lily-pond.' Next night the colonel spoke of Ireland, before returning to hunting.

What was to be the framework of Berners' life sketchily emerged. In 1920 he faded from the embassy. Among his last gestures was a reply to calm the Venetians. An Australian newspaper had said that it was sad to see a once noble city full of beggars; Berners wrote that it was all a mistake, a misprint: it was supposed to read 'buggers'. He bought the Palazzo Antici Mattei in the Via di Funari, not a palace but 'a delightful apartment. I like it more every day. It has an enormous room with a lovely view. I have already [May] given two dances which were great fun – one for Toby Elcho and Mrs Dudley Ward just before they left.' He drove out to Rome in the spring each year at a leisurely pace and returned no faster in the autumn. The car would be hoisted on to the ship at Newhaven by crane. (His mother noticed the GB plate and asked him why he had had the car initialled.) For almost twenty years these were some of his most agreeable days.

There was, and had been for some time, an English musical renaissance. Berners did not join it. The English set themselves against copying foreigners, instead looked for inspiration in English literature, English countryside, earlier English music. Many had a sense of mission, an almost political wish to bring music to the masses. In 1904 Elgar had been knighted, doubtless to the approval of Berners' mother, and in 1905, in a series of lectures, expressed his faith in the seriousness, earnestness and sincerity of the younger men. Berners was not to be one of them; indeed, in a book on the subject he is instanced as the exception. Arthur Bliss, Arnold Bax and Ralph Vaughan Williams, with his particular interest in folk music, were nothing to him and Vaughan Williams' description, written later, of what to avoid, might just as well be a view of Berners: 'I have known many young composers with a genuine native invention who have gone to Germany or France in their most impressionable years and have come back speaking a musical language which can only be described as broken French or German. They have had their native qualities swamped and never recovered their personality.'

It would, however, be a mistake to think of Berners as an English composer – he was from the first a European. The names of those who influenced him are foreign. Stravinsky and Casella are said to have persuaded Berners to relinquish his job, but this must mean that they gave him the confidence to think of himself as a composer. It was his inheritance that had made his diplomatic career superfluous; feasible while he was in Rome, but a posting outside Europe was now unthinkable and unnecessary. He continued to write, to make advances and to be performed.

In March 1919, he reports 'a most successful weekend at Manchester – my pieces very well played and conducted. I think the Manchester people were a little surprised.' This was the first performance of his work in England, *Three Pieces for Orchestra* conducted by Eugene Goossens. Paris, however, was the centre of all that he aspired to, so it was even more exciting when, on 17 June in that city, at a concert of English music, under the patronage of Lord Derby, Ernest Ansermet conducted the same *Three Pieces* for Diaghilev (he did so again the next day at the Alhambra in London). They were well received, but not by Ernest Newman in the *Observer*, who called them: 'The very latest things in British music (if I may apply that convenient expression to what is not really British and is hardly music)'. The narrow French, he continued, do not appreciate Elgar or understand the British character.

Newman returned to the attack and George Moore wrote, either with malice or without tact, to Berners' friend Lady Cunard, 'What a splendid article Newman contributed to the *Observer*, "Lord Berners' crucifixion". It is the only real piece of criticism that has appeared in the English language for many years.' Berners protested and received another onslaught headed 'Our Modern Creed'. Initially, Newman had welcomed Berners' work as 'nonsense but logical nonsense', which was 'inexpressibly comic', and had compared it favourably with 'mere harmonic absurdity, in the style that Erik Satie often affects', which 'is so easy that it is not worth doing'. This was more perceptive.

In Paris, six young composers who shared a liking for the light and deft, and a dislike of pretension, had come together as friends and gave concerts as 'Les Nouveaux Jeunes'. In January 1920 they were dubbed 'Les Six', but like any such group were later to protest that their differences made the label absurd. Francis Poulenc said:

The diversity of our music, of our tastes and distastes, precluded any common aesthetic. What could be more different than the music of Honegger and Auric? Milhaud admired Magnard, I did not; neither of us liked Florent Schmitt, whom Honegger respected; Arthur [Honegger] on the other hand had a deep-seated scorn for Satie, whom Auric, Milhaud and I adored.

Germaine Tailleferre and Louis Durey made up the six. In spite of their differences, they were a more coherent group than existed in England and there is an intriguing entry in Berners' engagement book in 1920, 'Dine, les Six'.

Honegger's contempt notwithstanding, Satie was their precursor, their godfather. He had set himself against German Romanticism and the expression of intense personal feelings and, as part of his technique of deflation, inserted comic little directions into his music, like 'Slow down politely' or 'Very seriously silent' and went in for odd titles, such as *Three pieces in the Shape of a Pear*. It is possible to see why Berners was referred to, even so early, as 'the English Satie'. The Frenchman, however, was not pleased and retorted to a third party that Berners was a professional amateur, which was patronising but not entirely unfair (Stravinsky had, on another occasion, said that he was an amateur but not at all amateurish). The spokesman, almost the publicist, for 'Les Six' was Jean Cocteau, a friendly acquaintance of Berners, who occasionally sent him postcards of congratulation.

Chapter VII

London's Darkest Drawing-rooms

Diaghilev had, inevitably, had a difficult war, much of it in America, South as well as North. The Ballets Russes had survived, which was a triumph, but was diminished and bankrupt. In 1918, Diaghilev, like Berners, came to an England he had not visited for four years, hoping to raise some money. He did so, but only by descending to 'the halls' and presenting dance sandwiched between comedians and ventriloquists. An almost continuous run of sixteen months, the longest he ever played anywhere, restored the company's financial position. Its character, however, had changed. Léonide Massine replaced Michel Fokine as chief choreographer until 1921, and modernism now dominated. 'Diaghilev's encounter with this [the Futurists'] dynamic avant-garde in wartime Italy was an event of the first magnitude, a major catalyst of the transition to modernism.' Berners' encounter with the same people meant as much, and more, to him. A new aesthetic evolved for the ballet, which included brevity, no narrative, speed and simultaneity, and non-objective forms of representation. Berners could understand and sympathise with such ideas.

Diaghilev was never at ease with the English. He 'regarded them with mingled condescension and mistrust'. In return they adored him; society had adored him before the war and now this feeling spread to the masses and the intellectuals. He created an audience for ballet that has never dispersed, and simultaneously attracted so many writers and artists that the Ballets Russes represents a landmark in the cultural history of England, as it does not quite elsewhere. Before the war, Sir Thomas Beecham had acted as the impresario's impresario in England, but they had fallen out. So Berners, an honorary European, and met under circumstances that presented him as part of the new, was a natural ally in a dubious land. He was also a composer to be supported. 'Although in 1921 during intervals at the theatre people did not flock to the bar as they do nowadays, most wanted to talk. That Diaghilev should have attempted to silence them – for ten minutes at least – in the interests of young or unfamiliar composers, seems remarkably quixotic.' He gave an airing to brief bits and pieces and Berners was one of the composers who benefited. When Diaghilev wanted a socially impressive line-up for *Les Biches* in Monte Carlo, one of the reserved chairs was for him. Diaghilev did not cultivate Berners because he could open desirable doors for him – there were many who where eager to do that – but his social position would have been an added attraction.

The agreeable spot in English life where society and the arts met was Berners' natural home. Maud (she later renamed herself 'Emerald') Cunard, Beecham's lover and champion, was another resident and Berners and she were already friends. She is always described as a bird, presumably because of her beaky nose; Lord Drogheda saw her as a 'canary of prey'; Cecil Beaton tried variously: 'her legs had the fragility of a sparrow's', 'an amusing-looking little parakeet in her pastel-coloured plumage', and 'hair as pale yellow and fluffy as the feathers of a day-old chick'. She was never dull or pompous, she brought together amusing people and spurred them on to perform, as hostesses then did. So Beaton forgave her clothes: 'She would choose too hastily and was impatient at fittings, so that the finished garment often proved a failure.' Not everyone was captivated, however. Lady Diana Cooper, more a friend of her difficult daughter, was forthright in a letter: 'Maud Cunard is a pest. She really is unbearable, always in a towering rage and threatening to go that night if the wasps won't leave her alone . . . Gerald Berners is always shrieking "O I've been stung" and sucking his finger, while Maud swallows the bait without fail.'

It is Sibyl Colefax's misfortune to be yoked to Emerald Cunard through eternity as the 'other' hostess of the 1920s, and then compared unfavourably to her. James Lees-Milne remembered Berners too making a comparison of their social style: 'the first [Cunard] was a gathering of lunatics presided over by an efficient, trained hospital nurse; the second a party of lunatics presided over by a lunatic.' Lady Cunard talked to her guests as equals and made friends; Lady Colefax did not know how to talk to them and made a fool of herself, but was a kind-hearted, decent fool and a resilient one. Berners became fond of her, but she remained an ideal butt for his quips and jokes. Complaining of insomnia, he said that he had had a room next door to Sibyl Colefax 'and she never stopped climbing all night'. One of his best-known teases was to send her a note asking her to dinner, with 'the P of W is coming' scribbled at the bottom. Always over-excited by the mere thought of royalty, she dropped everything and came, only to be introduced to the Provost of Worcester. The story has been told often, but Lady Mosley doubts that it ever happened; Berners might enjoy ridiculing his friend but would not involve the innocent provost.

In London after the First World War it was the heyday of such hostesses and a time for half-baked optimism. Monsieur Coué, a short Frenchman, gave lectures at which the audience was encouraged to chant, 'Every day in every way I am getting better and better.' It is true that Berners was heard muttering 'worse and worse', but that was not really his or the dominating mood. The gap between generations was more distinct than usual, sometimes even dividing brother from brother, rather than father from son. Alec Waugh, who had fought in the war, seemed remote from his younger brother Evelyn Waugh, who wrote *Vile Bodies*. Those who had been too young for the trenches blamed the slaughter on the older men; those who had been part of it were sometimes as much muddled as shattered and resentful of an only slightly younger generation that had escaped. Berners, however, as old as the veterans but unscathed, found the ideas and iconoclasm of the young attractive. Having made few friends of his own age and still unskilled in intimacy, he now made a greater number of acquaintances among a younger generation.

He had left a society that had no place for an artist – and in particular no place for a composer. Music was something that was written and usually played and sung by foreigners or, amateurishly, by women. Tiny inroads on this solid philistinism had been made; more were to come. On the very day that peace was declared, the Sitwells presented themselves as an almost unnervingly dynamic but benevolent force in the exact area in which Berners was most interested. A party was given by Monty Shearman, a barrister and friend of the painter Mark Gertler, in his flat in the Adelphi, which brought the Ballets Russes face to face with Bloomsbury. Of course many of that group had already seen the company – some had liked it, a few had even been enthusiastic; but Osbert and Sacheverell Sitwell had both been bowled over by it before the war and now moved among the crowd introducing Clive Bell, Roger Fry, Duncan Grant, Augustus John, Dora Carrington, D. H. Lawrence, Nina Hamnett, Jack and Mary Hutchinson, Maynard Keynes and Ottoline Morrell to Massine, who had dined with Osbert in Swan Walk, to Diaghilev and to Lydia Lopokova (who had met Keynes at an earlier

Shearman party, and was later to marry him). Osbert later recalled Lytton Strachey 'jigging about with an amiable debility. He was I think unused to dancing.'

Bloomsbury hesitated still, then next year became enthusiastic about the ballet. About the Sitwells they remained less certain and the doubts were reciprocated. In his account of this party, for instance, published in 1949, Osbert refers to some of the Bloomsbury women being dressed in clothes 'smacking of Roger's Omega Workshop, wholesome and home-made', while several of the men were dressed 'in ordinary clothes, if ordinary is not perhaps a misnomer for so much shagginess'. Circles are awkward things, always overlapping, never quite round, but the two groups remained – jealous, critical, suspicious in spite of individual friendships.

Berners, fond of jokes and of being shocked, as well as of the arts, might have seemed ripe to become at least an associate member of Bloomsbury; he never did. Diana Mosley says that he was too fastidious, too neatly dressed and fussy about his food: 'When he dined with Clive Bell and was told "I hope you like oysters. I've got some from a dirty little shop round the corner" he was quite rightly terrified.' Through Harold Nicolson and Vita ('Wry Vita' he called her) he had dinner with Virginia Woolf in 1924 and did not impress her: 'This Lord is as Siegfried Sassoon says a Kilburn Jew; round, fat, pale – no, fairly chubby, a determined little man, whose rank, I fancy, gives him some consistency not otherwise his.' Sassoon, of course, knew that Berners was not literally a Kilburn Jew and it is not clear what qualities are being suggested, only that they are not good ones.

Two years later at Clive Bell's house she found him 'stockish, resolute, quick-witted', but she also persuaded him to speak about himself, his parents, his struggle to become a composer. 'So, he said, he was inhibited as a musician. His talent clung (I think he said) like a creeper to the edge of a cliff.' This uncharacteristic self-revelation was not, however, the beginning of a friendship. Berners asked her to dinner, but she said she had a headache, and nothing much followed. He does get a mention in the preface to *Orlando*, published in 1928, among friends who have helped: 'Lord Berners whose knowledge of Elizabethan music has proved invaluable'. Lytton Strachey recorded 'a particularly mad lunch party at Lord Berners' . . . A desperate antique hag (by marriage an Italian princess) dressed in flowing widow's weeds, and giving vent to a flowing stream of lightly veiled indecencies, kept the table in a twitter.' Rex Whistler Berners knew better, and Lord

David Cecil much later became a friend. He knew the central figures a
little, some peripheral ones well, but he came to like rather smarter
society, and Bloomsbury was always more overtly serious. There was no
great antipathy, just not a strong enough attraction.

The Sitwells, on the other hand, were a great influence. They had
long declared themselves for art and against philistinism, for Modernism and against the shackles of the Victorians. Well, Berners too in his
less flamboyant style was rebelling against his Victorian youth and he
too liked to startle, both in music and in life. He valued mockery,
originality and experiment, though with him they were more likely to
lead to amusement than outrage. The Sitwell stand seemed more
dramatic then than it sounds now and they were heavily outnumbered;
Berners gave welcome and congenial support. They were only a few
years younger than Berners, but mingled with their juniors. Class too
was an important link. Osbert said that 'in the years between the wars
Berners did more to civilise the wealthy than anyone in England.
Through London's darkest drawing-rooms as well as the lightest he
moved . . . a sort of missionary of the arts.' He might have been
referring to himself, except that he was so much more conspicuous in
the newspaper columns.

The Sitwells' passion for publicity was not entirely alien to Berners,
but he never developed quite their flair for it. When a group consisting
of Osbert, Sacheverell and Edith Sitwell, William Walton, Aldous
Huxley, Augustine Rivers[*], Alan Porter[†] and Berners decided that
they represented 'The Poets of England' and presented the soprano
Luisa Tetrazzini with a chaplet of bay leaves at the Savoy in December
1921, photographers and journalists had been alerted and it is easy to
guess who the organisers were.

Bloosmbury too, of course, supported art and the new, but when
Strachey was asked what the most important thing in the world was, he
squeaked 'Passion'. Berners never attempted to put passion into his
work nor, as far as is known, into his life. Osbert Sitwell, in his
perspicacious account of his friend in the 1920s, wrote:

[*] Sir Reresby Sitwell, son of Sacheverell, suspects that Augustine Rivers never
existed: 'I believe he was a fictitious literary critic who always gave the Sitwell siblings
wonderful reviews but was a figment of the imagination created by Osbert'. This would
make the presentation into more of a joke and make Scott-Moncrieff, who accused the
group of conceit in choosing themselves to represent poetry, look rather portentous.
[†] Alan Porter, 1899–1942, communist, poet, literary editor of the *Spectator*.

He was in fact a dilettante but in the very best sense: for he aspired to be nothing but what he was. He talked well and amusingly; painted and wrote well, even with talent of an order. He often asked me to read what he had written, and occasionally, very occasionally, I thought I could detect another quality ruffling the surface of it, something sad and understanding that, it might be, he was at great pains to hide. So it seemed to me. Yet when others averred that he was artificial, cynical and heartless, these were accusatives difficult to rebut, for such sayings and tastes of his as we have detailed lent some colour to them. People wondered if he had ever loved, loved anybody or anything, had ever really cared? And what could one say, for as he sat in his drawing-room, smoking a cigarette, laughing – his usual mood – and surrounded by his, it must be admitted delightful, toys and musical boxes, it could but appear to the casual onlooker rather as though he was engaged in keeping life at arm's length.

Yet if this were so, there must – and this his enemies could not comprehend – be some very good reason for it. It is easy, of course, to credit people with too much feeling, but had not something, I wondered, wounded him very deeply in early life?

Although Sitwell belittled his talents and almost omits his composing, this is generous as well as shrewd and he is after all presenting the character as fiction. Edith found him 'a real eccentric' and quoted instances of his 'superb power of retort':

One of his acquaintances was in the impertinent habit of saying to him 'I have been sticking up for you.' He repeated this once too often, and Lord Berners replied, 'Yes, and I have been sticking up for you. Someone said you aren't fit to live with pigs, and I said that you are.' A pompous woman of his acquaintance, complaining that the head-waiter of a restaurant had not shown her and her husband immediately to a table, said, 'We had to tell him who we were.' Gerald, interested, enquired, 'And who were you?' On one occasion when my brother Sacheverell, my sister-in-law and I were lunching with Gerald, his stately, gloomy, immense butler, Marshall, entered the dining-room bearing a huge placard. 'The gentleman outside says will you be good enough to sign this, my Lord.'

Gerald inspected the placard and wriggled nervously. 'It wouldn't be any use, Marshall,' he exclaimed. 'He won't know who I am – probably has never heard of me.'

It transpired eventually that the placard was 'An Appeal to God that We May Have Peace in Our Time'.

Sacheverell, the least bizarre and quarrelsome of the family, was to become the closest friend, staying with Berners often and working with him on a ballet. Though he was a hard man with whom to sustain a feud, Berners did not escape the Sitwell rows entirely, and to offend one was to offend all. That feelings never became too bitter may have been because he posed no literary threat, which was what most easily stirred up the nest of tigers. When they drifted apart, it was more due to a divergence of style. Many of Berners' friends eventually came to find him silly; he came to find a lot of them pompous. Even in the early days when Osbert kept a great bowl of ever-replenished press cuttings in a sitting-room of his house in Carlyle Square, Berners placed an even larger bowl in the hall of his London house and put in it a solitary, minute cutting from *The Times* announcing only that he had returned from abroad. Much later, when Sacheverell and his wife were staying at Faringdon, the talk took a gloomy turn, suicide being discussed. The guests retired early but, on hearing a sudden explosion, Sacheverell rushed into the corridor only to find Berners giggling with a burst paper bag.

Meanwhile, as Evelyn Waugh said, 'The Sitwells had declared war on dullness' and Berners was happy to follow where they led. He supported skirmishes against their detested father, too: 'Every night at Renishaw, William Walton and Berners played wild cacophonous duets, at Osbert's request, to drive Sir George Sitwell to bed.' Walton had been born in 1902, so he was a generation younger than Berners, but he had got off to a much quicker start. His father had laboured in an iron works in Lancashire but described himself as a teacher of singing and managed to get his son to Christ Church Choir School in Oxford. Sacheverell Sitwell met him after the war, tall, pale and silent, and decided he was a musical genius. In 1919 he was introduced to Edith and Osbert and 'adopted' for the next fifteen years. There was even a faint physical resemblance to Edith – the same long, thin nose – which made some think that he might indeed be one of the family, an indiscretion on the part of Sir George perhaps. Osbert made a pass, was rejected, but 'it did not make an awkward situation'; Walton was referred to as 'Osbert's fag', but in the English public-school sense, not the American one.

The Dean of Christ Church, Berners and the Sitwells guaranteed Walton an income of £250 a year, enough to live on without a job. His widow has written that 'to survive, William became a scrounger', but those concerned remained unconcerned. For Berners it was generous only in that he might have been subsidising a rival, for the boy was ambitious in some of the same areas as himself. Otherwise they could hardly have been more different, Walton driven by the fear of being returned to his home town of Oldham, Berners eager to enjoy other things and not, as it turned out, driven at all. In 1922 the first International Festival of Contemporary Music was held at Salzburg; in 1923 Walton's String Quartet and Berners' *Valses Bourgeoises* were performed there, as were Berg's String Quartet, Bartók's Second Violin Sonata, Janáček's Violin Sonata, Hindemith's Clarinet Quintet and Bliss's *Rhapsody*: an impressive list. Berners went both years. In 1922 he also went to the music festival in Munich, which transformed an acquaintance into a friend.

The details are charted in the diary of Siegfried Sassoon:

> This afternoon Ottoline [Morrell] drove us to the station; I called at Half Moon Street (with a cheese for Burton) and had tea with Berners. Of Berners one can always be sure. He wears the same mask (if it is a mask) and is, to me, consistently inhuman, and unfailingly agreeable. To-day he was relishing his new Rolls-Royce – a superfine vehicle – and some atrocity literature, *The Terrific Register*, a thesaurus of violations, eviscerating murders and miscarriages of justice.

Sassoon had borrowed another unpleasant book from Berners the year before, *The Autobiography of a Child*, 'which I sat up late to read; it is full of revolting physical details'; this anonymous work, which claimed to be written from the psycho-sexual-analytical viewpoint, was banned and described at its trial as having no scientific value and being only likely to be read by dirty-minded schoolboys.

Sassoon continued for a time to find Berners 'unreal, appallingly distant and exclusively intellectual'. As Osbert Sitwell suggests, that is how he must have seemed to many who never got to know him well, a façade constructed to avoid giving offence – lacking emotion or spontaneity, perhaps concealing nothing. When, in September 1922, they met by chance in Munich, Sassoon was with a young man of twenty-five, Berners alone. At first Sassoon found himself 'automatically dropping into a bantering kind of chatter. "I'm reading St Augustine's *Confessions* in bed. What a bloody bore the City of God is," and so on. Quite artificial.' Calling on Berners later, he found 'two gorgeous apartments (one occupied by his blue-eyed charioteer). Clavichord on table; he played a couple of Bach Preludes, but is

suffering from the remains of a heavy cold. Talked volubly. I felt quite
pleased to see him. Score of new Schoenberg work there. Mad-looking
thing.'

Sassoon bought a ticket for that evening's Beethoven concert but: 'B
said "Nothing will induce me to go and hear the Ninth Symphony",
which rather damped my ardour.' In the event Sassoon went alone and
found it 'glorious'. Three days later he went to see Berners after
breakfast – 'he tinkled the clavichord a bit, and gave me immense
pleasure by his little snatches of various composers, ancient and
modern, from Handel to Schoenberg' – and they dined together the
next day. This did not go well:

> Too much to eat, but not much wine, mercifully, only some good claret.
> Dined very late, sat in the restaurant 9.30–11.30. It was a place I'd never
> been to before. The conversation was mostly semi-scandalous discus-
> sions of people I don't know. Of course B brought in the Sitwells and
> Firbank and Violet Trefusis (who was here last week). But the dinner
> was not a success. Berners (who was tired) kept darting from one subject
> to another in a truly Osbertian way. It was a relief to come back here and
> read Dickens in bed.

More successful dinners followed, however; Berners played Stravinsky
and bits from his own opera, and friendship ripened. There was another
sticky evening when the Sitwells, with whom Sassoon had had a row,
again intruded, this time in the flesh, with William Walton (whom
Sassoon had known before they did). After dinner, Osbert and
Sacheverell talked to Berners, and Sassoon felt 'extremely uncomfortable but I suspect that O and S felt much more frightened. Neither of
them looked in my direction.' Next week when he was leaving, Sassoon
judged that 'B is now firmly established among the people I consider
worthwhile.' Two years later in London he was wakened with the news
that Berners was very ill indeed. 'I found myself thinking (and probably
muttering) "This makes me realise that I have very few friends. If
Berners dies it will make a great difference to me".' He imagined letters
of condolence, 'I even fabricated a deathbed reconciliation with O
Sitwell – the expiring peer, with a final flicker of his characteristic
humour, amiably reuniting us at the moment of his own dissolution!' It
was all a misunderstanding. Berners merely had influenza and was
propped up in bed with a pile of books, this time respectable ones,
George Moore, Jane Austen, Congreve, and with the clavichord on the
counterpane. Sassoon says that they lost touch after 1926 – 'Lord B

soaring above me socially' – but there are fond letters during the Second World War. These are still much concerned with the same feuds: 'You must hastily draw some caricatures of Alfred Noyes, Noël Coward and other enemies of the Sitwells,' wrote Berners, 'so that you may produce them if the matter is pressed any further. I will willingly appear in the witness box as you know I welcome any publicity however dire may be the consequences.'

The 'blue-eyed charioteer' to whom Sassoon had referred was William Crack, who had become Berners' driver early enough to visit Stanley Hall before it was sold. He was noted by several of Berners' homosexual acquaintance, his eyes sometimes described as violet; to Harold Nicolson he was 'William, the Adonis chauffeur'. At first William drove the Lancia, bought for about £1,500 in 1920 but 'very old and we only had two wheel brakes'; soon it was a Rolls-Royce, the 'superfine' vehicle that Sassoon saw. This was given a new body and driven to Rome, where it won a prize for elegance from the Italian Automobile Association, William receiving a tiny blue rosette, Berners a gold medal. Barbara Cartland says that the lining in the back was stencilled with butterflies.

William was in a position to give the authoritative account of one of the stories most often told about Berners, that he had a piano, even a grand piano, in the back of his car. The story first appeared in the papers in 1923, though his mother had noted an instrument there in 1922. The truth is more compact. Made in Haslemere by Arnold Dolmetsch, an expert on early instruments, it was a small $4\frac{1}{2}$-octave clavichord, adorned with flowers and butterflies, painted in tempera for £25 extra. Crack: 'You know the length of the car, under the front seat, it was as long as that. About 18 inches or two feet and about 18 inches wide. It hadn't got any legs on. You just picked it out and carried it. Usually with a Rolls you put all the tools under there.' Nor did the eccentric peer strum and tinkle as he was wafted about Europe: 'You had to stop to get it out.' This installation, however, was not made until after the car had been protected from some little local difficulties: 'When Mussolini came I locked the car away because they took all the cars, and took the float out of the float chamber so they couldn't take it.' In October 1922, Mussolini, now Il Duce, appeared, spattered with mud, on the balcony of the Quirinal Palace with King Victor Emmanuel after 24,000 people had marched on Rome from Naples. 'We couldn't go out for three days. The fascists would pull you up in the street if you didn't wave your hat when they marched by.'

The house in which they were holed up was no. 8 Via Varese. Sassoon had dined there earlier in the month and Mario Panza, who was to be Mussolini's secretary, had warned that the city might be occupied. Berners was, and remained, a political innocent – or, less kindly, ignoramus – with the right-wing instincts that might be expected of a rich peer; many of his friends and acquaintances were less naïve and held extreme views. It is hard to decide how often a decent man can sup with monsters, doubtless assenting to, or at least smiling toleration of, their opinions, without contamination; Berners went further than most, but then he was unusually impervious.

Harold Nicolson had been sightseeing in Rome, perfunctorily, and Gerald Wellesley in a more informed and serious manner. Violet Trefusis also came; Berners had known her in Constantinople as Violet Keppel, where she had been engaged for a time to Wellesley. She liked to suggest royal descent, but Nancy Mitford wrote briskly years later: 'We all know it was Lord Grimthorpe. She used to admit it herself in the old days. But I daresay Edward VII would be considered more chic in Paris.' In 1919 she had married Denys Trefusis and told him on the honeymoon that she had never cared for him and that she planned to run away with Vita Sackville-West. Fortunately their visits did not coincide.

Though people refrained from answering the telephone when she was known to be approaching and hid behind the furniture when she actually arrived, somehow Violet Trefusis continued to wind her way in and out of the lives of many, including Berners. He liked anyone who made him laugh, he liked elegance; she scored in neither of these categories. She used to tell him tediously lengthy stories at lunch about the love-life of their friends, but he claimed that he got revenge by telling them back to her at dinner. He certainly did not like anyone who gave themselves the pretensions of being a serious writer without having the talent; of this she was guilty. He also had, however, a weakness for spectacular monsters and her impulsive flamboyance, her lack of fear about the feelings of others and her energy won her a place here. It might be more enjoyable to recount her visits after she had gone than to actually experience them but, one way or another, she made life less boring.

In 1923 Violet Trefusis met the Princesse de Polignac and began an affair that was to last about four years, with her husband included as a friend. The princess has been described as 'a rather splendid-looking American lesbian with the profile of Dante'. She had been born in 1865, Winnaretta, the daughter of Isaac Singer, who propelled himself from poverty to enormous wealth by way of Singer Sewing Machines. At the age of two Winnaretta was transferred to Paris, where her mother created a salon. At twenty-two she followed tradition by marrying a bogus prince. That did not last and six years later she married a real aristocrat, though his title too was disputed. Prince Edmond de Polignac had many other good qualities. He was charming, witty, fifty-nine, homosexual and musical. His opera had been placed above Bizet's in a competition. It was a marriage of the greatest possible convenience until his death in 1901. By then, and for decades to come, 'Tante Winnie' had decided to devote her life – and a great deal of money – to the support of art, particularly music. She became the most important and discerning musical hostess in Paris, supporting Fauré, Debussy, Diaghilev as early as 1909, Satie and Stravinsky; she knew Proust, Colette and inevitably Cocteau well. Many important pieces were first heard in her drawing-room on the corner of avenue Henri-Martin and rue Carambert and she was friend as well as patron, though it is difficult to be precise about affection when each had so much to gain. She was grand, exclusive. When asked at the first hearing of the music for *Les Noces* why she had not asked Chanel, she replied, 'I don't entertain my trades people.'

Berners could not have failed to meet her soon, another link being her niece, Marguerite Decazes, who was to become Daisy Fellowes. (Winnaretta's sister had followed her into the French aristocracy by marrying the Duc Decazes, but had then died, so little Marguerite was a frequent visitor.) Less predictable was that he should have struck up a lasting friendship with the Princess. Fine-looking rather than friendly, she said little, and then 'her way of speaking slowly through her teeth gave what she said a brusque quality'. She was intimidating, which, her friends explained, as friends do, was only because she was shy. Much of this could also be said of Berners himself, but it was not what he looked for in others; and no one has suggested that she in turn cared much for jokes. As Violet Trefusis replied when asked what Winnaretta and her husband did together, 'I can only suppose they talked about music'; if so, it was enough.

In 1923 Berners set out for Italy once more, this time with the Duff Coopers. Lady Diana was on her way to the Pyrenees for a 'tonic-cure' that would enable her to produce a son (John Julius was not in fact born until 1929). It was a gay drive, commemorated in a poem written for his wife by Duff:

> Lest we forget, by any chance,
>   The happy days we spent together,
> Travelling through the fields of France
>   In sunshine and in cloudy weather.
>
> Lest we forget the ruined keep
>   That Richard set above the Seine,
> And how we climbed the castle steep,
>   You, I and Berners in the rain.
>
> How Berners left us for Montmartre,
>   And how we took the road once more,
> And didn't care to stop at Chartres,
>   Because we'd seen it once before.

Lady Diana says that William Crack drove into someone, but he denied it. On another occasion he admitted that they were stopped – 'they wanted to fine us' – but Berners feigned ignorance of all known languages and escaped. They may have visited Montmartre but probably stayed as usual at the Ritz, where there was a special room set aside in which up to a hundred valets, maids, couriers and chauffeurs could eat; William found the food excellent. (He usually complained.)

Within a few weeks, they were all together again in Salzburg, Lady Diana auditioning nervously for Max Reinhardt, to secure the role in *The Miracle* that was to dominate the next years of her life; Berners with the Sitwells and Walton. His own *Valses Bourgeoises* was to be played at the music festival and Walton's String Quartet was the only other official British contribution. The waltzes were described in the *Musical Bulletin* as 'one of the most directly successful items of the Festival', but Walton's piece, which came at the end of a long programme, was thought, at least by Osbert Sitwell, to have been a disaster: 'Those poor good English girls dressed in turquoise tulle put up an abominable performance', and the cellist contrived to press some stage device so that she sank from view and then re-emerged, still gamely playing and smiling. The audience roared with laughter. There was compensation to be found, however, in meeting and making musical acquaintances. Ansermet was on the jury, Casella a member of the Italian committee

Gerald with his mother

'Arley', an idealised Apley Park with an idealised Gerald in the foreground, drawn by Berners as a frontispiece for his autobiography, *First Childhood*

Aged about twelve

In Hamburg, April 1905

Serge Diaghilev

Osbert, Edith and Sacheverell Sitwell
before a performance of *Façade*, June 1926

Igor Stravinsky
at Faringdon

Berners, drawn by
Max Beerbohm in 1923:
'Lord Berners making more
sweetness than violence'

3 Foro Romano

Diana Guinness
in Rome, *c*.1932

Berners painting outside Rome

Lady Diana and Duff Cooper

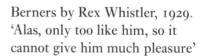

Berners by Rex Whistler, 1929.
'Alas, only too like him, so it
cannot give him much pleasure'

Phyllis de Janzé
and Doris Castlerosse

Cyril (standing), and
clockwise: Algernon, Robert
and Alan Heber Percy

Robert Heber Percy
painted by Berners

Kathleen Merrick
with Robert Heber Percy

Lady Dorothy Lygon
with Robert Heber Percy

Faringdon from the north: 'Plain and grey and square and solid'

William Crack with the Rolls Royce, which won a prize for elegance from the Italian Automobile Association

Berners feeding the fantails

'The last folly to be built in England',
1935. 'Gerry Wellesley built it classical
up to nearly a hundred feet ... Gerald
insisted on the top bit being Gothic'

Rex Whistler at the party for the folly

Lady Mary Lygon;
Loelia, Duchess of
Westminster; John
Betjeman and
Robert Heber Percy
before the opening
of the cinema in
Faringdon

Penelope Betjeman with Moti in the drawing-room at Faringdon.
'Gerald loved having him there. He was domesticated.'

One of Berners'
illustrations for *The Camel*

(which, however, walked out). Alban Berg, to whom Sitwell presented Walton as 'the leader of atonal music in Britain', was either kind or interested enough to take him and Berners to meet Arnold Schoenberg.

Schoenberg was now fifty, but only that year had adopted his provocative 12-tone technique. The details of the meeting vary. Berners, when describing the sort of room he needed in order to compose, insisted on the presence of a piano. He continued:

> I have noticed a tendency among composers to pretend that they work without a piano. Yet, say what they will, nearly all modern composers do in fact compose with the help of a piano, and if, from an undue sense of virtue or because of something Bach said many generations ago, they refrain from doing so, that is their misfortune. A very celebrated composer told me he never worked with a piano but, happening one day to enter his work room unexpectedly, I noticed music paper on the piano together with a pencil and india rubber. As invariably happens on these occasions I felt as ashamed of my detection as he did of having been caught out.

This was Schoenberg. Some say that Walton and Berners arrived early and were sent for a walk (to remove the embarrassing evidence?). Certainly conversation, as translated by Berners, was stilted and concerned just that subject – composing at the piano. Walton, however, reports Schoenberg as being in favour. Later Berners wrote, 'The violent interest I took for a time in Schoenberg was I fancy the interest of an explorer. He had opened up for me the new territory of atonal music but this territory, that at one time seemed almost a promised land, has proved itself infertile, an enclosed, dry, rocky academic valley with no issue.'

Berners had continued to write songs. *Trois Chansons*, 'in the French manner', was written in 1919 and published in 1920. The almost untranslatable texts are by Georges Jean-Aubry. The critic Ernest Newman, now on Berners' side, wrote, 'If one wants to see how bizarre a harmonic scheme can be made to sound natural . . . he can hardly do better than turn to Lord Berners' *Trois Chansons*. Here we have the thing done with such ease and assurance that it comes off brilliantly.' Not to be confused with this are two sets of *Three Songs*, written in 1920 and 1922. The first comprises a loving treatment of Thomas Dekker's 'Lullaby', followed by an indignant and mocking 'Lady Visitor in the Pauper Ward' by Robert Graves and 'The Green-Eyed Monster' by E. L. Duff, in which the singer laments:

James gave Elizabeth a Dodo.
He only *offered* one to me.

The second set concerns the sea, with John Masefield's 'The Pirate King' and two shanties, one gentle, one rollicking. A song by itself, with words credited to Ned the Dog Stealer, 'Dialogue between Tom Filuter and His Man', concerns the repayment of a debt and seems suddenly in line with the folk-songish fashions of the time; but from Berners? It is so slight that perhaps there was no intention to mock or support, perhaps it was just a trifle thrown off. For the most part Berners' music had from the beginning its own character. He did not progress so much as present different facets of what was recognisably the same talent. If he tended to write longer pieces on a larger scale as time went by, this was a reaction to circumstance, to what was asked of him, to his audience. In Italy he had been composing for a small professional circle very much headed by Stravinsky. In England his manner was less avant-garde and might be thought almost tame by comparison.

Eugene Goossens had decided to organise things his own way and put together an orchestra, which in 1921 played the first concert performance in England of Stravinsky's *The Rite of Spring*. Other pieces included Berners' *Fantaisie Espagnole*. Stravinsky, Diaghilev and Massine were late but the whole evening was a triumph, with Berners playing a modest part in it. In 1924, he wrote his last work for the concert hall – his *Fugue in C Minor*. This is surprising from him, written in conscious response to those who found his music lacking in technique and form. (Years later he was to take lessons in counterpoint, tacitly admitting that such a lack existed.) At six minutes it is long by Berners' standards, and attention is held by invention rather than the feeling that the piece is an organic whole. As one would expect, it is full of the unexpected, including a xylophone and an end that is inconclusive. There may be a comment intended on the heavy orchestration of Bach by Elgar, among others, which was prominent in the first quarter of the century. The Fugue was popular, joined Diaghilev's interval pieces, and in 1926 Berners received a telegram: '*Jouerai votre magnifique fugue mercredi, espère seriez présent, amitiés Diaghileff*'. Berners did indeed attend, Goossens conducting.

In 1919 and 1920 Berners had also planned to write a ballet 'after Rowlandson', called *Portsmouth Point*, and he completed a piano solo version, his longest piano piece, and some fifty bars of orchestral music, but then abandoned it. He did not choose to have it published in this form. (In 1925, Walton had a great success with an overture of the same name, dedicated to Sassoon, but there was no connection between the two.)

Meanwhile Berners had moved on to a larger work, and had indeed completed an opera. The 'book' he chose for the plot had been, until recently, extremely obscure. Almost a century earlier, Prosper Mérimée had written a light ironical play, *Le Carrosse du Saint-Sacrément*, which opened to immediate – and continuing – failure. For twenty years no one mentioned it. Revived in 1848 after the revolution, it was roundly hissed; Mérimée, arriving late at a performance, asked what was going on and, when told, said, 'I am going to hiss too.' This time it managed six performances. In 1917, however, it appeared successfully in London with Yvonne Arnaud, and in New York and Paris. In an interview that allowed Berners to speak in unconvincingly elegant sentences (perhaps because it was conducted in French and translated), he described how friends took him to the theatre in Paris: 'I was at once fascinated by the grace, the spirit and the character of this little work . . . It is true that a piece whose charm lies almost entirely in word and dialogue, where the action, materially speaking, is reduced to the very simplest expression, did not seem to me particularly suitable for musical treatment.' Nevertheless he began work:

> Although this is a comic opera, or if you prefer it, a *comédie musicale*, I have laid aside the traditional overture or prelude, the utility of which I fail to see . . . As regards style you will see that I have not adhered to the old tradition of different airs and scenes following each other, and bound together by the different turns of the intrigue; Mérimée's comedy unfolds itself in too continuous and concise a manner not to induce me to follow its line by a musical development that is held together in the style of a symphonic poem.

Mérimée's intrigue is set in Peru, and concerns a temptress and a viceroy, whose gout is too painful for him to go to a great church celebration. He gossips about La Périchole – his mistress and, it emerges, that of others. She arrives, persuades him to ignore all this idle accuracy, and to give her a carriage to go to church. From his window the viceroy watches her adventurous progress, which leaves a wake of accidents and fights. Unfortunately an influential marchioness is overturned. Complaints are made, but when the bishop is announced, which sounds like more trouble, he enters hand in hand with La Périchole. She has given the carriage to the Church, gained an ally, and so triumphs; in future the carriage will take the last consolation to the dying. (It is a true story. As a boy in Peru, Frederick Ashton met a man who had seen the coach.) Berners left the text in French, cut particularly at the beginning, and the result played for an hour and a quarter.

As early as December 1922 there are letters to Diaghilev about precise cuts, but it was not until 24 April 1924 that *Le Carrosse* was presented at the small Théâtre des Champs-Elysées in a bill with *L'Histoire du Soldat*, for which Stravinsky had written the music, and *La Chatte*, a ballet by young Henri Sauguet (there was a plan to drop this, but Berners said they could not have *Le Carrosse* if they did). Choreographer Serge Lifar mentions that Berners' piece had been much in Diaghilev's mind. The composer's, too. The day before the première, a journalist reported him as walking up and down the foyer of the Ritz waving his arms in despair.[*] '*Mais le décor*. It will spoil everything . . . Last night after rehearsal I had dinner with the *chef d'orchestre*, M. Ansermet, and we simply sat and wept. We did really . . . Those awful red curtains. Oh I wish tomorrow night were weeks off.'

In the event *The Times* reported 'an unqualified success . . . Lord Berners' music makes the work an unalloyed enjoyment. Only the fact that it leaves no opening for applause, that it flows on sustaining, illustrating, emphasising the text with unflagging wit and varying sentiment, prevented the work from being interrupted several times by appreciative cheers.' The composer appeared on stage and was personally applauded for several minutes. The French critics were less enthusiastic but the public, in spite of there being a lack of 'tunes', liked the whole evening and attempts to find a theatre in London were made, unsuccessfully.

The opera has never been staged again, although Constant Lambert salvaged some of the interlude music by arranging it into *Caprice Peruvien*. Nor did Berners complete another opera, though he had already mentioned another project ('I am anxious to embrace a work of a serious character'). There are no references either with pride or regret. Perhaps the back-stage dramas were too intense, the success too localised and brief for the two years he had spent on it. Yet there seems to have been no revulsion, either. The next year, Berners lent George Moore a volume of Mérimée's plays, presumably so that he could read

---

[*] A. L. Rowse says in *Friends and Contemporaries* that Berners once shared a house in Paris with Stravinsky and Diaghilev. This seems the most likely time, so perhaps he was only lunching at the Ritz.

the original text (on which Moore commented to Emerald Cunard, 'It is altogether without emotion and I always understood that emotion is the soul of music'). It had been a slight work by operatic standards, but the largest by far that Berners had attempted and, in the same way, if its success was limited, it was the greatest success he had yet had. All the same, opera had proved not the way ahead, but a cul-de-sac.

Chapter VIII

The Triumph of Neptune

Mrs Tyrwhitt had feared that music might distract her son from his career. The danger now was that social life might distract him from his music. Glimpses of Berners' life are still vouchsafed by her diary. The Marchesa Casati walked round the lake at Faringdon in the January moonlight of 1921 with the Marquis de Bourbon and 'G'. In 1922, 'Mrs Trefusis and I went to church.' Siegfried Sassoon, Osbert or Sacheverell Sitwell, the Wellesleys and Nicolsons continue to appear; there is a lunch at Blenheim from which 'G brought Mr George Keppel', and one at Faringdon, which Lady Ottoline Morrell found terrifying, with witty remarks required but an undercurrent of nervousness. Norah Lindsay is always popping over from her own beautiful garden at Sutton Courtenay and the Asquiths come once from the Wharf, whose garden Lindsay also designed. In May 1922, she wrote expansively, 'Went to Academy. Then to his new house 3 Chesham Place, had tea and then took me to the station. Back to Swindon 7.35.'

This house Berners shared with his old friend Gerald Agar-Robartes. There was also room for a valet and, until he got married, for William Crack. Agar-Robartes had more than a Christian name in common with Berners. His family had lived in Lanhydrock in Cornwall since the sixteenth century, when it was a simple manor house; in the eighteenth century it got a bit smaller and in the nineteenth quite a lot bigger. Like Berners, Agar-Robartes left the diplomatic service and inherited considerable estates and a title, becoming Viscount Clifden. His tastes, too, were similar. A. L. Rowse, a friend, remembers him as 'a bit of a connoisseur, bought pictures, Boudin etc . . . Two superb bronze urns for Lanhydrock, which came from the Comte d'Artois' villa Bagatelle. When I told dear Gerald Berners he was pipping with envy. Actually those urns would go much better at Faringdon.' In Rowse's phrase,

Agar-Robartes 'went to the good' – good works, Liberal MP, against appeasement. He was one of ten children, only one of whom married, so that he ended up living in the great house with two sisters. The title is now extinct.

Berners at this time seems more like a man in his early twenties than in his early forties, curious but a little cautious. While not rebelling against his inheritance, he was determined not to be controlled by it. He tried on bits and shook them off if they did not appeal. Diana Mosley asked him if he had ever been to the House of Lords and he replied, 'Yes I did go once but a bishop stole my umbrella and I never went there again'; indeed, he took his seat in December 1923 but it is more likely that it was the debate about widening the powers of the Mersey Docks than a thieving prelate that discouraged him from returning.

To inherit wealth publicly is to receive begging letters and Berners responded to one from Clive Bell, on behalf of the ageing Walter Sickert, with twenty pounds, adding, 'I wish I could make it more but I will help again later if necessary.' He cheered up another distinguished old man when Sassoon took him and his clavichord to visit the Poet Laureate, Robert Bridges, and later Berners was among those who contributed to buy such an instrument for the poet's eightieth birthday. Curiously, as he was not to publish anything for ten years, Berners joined the Society of Authors: thirty shillings for a year's membership, the same for the pension fund.

He had also made a younger literary friend. Sir Coleridge Kennard had been introduced to Ronald Firbank before 1907. Presumably it was Kennard who introduced his own mother to Berners. Widowed, remarried and widowed again, she was now Helen Carew. In 1918, she arranged for Firbank to meet first the Sitwells and then Berners by the same technique: Firbank was assured that they were fervent admirers, before a visit to his rooms opposite Magdalen College, Oxford was permitted.

All of which may seem a remarkable fuss about meeting a novelist who was not widely known or admired, but such a meeting was indeed remarkable. Firbank, then as ever, had scarcely any friends at all. Berners had been aware of him for some years. He had seen him at the Ballets Russes, seated more or less upside-down. When they had actually met, Firbank had been so incoherent as to appear drunk, and Berners, sighting him later in Piccadilly, thought it best merely to shout, 'You are my favourite author,' and pass on. They had other things in common: Firbank had been born in the 1880s into a 'tame,

conventional and rather pompous milieu', though *nouveau riche* rather
than aristocratic. He too had been packed off to Europe and Scoones's
in the hope of turning him into a diplomat. Osbert Sitwell remembered
him as surprisingly but not consistently well read, a result of his
selecting books for the beauty of their bindings rather than their
contents, as Berners occasionally did. He too dressed conventionally in
dark, well-cut suits but the effect was very different: 'his physique,
however, invested these accoutrements with an element of fantasy, and
with his serpentine wriggling, his arch gestures and perpetual giggle, he
had the equivocal air of a female impersonator'. In modern terms
Firbank was outrageously camp, while Berners was still in the closet.
Firbank was greatly influenced by personal appearance and once
retreated from an introduction muttering all too audibly, 'Oh no, he is
much too ugly'. He made an exception of Berners and it may even have
been that their shared lack of good looks was an unspoken bond. The
outbreak of war in 1914 shattered Firbank, as another war was to shatter
Berners in 1939, and each retreated to Oxford. There Firbank talked to
no one, almost literally, and wrote. In these years each was a modernist,
working out his own style and producing work that, admired by a circle
of sympathetic fellow-artists, led to great interest as to what they would
do next. What Firbank did next was publish his best-known novel,
Valmouth, at his own expense in 1919. It contains the sentence 'the
maître d'orchestre had struck up a capricious waltz, an enigmatic au
delà laden air: Lord Berners? Scriabin? Tschaikovski?'

What this account only hints at is Firbank's shyness. Berners wrote,
'To become a friend of Firbank was no easy matter. One had to take a
good deal of trouble. There was one's own shyness to be overcome as
well as his.' Berners was shy in an ordinary way. Like Firbank, he
gained a reputation as a wit by occasional brief interjections rather than
by holding the table, as Wilde could. Like Firbank, he was attracted to
society, but unlike Firbank he found it easy enough to move among
acquaintances in a formal way, as long as nothing more revealing was
required. When self-conscious, he merely gave 'little quick blinks of
both eyes – very endearing'. Firbank's affliction was altogether more
intense and it is fair to say that it dominated his life. It seems likely that
the instance Berners gives here was of Helen Carew: 'A lady who was
one of Firbank's earliest friends and admirers told me that often when
she used to visit him while he was living in Oxford (at his own
invitation – there was no question of intrusion) she would find him in
such a state of nervous diffidence that he would only talk to her with his

back turned and looking out of the window.' His was the sort of shyness that drew attention to itself, so that once at least he hid under the table rather than face a head-waiter, thus giving himself something to be shy about.

The friendship flourished in Rome and Berners became skilled at dealing with Firbank's elusive style:

Conversation with him was like playing tennis with an erratic tennis-player. You never knew in what direction his thoughts would fly. After a time a sort of technique could be acquired. It was no use for instance ever asking him a question, or, at all events, to expect a reasonable answer. He seemed to dread being pinned down to any assertion of even the most simple nature. 'Where does so-and-so live?' one might ask. 'Why should one live anywhere?' he would reply, and go off into peals of convulsive laughter generally ending in a paroxysm of coughing. The phrase 'I wonder!' was constantly on his lips, and uttered in a tone that seemed to evoke all the unsolved riddles of the universe.

Berners, like Sitwell, discerned a certain steel beneath the silliness, which fits in with Firbank's surprising ability to look after himself, or at least survive when travelling; Berners even records that Firbank, 'in the course of an expedition down the Nile on a dahabeah . . . succeeded, single-handed, in quelling a mutiny.'

There was one curious hiccup in their relationship. In October 1923, Firbank lunched with Berners and they condemned together the ugliness of a plaster cast of Psyche in his house. Next day there was a larger lunch and the guests, presumably led by Berners, who must have brought up the subject, decided to send the offending statuette to the one who so disliked it. First they all signed: Berners, Edith and Sacheverell Sitwell, William Walton, Geoffrey Lovelace, Aldous and Maria Huxley, Evan Morgan, Harold and Vita Nicolson. Then the butler took it round in a taxi. The gesture seems less amusing than obscurely offensive. Firbank was in fact mildly amused and mildly offended, but he bore Berners no grudge.

A lunch the next year led to another unsuccessful joke:

Thinking I heard Ronald approaching the house, a sudden impulse seized me to put on a Negro mask and surprise him by appearing at one of the windows. However it was not Ronald after all. And a small boy who happened to be passing on a bicycle looked up and was so frightened that he fell off and was run into by a motor. He was luckily unhurt, but a crowd collected. At this juncture Ronald himself arrived, and when I explained to him what had happened, he said, 'That will teach him to concentrate in future.'

Berners liked and possessed many masks, some, designed by Oliver Messel, less terrifying than the negro one seems to have been. The story grew, perhaps from this incident, that he wore them when being driven and would look out of the window to frighten passing children. He said once that they made a great impression in France and Italy, but in England people thought it was the squire out for a drive. Beverley Nichols makes slightly more than most others of this:

> Of late, certain tourists on the main roads of France and Italy have returned to their native lands with startling stories of an Apparition. These stories have variations but the main theme is always the same. It concerns a masked figure that flashes by them in a high-powered car. Sometimes the figure wears a chalk-white mask with a shock of orange hair; sometimes the mask is negroid, with staring eyes and cherry-coloured lips; sometimes it is a mask with a broad forehead and a heavy jowl, bearing a singular resemblance to Beethoven. And always it sweeps past swiftly, leaving only a cloud of very real dust to persuade the spectator he has not seen a ghost . . . in Lord Berners' own words, 'I get very bored with my own face. To go through the world with the same face is quite as wearisome as to go through the world with the same suit.'

Once more driver William Crack is a convincing if diminishing witness: he never saw him wear a mask in the car, though curiously, 'he'd put a different hat on going through a town'.

In November 1924, Firbank was in need of a place in Rome and would have moved into Berners' house if his cook could have been moved out. This was six months after the death of his mother and he was still distraught. His health was worse, he looked terrible, and after he had seen a doctor in London he was found drunk at the Café Royal exclaiming, 'I don't want to die'; presumably the doctor had raised the possibility. He was at last enjoying some success with his novels. *Prancing Nigger* was much talked about in New York and he thought he might set his next one there, though he had never been. He went to Egypt, quelled an uprising perhaps, and returned to Rome in 1926.

Berners motored out with him to Lake Nemi and watched him 'ambling down the precipitous streets of Genzano followed by a crowd of children shouting "Ridolini! Ridolini!" [a popular Italian comic film character]. From time to time Firbank would stop and scatter handfuls of nickel coins, a proceeding which only tended to aggravate this situation.' Less than a week later Berners got a telephone summons to the Hotel Quirinale. The doctor said that Firbank was ill but better, and had sent away his nurse for the night. Berners went round in the morning and found that he had died.

Muddle ensued. Firbank's passport had only an unhelpful address in Monmouthshire. The death had taken place at the beginning of a bank holiday. By luck, the address of his solicitors was found on a crumpled piece of paper, a lease that had been sent to him to sign, and eventually his sister Heather was reached by telephone. She said that he should be buried 'suitably' in Rome. Berners was asked by the British Consulate to make arrangements and on 1 June, ten days after his death, on 'an early summer morning under a cloudless Italian sky, amid the cypresses and roses and singing of nightingales', there was a funeral service and Firbank was placed in a vault in a double shell casket with silk lining, in the Protestant cemetery. Unfortunately it then emerged that he was a Roman Catholic. Heather Firbank, with some difficulty, transferred the body to the Catholic cemetery at Verano by late September.

Sometimes this error, more Orton than Firbank, is recounted to show Berners as a hopeless innocent, protected from the world by his money and incapable of organising anything; this is unfair. As he wrote to Jocelyn Brooke, 'To know Ronald Firbank doesn't mean that one got to know very much about him, at least I didn't.' Firbank had once said to him, 'The Church of Rome wouldn't have me so I laugh at her', which Berners had taken to mean not, as was in fact the case, that Firbank had wanted a job in the Vatican, but that he had considered conversion but nothing had come of it. In fact he had become a Roman Catholic in 1908. There had been no mention of priests or last rites at the hotel. In any case, Berners maintained, Firbank would have preferred to lie with Shelley and Keats rather than among a crowd of Italian bourgeois.

Berners appreciated an unusual man and writer as few others did, and their eight years of friendship reflect credit on his tact and sensitivity. His own writing was not at all influenced, as many others were, by Firbank's original way with dialogue and plot, but he continued to read the novels, sometimes aloud to his friends. Years later he made some jottings towards a defence of Firbank's position (which would have shielded him too), but they never quite cohere into an argument:

Ronald Firbank is frivolous par excellence. Frivolity combined with

beauty, humour and fantasy. One should not expect to find in his work
any weighty sociological or philosophical judgements, any more than one
would in the books of Edward Lear . . .

There is a good deal to be said for frivolity. Frivolous people, when all
is said and done, do less harm in the world than some of our
philanthropisers and reformers. Mistrust a man who never has an
occasional flash of silliness . . . One contemporary reviewer said of him
that he was essentially a second-rate artist. Now that is one thing that
Firbank was essentially not. He was a minor artist perhaps but never a
second-rate one. There is obscenity at moments but never vulgarity.
Silliness, yes, but never triteness or stupidity.

It is all too negative, too much on the defensive. The distinction
between second-rate and minor is well made, and he might have
continued, for himself at least, with frivolous but not trivial, silly but
not foolish, serious but never solemn. In one draft he did include:
'There is a legend that our Lord said "Blessed are the Frivolous for
theirs is the Kingdom of Heaven" and that it was suppressed by St
Paul.' Even so, Berners was only frivolous if frivolity is allowed to be
compatible with a willingness to work, to study consciously and
conscientiously the techniques required. Certainly his flight from
Victorian heaviness and emotion, his refusal to preach, his fear of
boring, let alone becoming pompous, stripped him of the trappings of
seriousness; but that is not quite the same thing. While such a man as
Berners is not taking life seriously, he may have time for anything, from
the latest gossip to arcane scholarship. It is engaging for someone to
make light of all problems, including his own – at least for a time.

Berners had the financial and emotional independence not to have to
grow up, and does not seem to have had any wish to do so. He was in a
position to avoid what he found unpleasant. Never ambitious, he made
the decision against profundity early on and stuck to it. Generous Lord
David Cecil described him as 'very boyish – not even a youth'.
Speaking of a much later time, he continued:

He was a light-weight talker but that is a very nice kind of talker. It
didn't involve intellectual discussion or even complex analyses of
character or anything like that, but it was full of taste and humour in
such a light vein. And it was relaxed, it wasn't artificial, it was
spontaneous . . . I think it wasn't that he had a macabre sense of humour
so much as that I think he was so anxious not to be upset by anything
. . . If something rather horrible or painful came up in the war he'd sort

of make a joke about it and then change the subject. It was a slightly inadequate reaction.

Cecil uses 'childlike' rather than 'childish' and found that 'In spite of all these extremely sophisticated and rather hard-hearted people he must have seen a lot of, I would have said he had a sort of innocence in a way. It was incurable.' There are parallels with Max Beerbohm, whose biography Cecil wrote. They shared many acquaintances, a few friends and a taste for parody; they liked each other's humour and style – not quite unkind, but mischievous, impish.

Beerbohm left London for Italy before the First World War but he and Berners became friends after it, in spite of geography. In 1923 Beerbohm did a sketch of Berners; in 1924 Berners called on Beerbohm in Rapallo on his way home; in 1926 the visit was returned when the Beerbohms came to Faringdon and left with a goose. When Berners' letters stray from dates and train times, he is almost excessively polite:

My Dear Max,
    A thousand thanks for your wonderful gift [a book] – I shall certainly not put it in the guest room – it would inevitably be stolen – rather shall I keep it on my own bedside table – chained, as were bibles in the olden days, or, as, in more modern times, was, in the washing-room of the Grand Hotel in Bologna – the soap. I don't know which among the illustrations I like best. I am very fond of the sentimental 'Twilight in the Old House' but for sheer elegance of posture I think 'By the Fireside 1915', fairly takes, as H. James might have said, the cake.

Berners was the junior partner, not only by eleven years in age but in reputation and talent; he liked the role, and the friendship lasted. One idea he may have taken from Beerbohm was that of cutting up and emending pictures, though he had added moustaches to the portraits of his ancestors before they met.

Another taste in common was for masks. Discussing the great importance for Beerbohm of wearing one, Cecil writes, 'Half a child, wholly an artist, he could fulfil himself only in the universe of his imagination'; Berners, with the proportions reversed, played with masks literally, if not in cars, and it seems almost too obvious, too heavy-handed an interest for a shy man. It is true that there were more opportunities for wearing masks then. Lady Diana Cooper wrote to her husband that, at yet another fancy-dress ball, 'the rest of us were porters. We thought we were pretty funny all dashing into the room,

shouting "Porteur, porteur". Gerald Berners was good as a hunting
man with a marvellously funny mask by Oliver Messel, who had
announced his intention of going as Nurse Cavell but was dissuaded.'
Masks were Oliver Messel's way to success. In 1925 Diaghilev used
some for a ballet called *Zephyre et Flore*. C. B. Cochran asked Messel to
design his 1926 revue, and in 1928 he scored a spectacular success with
more masks worn for Noël Coward's 'Dance Little Lady' in *This Year
of Grace*. His career subsequently rarely faltered and he became the
leading stage designer of his day. Messel was one of the most noticeable
and charming of several young men born just after the turn of the
century and often connected with the arts who formed a set that Berners
found congenial.

In 1921 Diaghilev had unexpectedly changed direction and, instead of
laying down the rules for the future, dived into the past. *The Sleeping
Princess* (later *Beauty*) was an immensely opulent production of Petipa's
greatest classical ballet. When things went wrong on the first night,
Stravinsky recorded, Diaghilev had a nervous breakdown and sobbed
like a child. It was the most expensive failure of his career and he left
England with unpaid debts and thus without his scenery and costumes.
The intellectuals hated it; Raymond Mortimer spoke for Bloomsbury
when he described it as 'a ballet all clothes and three hours long, a ballet
that delighted those who hated the *Sacre*'. Lytton Strachey told
Sacheverell Sitwell that it made him feel sick. It did not, however, make
Sitwell feel sick; on the contrary, he became fascinated by the theatrical
past, particularly the Victorian past.

Diaghilev recovered in Monte Carlo. In August 1924 he made the
acquaintance of Lord Rothermere, the proprietor of the *Daily Mail*,
who had a house nearby at Roquebrune. In November Diaghilev was
back at the Coliseum in London and, though in diminished form, was
received with delight. Both the company and its audience, however, had
changed: 'the whiff of artistic fashion and aristocratic pretence that
hung about its repertory appealed to a different clientele than the
catholic works of high modernism. With the failure of *The Sleeping
Princess* Diaghilev cast in his lot with High Bohemia.' Berners could
follow him there.

After further financial success, Diaghilev grasped that there was more
money to be made in London than anywhere else in the world. He
began to look for an English backer. Having failed with Lord

Beaverbrook, he remembered Lord Rothermere. The elaborate courtship that followed included a bombardment of telephone calls, supper,
beautiful ballerinas ('in spite of his tallness and corpulence,' said one,
'Lord R. danced with remarkable lightness and a great deal of rhythm'),
and the promise of an English ballet using English talents. But whose?
William Walton had made just the right kind of *enfant terrible* splash
with *Façade*, first performed in the Sitwells' drawing-room in 1922, but
he was rejected. He played his boisterous overture *Portsmouth Point* to
Diaghilev at the Savoy Hotel, but played it badly and made the mistake
of bringing his friend Constant Lambert, who played his own work
better. Lambert is said to have been commissioned with the words, '"I
like your ballet. I'm going to produce it but not with that silly title." He
[Diaghilev] took a big red pencil, crossed out *Adam and Eve* and wrote
Romeo and Juliet over it. Constant burst into uncontrollable tears.'

Tears do not sound like Lambert, who was extraordinarily young
(twenty) but formidable; it is true, however, that the *suite dansée* that he
had written with Angus Morrison became the 'more English' *Romeo and
Juliet*. Lambert was the son of a well-known Australian painter and had
simply turned up on the doorstep of the Sitwells one day, uninvited but
welcome. Soon Osbert declared himself in love with 'the fast-talking,
cigarette-smoking, outspoken job lot Apollo'. Lambert became a close
friend of William Walton, though also his rival. When it had been
decided that some poems of Edith's should be set to music, the Sitwells
naturally turned to Walton; but he was reluctant. The merest suggestion
that in that case young Lambert might like to try his hand changed his
mind. *Façade* went through many changes and gradually more public
performances, and when it scored a great success in 1926, Lambert, to
whom it was dedicated, acted as copyist. He had composed a few bars
and took over as reciter – at which role, Walton later pronounced, he
was the best ever.

Before that there had been a row over the sets of *Romeo and Juliet*,
and Lambert – unestablished and scarcely more than a boy – had
insisted on seeing Diaghilev, all-powerful as well as personally
commanding, and wrote later, 'he became very angry . . . I naturally lost
my temper . . . it was rather a dreadful scene.' Though not sharing his
wildness, or his pronounced enthusiasm for wine and women, Berners
agreed with this daring youth about song. Lambert 'abominated the
fabricated nationalism of their immediate forebears', as did Walton.
Lambert appeared flippant, admired the modern French composers,
was drawn to ballet, wrote well, and above all was wonderful company,

funny and stimulating. He became the musician whom Berners knew and loved best. On his side, Lambert, who disliked high society, relished Berners' jokes, admired his music and quick musical intelligence and became something of a champion on his behalf – in time an extremely influential champion.

Diaghilev, the man of action, once said to Berners, 'One always ends by getting what one wants. It is only a question of wanting it sufficiently.' Berners, passive, stoical if need be, commented, 'Yes – but one often gets things one doesn't want. However little one may want them.' Diaghilev wanted a British ballet and for his second and, as it turned out, final commission of a ballet score by a British composer he selected Berners. In January 1925, Berners wrote in the *Evening Standard* that Diaghilev had suggested the policemen's strike as a theme: 'The subject frightened me. One does not want to offend the police. I also felt that the subject was too topical and transient and of too local an interest.' He preferred such unchanging British customs and institutions as bank holiday on Hampstead Heath, cricket matches at Lord's, the Henley Regatta, the Derby, and the Lord Mayor's Show. Pondering with elaborate but perhaps real modesty on why he had been asked, he could 'only suppose that the kind of English ballet he [Diaghilev] has in view is not to be a serious one, and that it will be satirical rather than romantic.'

In fact no one seems to have had much idea of what it should be. Berners wrote some music, which Diaghilev liked but, having once wanted a modern subject, he now favoured an adaptation of *The Merry Wives of Windsor*; or maybe *As You Like It*. Edith Sitwell once more wrote some verse, as she had for *Façade*. Then Sacheverell Sitwell, still very much the younger brother but more interested in ballet than his siblings, took Diaghilev to Benjamin Pollock and H. J. Webb, a famous shop where the impresario examined, and indeed bought, some of the 'Penny Plain or Twopence Coloured' sheets that were used as sets in model theatres for children. They could be adapted for the real theatre and could solve the problem that Diaghilev's pronounced lack of enthusiasm for English painters had created. Pollock and Webb were duly credited for the sets in the programme. Sitwell enthused about the whole tradition of spectacular English pantomime, then still very much alive. Diaghilev commissioned him to write the book in their spirit.

On 14 September, Diaghilev summoned his new choreographer, George Balanchine, to the Palace Hotel in Florence. Soon they, Sacheverell Sitwell and Berners were at Montegufoni, Sir George

Sitwell's castle outside the city. Sitwell wrote to his wife, 'Diaghilev is charming, Berners rather less so', and later complained that his composer was 'too busy with Lady Cunard to think of anything else, and is really rather hopeless'. Berners, writing to Diaghilev in French, perhaps corroborates this: 'I don't feel very inspired at the moment. However I bought a very pretty Renoir this morning and I hope things will now go better.' Diaghilev took Balanchine and Serge Lifar, who was to be the leading dancer, off on a cultural tour of Naples and Pompeii, while Berners got on with the score at his house in Rome. When the others went to Capri, Balanchine came back to Rome. Later they all rehearsed in Paris. Some of the music was written while crossing the Channel, some while Berners had influenza. Berners admitted that the score was as 'variegated as a Christmas tree. You will find a little of everything in it from Tchaikovsky to Léo Delibes. And above all it is not in the least "modern".' Unlike his hero, Stravinsky, Berners was growing more accessible with age. This was perhaps due to the influence of his audience: *Le Carrosse du Saint-Sacrément* had been written to be performed in Paris; this was to be premièred in London.

Berners had had little idea how to compose for ballet and it is not surprising if some Tchaikovsky crept in: he had been given a score of *The Sleeping Princess* as a model. Lambert and Walton gave advice. Among Berners' unpublished papers is an essay entitled 'The time-element in music'. In it he writes:

> There are no hard and fast rules to determine the exact length a piece of music should be; nor are there canons to govern the timing of entries, the length of development or the exact amount of suspense to be inflicted on the ear before it is relieved by resolution. These are matters which depend on the tact and sensibility of the composer. If he is lacking in this sensibility, the music that he produces is apt to be unsatisfactory in that, if he errs on the side of length, it will seem to drag; if on the side of brevity, it will appear spasmodic or trivial.

Berners was never one to outstay his welcome. Indeed, 'My own point of view is that it is better to err in the latter respect, for music is not like a book in which we can skip passages when they begin to get boring.' He considers opera for a moment, then adds, 'In ballet music the time question is happily settled by the exigencies of choreography.' In another note he admits that choreography is master: 'Bad choreography may spoil good music but good music can never save bad choreography,' and he continues:

Time measurement in choreographic music is different to that of
symphonic music. A solo dance lasting two minutes is quite an
important affair. The eye and ear combined seem to tire more easily than
when the ear alone is concerned. Thus it happens that when music
destined originally for symphonic purposes is used for ballet, it often has
to be arranged, transposed and hacked about, so that if not performed by
a skilful hand, it is liable to suffer. On the other hand too profound a
respect for the composer may impair choreographic perfection.

It was in connection with this problem that Diaghilev once confessed
how, in the depths of the night behind locked doors, he had cut out four
bars from one of the scenes of *L'Oiseau de Feu*.

Sitwell had come up with twelve suitable scenes rather than a story
for the ballet. Among the twenty-six characters (apart from fairies,
harlequins, pages, ogres and attendants on Neptune) were the two
heroes, one rather surprisingly a journalist, the other Tom Tug, a sailor
danced by Serge Lifar. He sees Fairyland through a magic telescope and
decides to explore with his friend. They are shipwrecked (Berners
supplies percussion only, an original effect) but rescued by a god. Then
the story pauses for a scene in a newspaper office and another in The
Frozen Wood (known to facetious stage-hands as 'Wigan by Night'),
where fairies glitter and fly in the moonlight. In Act 2, Tom's wife does
a polka with a dandy, but as they are about to embrace romantically, a
giant hand with a knife appears – the sailor's spirit. Then there is an evil
grotto with giants, through which the travellers battle, only for the
journalist to be seized and sawn in half at the ogres' castle. Back on
London Bridge a drunken negro upsets and breaks the magic telescope
but, in the end, it does not matter: Tom becomes a fairy prince and
marries Neptune's daughter. The whole lasted forty-five minutes and
was called *The Triumph of Neptune*.

This conglomeration of incident and characters might seem the last
subject in the world for Balanchine, the greatest of all abstract
choreographers. He was, however, only twenty-two and had been in the
West less than two years. Diaghilev had taken him on after asking, 'Can
you arrange dances for operas?' 'Yes.' 'Can you do it quickly?' 'Yes.' So
Balanchine was still willing to turn his extraordinary inventive talent to
anything and, though the fairies were given curious jerky movements
and had to hold angular positions of the arms above the head (possibly
because he mistook faulty drawing for authentic pose), he made a great
success of it. In particular, he created 'a wonderful negro dance' for
himself as Snowball, his last dancing role for Diaghilev.

Lydia Sokolova complained as late as the orchestral rehearsal that her part was inadequate. Diaghilev sent her to Berners, who was on stage, 'looking with a hint of mockery the quiet kind of dandy he was'. After lunch she was given a sort of reel, danced to the music of a hornpipe, created with amazing speed by Balanchine and, in spite of an immensely heavy costume, as a 'kilted Britannia' she stopped the show each night. The sailor's wife and the dandy were interrupted by a drunk singing 'The Last Rose of Summer'. This is a characteristic joke, but was not disdainful – Berners chose it as his favourite song in a questionnaire that year.*

It was the only new offering of the season and the largest ballet that Diaghilev had presented since the disaster of *The Sleeping Princess*. It was also different in tone from the airy impressionism of his other ballets – 'a Frith among Whistlers'. As usual, it was born in chaos: 'Once again the scenery was actually being completed during the playing of the overture.' It had been intended to open the season, but emerged only just before the end. Nevertheless, the first audience at the Lyceum on 3 December 1926 applauded practically everything. Sacheverell Sitwell, with William Walton (who had helped out in the rush by orchestrating 'four large numbers') and his beautiful wife Georgia, wearing pink flowers on her white ermine, looked rather pink and nervous himself at first.

At the end flowers, hats and objects of one kind and another were showered on the stage and there were innumerable curtain calls. Lifar caught several wreaths, one of which he flung round the shoulders of Berners, who, when asked to take a curtain call by Diaghilev, refused – it was quickly being repeated everywhere – on the grounds that his aunt had threatened to disinherit him if he ever appeared on the stage. Nevertheless, Beaton, who had himself been 'quite sick with delight', described Berners as 'like a bald wax figure in a cheap clothes shop, bowing and smiling – and the curtain of course came down on his bald pate'. Sitwell, no more at ease, accepted, but losing his sense of direction made his entrance with his back to the audience and tried to pass through the scenery.

---

* Berners' other selections were: 'My favourite composer, Bach; my favourite tune is the third of Schoenberg's six pieces for pianoforte because it is so obscure that one is never likely to grow tired of it (which you must admit is as good a reason for preferring a tune as any other); and if by 'singer' you mean any kind of singer, then the one I prefer is Little Tich. But, on the other hand, if you mean concert singers, please substitute Clara Butt.' *The Gramophone*, December, 1926.

Though there were dissenting voices and even boos from the cheap seats, broadly speaking *The Triumph of Neptune* was a triumph for all. It was repeated nightly and at Monte Carlo the following year, when '*le public fait une ovation à Lord Berners*'. A few changes were made; the ogres were dropped and Berners added some music for a fantastic cupid, who had red and silver roses on his head, a pink shirt, blue stockings and white breeches, as well as the identifying bow and arrow. He was also able to revise and re-orchestrate the whole score himself, which he conscientiously did. Antwerp and Paris were less charmed by this farrago of Englishness – 'the puerile romanticism of a race of grown-up, laughing children' – and the Americans were later unimpressed, although galas were graced by King Farouk of Egypt and King Alfonso of Spain. The music became popular in its own right. It has been recorded four times (complete once, the suite thrice), twice by Sir Thomas Beecham including *Mr Punch and the Street Party* (1979), and other ballets have used much of it. Berners had conquered a new and congenial world, had combined with the greatest talents of his time to happy effect, and had extended his range, to which it now seemed no limits should be set. Sachevell Sitwell came to find Berners charming, and dedicated *Spanish Baroque Art* to him in 1931. He even brought his family to stay at Faringdon when hard up, and borrowed Berners' London house.

Yet Virginia Woolf had recorded in her diary in February 1925, before any of this had begun, how Berners had described his musical career to her:

> One day he wrote two [three actually and it is not clear they were his first] marches for fun. Stravinsky saw them, thought them good, and they were published. So he was accepted as a serious musician with only four lessons from Tovey in counterpoint. He had an astonishing facility. He could write things that sounded alright. Suddenly, last year, all his pleasure in it went. He met a painter, asked him how you paint; bought 'hogsheads' – (meant hogs' bristles) and canvas and copied an Italian picture, brilliantly, consummately, says Clive Bell. Has the same facility there: but it will come to nothing he said, like the other.

There followed more than ten years without a major work. Berners never again wrote music without being asked to, or without collaborating in ballet or film. He would have said that his muse had deserted him, which is close to what he told Virginia Woolf; that he simply did not want to compose any more. Others would say that if he had needed money and it was his only talent, he would have got on with it or that, more frivolously still, his rich man's life was too enjoyable for him to bother with the effort. Not long before his death he allowed, with disappointingly conventional regret, that there was some truth in this. Edward James described such distraction taking place in a literal way while he was still composing: 'I can always tell when Gerald's weekend guests arrive. There's a sudden cymbal clash.'

The men from Porlock were invited.

Chapter IX

The Painter

Lord Berners
Told a crowd of learners
That if they wished to compose
They should paint or write prose.

Anyone who knew that Berners had been a friend of the Futurists in Rome and was to be a friend of Edward James and Salvador Dali; anyone who had seen his portrait by Gregorio Prieto, in which, serious in a dark suit, he is holding up a lobster; anyone who knew his delight in a surprise or a joke or had heard his sharply contemporary music, filled with allusion and parody – any such person would have been confident in describing what sort of painter Berners would be: an English surrealist, not cruel, but mocking as well as whimsical. They would have been quite wrong.

Beverley Nichols recounted how Berners set about learning the technique of oil painting. He was talking in a tone curiously reminiscent of Nichols' own, of how he was confident that he would be a good cook: 'For what is the difference between taste and colour? . . . Once one had mastered the elements of cooking one would be as unlikely to put too much sugar into a soufflé as to put too much sentimentality into an aria.'

Nichols, writing in early 1927, continues:

As though to prove his point, he showed me some pictures he had recently painted. Two years ago he had never painted anything at all. Then suddenly he said to himself 'I will paint'. (Rows of mildewed tubes in my attic bear witness to a similar desire, frequently recurring, on my own part.) But with Berners the desire bore fruit. He summoned a Royal Academician. He said 'I must paint. What do I paint with and what do I paint on? In fact, how do I paint?' The Royal Academician (it might just as well have been a cook or an architect) informed him that one first spread an even layer of colour over one's surface, that one must then . . . but of course you know all this for yourself.

The fact remains that Berners' little pictures are good pictures. The first thing he did was a copy of a Poelenburgh. The anatomy of the lady in the picture is almost suspiciously accurate. The whole spirit of the picture, apart from its mere mechanics, is charmingly caught. There followed copies of Dürer prints, in which he 'put in' his own colouring, then suddenly an original interior, which, to me at least, is beautiful in colour and design. Now he is painting Cézannes. Or was painting Cézannes. For one day Diaghileff heard of this departure from his first love, and stormed into his Lordship's room, crying 'Je vous défends de faire de la peinture! Je vous le défends!' And since Diaghileff can be more terrifying than Satan, the paintings were put away, and our hero wandered back to the piano.

The music that Diaghilev wanted must have been for *The Triumph of Neptune* the previous autumn. The 'two years' since the summoning of the Royal Academician agrees with Virginia Woolf's diary that Berners had turned to painting more seriously in 1925, probably before the subject of the ballet was finally decided. The name of the Academician remained a secret that Berners would never divulge. Nichols was unaware that Berners had been sketching all his life and did not mention the painter whom Berners was to copy, rearrange and model himself on, to the exclusion of all others: Corot.

With slight qualifications, the faint praise of Berners' pictures by his friends can be allowed to stand. David Cecil found them 'lively but classical really, quiet and sensitive'. Harold Acton remembered them as conservative, conventional settings with pine trees, very charming but unremarkable. Berners himself confessed (his word) that he had been taken as a boy to the Royal Academy Exhibition, where he saw Lord Leighton's *Perseus and Andromeda*:

The experience stands out as one of the most exciting landmarks of my childhood . . . A buxom Andromeda occupied the centre of the canvas. Over her sprawled the dragon huge and ominous with jaws aflame and one wing outspread that covered her like an umbrella, while up above in the sky Perseus hovered on his winged steed. Andromeda was being very brave about the whole business, very British; indeed her phlegmatic attitude, given the alarming situation in which she found herself, almost makes one suspect that she knew all along that she was in the Royal Academy and that everything would come out all right in the end.

> Another picture in the same exhibition that impressed me very much
> was one called 'The Doctor' by Luke Fildes ... In a humble cottage a
> doctor was sitting by the bedside of a sick child, peering into its face
> with a very earnest expression; while the mother watched in an attitude
> of pathetic anxiety ... The doctor was wearing a very elegant morning
> coat and he must have been a far more expensive doctor than such
> humble cottage folk as these could afford; but he looked a very nice man
> and no doubt he was giving his services at a reduced fee.

So, just as his first interest in music had been stirred by the visual, his
first interest in painting was stirred by literary associations. This was,
however, the contemporary convention and by the time Berners wrote
about it, as is clear from his tone, he is well aware that such an approach
is now frowned upon. Indeed, he came to adopt the expected scorn for
the institution: 'An artist is never a bourgeois. Except a Royal
Academician. The Royal Academy is the bourgeois painter's spiritual
(and material) home.' The end of his 'confession' regrets that such
pictures are no longer shown, so that it is 'in vain that one searches the
modern exhibitions for anything really funny'.

There is nothing remotely amusing about the vast bulk of Berners'
own paintings, of which there came to be a great number, many of them
of the countryside round Rome. A hundred years earlier, Corot had
spent three years in many of the same places, producing at least 200
drawings and 150 small landscape paintings out of doors. He also
produced two large exhibition pictures indoors and, as he only showed
the other Italian work once during his lifetime, his growing reputation
rested entirely on his studio painting. Later, when everything had been
seen, opinion reversed itself: 'The view "that his early Italian landscapes
and late figure pieces represent his highest achievement" began to take
hold in the early decades of this century. By 1930, at least in advanced
circles, it was accepted as fact.' That this was Berners' opinion is clear
and recorded: in an uncharacteristically pompous note on their cultural
tradition, Berners listed the Frenchmen he admired: 'Voltaire, Balzac,
Flaubert, Stendhal, Renan, and Anatole France, Corot (the early
Corot), Delacroix, Géricault, Monet, Ingres, Sisley, Cézanne, Matisse'.
A later note makes the same preference explicit, 'Corot, finding that his
fluffy landscapes went down well with the general public, painted
thousands of them. But from time to time he produced exquisite
pictures in his early manner, the Belfry of Douai for instance, painted
towards the end of his life.'

So in admiring and emulating the Roman landscapes, Berners was showing taste, not entirely classical and conventional, and at least up with advanced circles. Oscar Wilde would have found his admiration natural. 'Corot seems to go with music,' he has Sir Robert observe in *An Ideal Husband*. Berners' own explanation is simple. The landscape he most loved was that around Rome and 'the directness and simplicity of Corot's early painting seems the perfect method of dealing with landscape'.

His first exhibition at the Lefevre Gallery in 1931 was pronounced by *The Times* to show 'greater warmth and variety of colour and a more deliberate emphasis in the design' than Corot, but Berners' range was close and he was aiming for the same atmosphere of calm. Sometimes he literally copied, at other times he moved things about. Often his problem was that he was in England, with a different light, the colours obscured by a grey or bluish haze, and on the whole these paintings are less successful. He also painted portraits, William Crack sitting twice himself and recalling that professional models were also hired. When Berners painted Penelope Betjeman on her horse and Diana Mosley at the Villa D'Este, however, he did so from photographs.

It is easy enough to keep the precise distinction between amateurs and professionals: a professional is anyone who is paid. In time, Berners sold some pictures, so he was a professional painter. Beyond that, however, is a widely held feeling that professionalism, or lack of it, depends on how much the work meant to the creator. Money comes into this – the amount earned against the amount possessed, or thought to be possessed. (It is possible, but not easy, for a well-known millionaire to be regarded in this nebulous sense as a professional poet.) Solemnity helps, and conspicuous industry and the evidence of such industry: very big or very long works. Singleness of purpose is an asset, and working-class origins may contribute. Passing time may drain away the memory of wealth or frivolity and leave only the work.

Berners fails by practically all of these tests. A noticeably rich peer, who moved from art to art and also had a spectacular social life, he earned little by his efforts, a paltry addition to his income. His music, slight and frivolous though much of it appeared, has however been augmented by the passing years. He usually rates references, rather than chapters, in a history of twentieth-century British music, but he is there as a professional composer. By these whimsical standards his more obviously serious painting is relegated to that of an amateur – a gifted, industrious, successful amateur – whose pictures are still attributed and

give pleasure but are somehow not those of a professional artist (in the
1990s they tend to cost a few, a very few, thousand pounds). Defenders
of amateur status rush forward to point out how sympathetic it is to be a
lover of the arts, but there clings to the word – and still more to
'dilettante', which has simply travelled further down the same road –
the suggestion of merely playing, which is not present when, for
instance, a steely old professional like Picasso dashes off a dove on a
tablecloth in a few seconds.

Berners himself, though eager for serious recognition, did not bother
himself about such categories. He mixed everything up without any
sense of strain and held that enjoyment was always his aim. He bought
serious pictures, which he naturally studied profoundly and sometimes
rejected: Alexander Reid of Reid & Lefevre (who had himself been
painted by Van Gogh) 'used to come down to Faringdon with some
Corots on trial for about a month', a friend remembers. Berners did not
often pay more than £100. He also acquired amusing rubbish, and
much in between, and his skill lay in juxtaposing them. He bought from
friends, he made friends with those he bought from, he made friends
with painters who worked with friends.

In 1925 Berners had met the rather wild young English painter
Christopher Wood in Rome, possibly through the Marchesa Casati.
Talented and attractive, Wood first hero-worshipped and got to know
Picasso and Cocteau but was already sure of his own style; 'lyrical and
slightly sinister' his biographer calls his paintings of boats, white houses,
stone walls, fishing nets. Wood heard that Diaghilev was interested in
an English ballet and made designs for one to be called *English Country
Life*. He approached Walton to write the music, then Berners and then
Constant Lambert. Nothing came of this, but by September 1927
Berners, who had already bought a large oil (*Winter*), was staying in the
South of France with Emerald Cunard and found that 'Kit' was next
door. Wood reported to his mother that Berners 'is a patron of mine,
takes me in his car to beautiful parts and we paint together. He has just
taken it up and the only fault that I find in his work is that it is just too
perfect. He does everything just as it should be done. He has bought
two flower pieces.'

Wood was yet another artistic young man of a generation below his
own that Berners came to know. Though Wood felt that 'Every intimate
friendship reduces one's particularity and one becomes less oneself',
unintimate friendship was becoming Berners' speciality and he is so
mentioned. Berners always liked company while at work. Staying in the

same house-party once was Winston Churchill and, as Churchill tossed away unsatisfactory canvases, Berners picked them up and used them. So underneath some of his pictures lie more valuable Churchills.

Berners' social round was still spinning merrily. In the absence of a diary, we get arbitrary glimpses of him when someone else writes an account of a meeting or party, or when the papers report his presence, as with the visit to the Côte d'Azure. The sun was now popular, though not with Berners. In 1923 Coco Chanel had descended the gangway of the Duke of Westminster's yacht, brown as a cabin boy, and 'I think she must have invented sunbathing, at that time she invented everything,' a fashionable prince recorded. Nice was 'good only for shopping', Monte Carlo had not really got going, Villefranche was artistic and scandalous. Berners stayed at Cannes. 'The bohemian artist Nina Hamnett came to Villefranche in a Chanel suit for two days, painted a picture and then went on to Cannes to join the smart set of Lady Juliet Duff, Lord Berners, Lord Alington and Daisy Fellowes.' The glamorous Blue Train, which was to inspire a Diaghilev ballet (costumes by Chanel), was running and the craze was to race it from Paris by car. In 1927, *The Times* warned that all driving on the Riviera was dangerous, but William Crack had no trouble.

Nina Hamnett was too bohemian for Berners, and may exemplify an apparently congenial world into which he did not often venture. More in his style was a visit down a salt mine with Oggie Lynn, a plump but tiny opera singer (it may have been Berners who speculated that her coffin would be a perfect square); or a fancy-dress ball in Venice in 1927, when William Crack stood on the stairs 'as a sort of page all dressed up' and Berners and his friends were not allowed in at first because it was unacceptable to wear masks in the presence of royalty.

That same year, Berners was apparently proud of owning a truffle-finding pig and had hopes (disappointed) of working it in England. In February his new acquaintance D. H. Lawrence, who had found him 'very nice', thought of asking to be driven to the Etruscan tombs outside Florence but decided, 'He's so rich – such a huge Rolls-Royce. It goes dead against my stomach.' In June the *Daily Sketch* writer felt, 'I can imagine no more pleasant way of spending a wet Sunday morning than at Coombe [Lady Juliet Duff's house] listening to Eugene Goossens playing his piano pieces and watching Lord Berners painting a still life – a corner of a room with a great vase of orange Emma White roses.' (Sir John Lavery arrived for lunch and civilly said that it was 'a really beautiful bit of colour'.) In July, 'Gerald and his nice friend [Mario]

Pansa' came to stay with his mother at Faringdon, and again 'They
walked round the lake.'

Apart from regarding a Matisse fixedly through his eyeglass at the
Contemporary Art Society, Berners then drops from sight until another
fancy-dress ball, this time given by the Duchess of Sutherland. If Lord
Wimborne, as Richelieu, was by universal consent the most successful
'of the humorous costumes, which were of course very plentiful, the
most amusing was that worn by Lord Berners – a white monkey bride;
in the monkey's paw he carried the prettiest little posy, and on his
monkey's head a most demure wreath and veil'. Duff Cooper was one of
the three blind mice.

Then Berners was off to Berlin for a complicated visit to Harold
Nicolson, who was rather taken with Ivor Novello. Berners was popular
there: 'He was the most appreciative of guests as well as the most
amusing. He was never bored and he never complained. He liked and
was liked by everyone ... The only fly in the ointment was that
Gladwyn [Jebb] did not care much for Ivor. Harold suspected that Ivor
may have made advances to him. He did, and was imperiously
rebuffed.' Cyril Connolly found a second fly:

> [Novello] worshipped culture and intelligence. His tragedy. For culture
> (Lord Berners) and Gladwyn Jebb (intelligence) didn't worship him.
> They found him a bore and said so ... At supper the band played the
> famous Berlin tango, Ivor raved over it and wrote the music down by ear
> on a bit of paper. We were impressed until Berners told us that he had
> looked over his shoulder and seen him get it all wrong.

Love is not love that alters when it alteration finds. Berners' love for
Rome did not waver, but he was not enthusiastic about alterations.
Sometimes he harked back to his original vision: 'I can remember the
Palatine as it was when I first came to Rome. A delightful romantic spot,
with shady groves of ilex and myrtle, the ruins appearing mysteriously
through clumps of cypresses and pine trees.' That was how ruins should
stay. In 1928 he bought a new house, 3 Foro Romano, which was to be
his home for over ten years, and his possession for much longer (though
he kept the house in Via Varese). It cost him '£9,000 or more' and he
added a garage. This was what led to his quoting other people's
memories of the days 'when the Forum was buried under pasture land
and large white oxen browsed on the desolate site: a shepherd boy lay
asleep at the foot of a lofty column rising out of the brambles', and

outbursts against archaeology, which 'with its prurient claws has grabbed up, torn down and scratched away the patina of time in order to expose a few ugly relics of the past'. His house had indeed 'a lovely big drawing-room with a balcony' which commanded a fine view of all going on in the Forum. Berners himself was satisfied: 'On a moonlit night it is pure magic.' The next year Rex Whistler came to stay and wrote to his mother that he could see the wonderful view while lying in his bath. A postcard of his bedroom notes, 'Isn't it delightful? The walls are dirty parchment colour and the bed, curtains etc. are crimson damask. The head of the bed is carved and gilt.'

A man was found to look after the new house, who was also 'a first rate cook'. Perhaps inevitably, Tito Mannini came to regard the house as his own. Edward James, who was meant to be staying indefinitely, found him so rude and unbearable that he left after a month, alleging that Tito used the front part of the house as an antique shop when Berners was away. Diana Mosley, on the other hand, rather liked him and certainly appreciated his skill:

> Tito bred canaries which sang all day and kept him company when Gerald was in England and he was alone in the house. An enemy opened the doors of all the cages and the canaries flew away into the Forum where they perched singing and twittering on bushes and trees. There was no food that day; Tito was in the Forum from morning to night coaxing and whistling to his birds. They all came back and even seemed pleased to find their familiar cages once again. He made delicious things, in particular there was a cake, hard chocolate outside and inside sour cream which I have often thought of since but never achieved.

Penelope Betjeman found Tito a bit tricky: 'He seemed rather out of sorts at first because of the short notice but I told him not to put all the carpets down as it isn't worth it. He had a bad throat . . . He also said his leg was very bad so I arranged that we should all breakfast in the dining room to save him carrying up so many trays.' But John Betjeman managed to get along, 'This is the first night in your house and I must write at once to thank you for lending it to us. It really is a bit of all right with that view of all those ruins and the charming Tito to whom I speak French, Italian, Deutsch or English very clumsily.' A honeymoon couple, to whom Berners also lent the house, had a less carefree time. Berners sent Tito a selection of the cards of famous bores, with instructions to leave one or two in the tray in the hall each day so that his guests might expect visits to follow.

Lady Dorothy Lygon's father, Earl Beauchamp, took the house for a couple of winters in the early 1930s, and then took Tito to the Palazzo Morisini in Venice in the summer of 1936. When Lady Dorothy met him in Rome in the war 'he was certainly wearing one of Gerald's suits'. Berners worried about him at that time, and even after peace returned, though he noted, 'I don't quite know what payment my servant Tito is getting. As I told you I find his letters very difficult to understand! I imagine the payment is adequate or I should have heard complaints.' In fact, Tito prospered, as king of the post-war black market, it was said, and Nancy Mitford reported in 1948 that Lady Rodd had given a cocktail party for 'your Tito, now a man of great importance, it seems'.

Rex Whistler was a recent friend. Another precocious youth, the same age as Constant Lambert, both impulsive and diffident, he was already making his way in the arts, having completed the mural in the Tate Gallery when only twenty-one. He and Berners had painted together before, the middle-aged amateur more diligent than the young professional: 'I tire of it after an hour while Lord B. can go on for two or three hours without getting up', but now Whistler came to stay for over a month, starting towards the end of June 1929.

He wrote home constantly, this time to Stephen Tennant:

This is how I spent my [twenty-fourth] birthday last Monday: I got up about 8.30 and had breakfast with B in the loggia overlooking the Forum – a breakfast of little hot rolls and butter and coffee followed by peaches and figs. At ten we drove to that spot nr. the Arch of Constantine and I began the picture which I have mentioned before. After lunch I rested in my dark and shuttered bedroom till 4 when we drove out of Rome to Frascati. A very beautiful place and high up above the campagna. We painted all afternoon in the gardens of the Villa Aldobrandini, full of old fountains and ilex trees, and a view across the plain which takes the breath away. In the faint haze of the afternoon sun it looks more like a vast expanse of *sea*, stretching away and away toward the horizon and the dim peak of Mount Soracte – and in the other direction the long silver gleam which is the real sea. We have been several afternoons painting. B had a written leave from the family. On Friday while I was painting I looked up and saw a sallow face peering down very hard at me from a terrace above. It was 'Il Duque Aldobrandini', just returned. Fortunately B was sitting not far away and Aldobrandini waved to him and came down and talked to us.

A postscript to his mother reads, 'I have done a small sketch portrait of Berners. Alas only too like him so it cannot give him much pleasure. He is so charming and kind.'

William drove them back to England, taking the usual leisurely two weeks. 'Berners does not care very much for Siena. He says it is rather grim and gothic with high battlement walls all around and deep narrow streets and those strange stark towers sticking high up above like factory towers.' They had spent four days at Aula: 'I painted two pictures and had a divine bathe in the river – with William the chauffeur! – so charming and handsome. B doesn't care much for bathing (*like some other misguided people I know*) I think, though he bathed with me once or twice in the sulphur springs near Tivoli.'

Whistler's enthusiasm lasted through France. It is hard to believe that Berners too had not enjoyed himself, taking pleasure in his ability to bestow so much beauty and luxury – the ducal gardens, the evening hush, the figs, the Rolls-Royce – on a congenial young companion. Yet they parted and remained friendly acquaintances rather than friends, let alone lovers. Later, when Whistler painted the dining-room at Port Lympne for Sir Philip Sassoon (a cousin whom Siegfried scarcely knew), transforming it into a blue-and-white striped tent, the real curtains blending with the *trompe-l'oeil*, he allowed vistas in which you can see, far away, Faringdon and a little boy waiting for a paddle-steamer, with a coroneted 'B' on his trunk; though more than twenty years his junior, Whistler too saw Berners as a child.

Back in London, Berners bought another new house, 3 Halkin Street off Belgrave Square. This was for him alone, quite modest, with only one spare room and a small drawing-room on the first floor in which he sometimes slept. In his proper bedroom was a four-poster with crystal columns from Peter Jones. Over the years the house was transformed, by Berners' idiosyncratic taste, into a metropolitan miniature version of Faringdon.

On 19 August 1929, Diaghilev died in Venice. It was a devastating shock to the world as well as to his friends – 'people ran from room to room to announce the news or shouted it from windows'. Whether Berners would have worked for him again must be a matter of conjecture; he had scored only two successes, but then few composers, apart from Stravinsky, did. In the event, the Ballets Russes collapsed more or less immediately. Of course its influence could not but continue. In England it was the classics and the work of Fokine that were prominently displayed; modernism largely crossed to America with Balanchine.

Amid the cries of despair bewailing the death of ballet could be heard a more positive voice. In February 1930, the Camargo Society was formed, which, though it was named after a French ballerina, had as its aim the gathering of the fragments of national talent to form a British ballet. Berners joined in December, Ashton was dancer and choreographer, Constant Lambert became its resident conductor. It was a crucial forerunner of the Sadler's Wells Ballet and so of the Royal Ballet itself.

For some, the death of Diaghilev marked the end of the 1920s. On 24 October 1929 came the Wall Street crash, which marked the real beginning of the 1930s for everybody. If Berners had not already bought his houses, he would not have done so now. He thought himself poor and behaved as if he were. William Crack and his wife came to live in Halkin Street for a time instead of being kept elsewhere and commented, 'he [Berners] couldn't afford to keep anyone there, he only had a butler and somebody in the kitchen', who presumably came in daily. In fact, all was fine; his income does not seem to have declined significantly but Berners, a hypochondriac, was also given to worrying about money. As Evelyn Waugh wrote later to John Betjeman, 'it may be that you are not bankrupt at all. It is an illusion that often affects the rich, e.g. Berners.' Beverley Nichols, less reliable with figures than with anecdotes, remembered Berners coming to stay in his cottage:

Then he sat down on the sofa, opened the Sunday newspaper, and almost immediately burst into tears.

'Whatever is the matter, Gerald?' He really was producing an extraordinary amount of quite wet tears.

'It is too terrible. What is to happen to us all?'

'But why? What is it?' I hurried over to see what he was reading. The paper was open at the financial page, and there was a rather gloomy leading article – the usual sort of thing. The pound was weakening, exports were falling, costs were rising, labour was striking, taxes were crippling . . . in fact the mixture as before.

'Where is it all to end?' sobbed Gerald.

I suggested that it would end as it always did, in nothing much.

To which Gerald retorted that *I* was all right. *I* had a profession. *I* could always keep myself. But what had he got?

I might have reminded him that he had, apart from many other possessions, £100,000 in gilt-edged securities, a sum which had hitherto evaded me. But he was beyond comforting and shortly afterwards he went to bed.

The absurdity of a meeting with Lord Beaverbrook in 1931 cheered Berners up. They agreed that ruin stared them in the face, Beaverbrook took him back to Stornoway House and the two rich men knelt down on either side of his bed and prayed that God should protect their money.

No one sympathises with the financial worries of someone richer than themselves but suddenly to have less is indeed to feel poor. Nevertheless, Berners' worries were neurotic and not much connected to reality. As has been noted, his annual income from the Berners Estate Company until 1935-6 averaged more than £7,000, without a trend downwards or serious inflation to make its worth dwindle. Indeed, the world Depression that was arriving made him all the richer; any other depression was his own.

In spite of death and despondency and painting, Berners was soon back writing ballet music, though on a reduced scale. Charles B. Cochran was a showman who put on everything from Shakespeare to prize-fights but, slightly to his own irritation, he remained best known for revues. In these he employed much first-rate talent, but in constricted circumstances. The stage at the London Pavilion was tiny, the only entrance so narrow that if hoop skirts were to be worn they had to be lowered onto the performers from the flies before the curtain went up.

Many of the Ballets Russes performers were unemployed, so here, in March 1930, Balanchine devised a piece called *Luna Park*, with music by Berners and décor by Christopher Wood. A barker shows four freaks in turn – a man with three heads, a juggler with three legs, a one-legged ballerina, a man with six arms. Each does a dance, the barker departs and then they reappear as normal people – they were fakes – and dance again before running away. The barker returns, pulls back the curtain and reveals the props: two heads, billiard balls but no juggler, an abandoned leg, four disconnected arms. It is hard to assess from one number how a show was received, but a young Cecil Beaton found it 'all very strange and in its peculiar way beautiful', and Bernard Shaw liked it. Serge Lifar, who danced the part with six arms, refers to the piece as *Frix*.

Berners' music, in recognition of the popular audience, was more accessible than anything he had yet written, pleasant and professional, including a sly parody of the Rose Adagio from *The Sleeping Beauty*. It was described as 'quick witty snatches tinged with melancholy'. The music was used again by Ashton with the Ballet Rambert in 1932 for *Foyer de danse* (sets and costumes 'after Degas'). At the Mercury Theatre, again tiny, the set took up the entire stage so that Alicia Markova would be trapped in her dressing-room, lit only by candles, the only exit down a staircase to stage centre; Ashton used to come round outside so that she could climb onto his shoulders and escape. Similarly, some of Berners' music from *The Triumph of Neptune* reappeared at the Lyric Hammersmith the next year in two short ballets. *Le Boxing* was found 'charming. With Miss Diana Gould [later Lady Menuhin] as a super-vamp, in a picture hat and little black shorts and an absurd wisp of a train . . . the Marie Rambert ballet gave one of the most pleasing and original performances that Londoners are likely to see. Lord Berners' other new ballet *Waterloo and Crimea* was also on the programme.'

If ballet was in crisis and promised few immediate opportunities, Berners' painting received its first public showing. At the Lefevre Gallery off St James's, thirty-eight of his pictures were on exhibition in 1931 'for the whole of July', as he wrote especially to tell Lytton Strachey, 'so you may perhaps find time to look in'. Many were landscapes of the countryside near Rome or of Rome itself, but there were also flowers, a still life, some English and French scenes, and a portrait of Osbert Sitwell. The foreword to the catalogue by Clive Bell begins, 'It is popularly supposed that Lord Berners took to painting only when he had temporarily given up music.' Berners wrote and asked for the 'temporarily' to be put in as he was working at the Lyric when he received a proof, but clearly news of *Luna Park* had not reached Bell. He continues:

> Indeed I begin to suspect that these experiments are not so much the gropings of one with a message in search of a medium as the adventures of a man in love with all subtle forms of expression and equipped for excellence in all. For here is exquisite painting; here is the craftsman's understanding of the uses of paint. Not that Lord Berners has nothing to say: only what he has to say is not at all like a message, but like a fine scent rather, or a flavour . . . We shall be told that he cannot sit down to paint Rome without thinking of Corot. Well, Corot could not sit down to paint Rome without thinking of Claude. I do not know that Lord Berners need feel abashed.

The review in *Apollo* was favourable, but 'One views his pictures with delight, only tempered by regret that being so good they are not just a little better . . . Lord Berners put Mr Osbert Sitwell into the doorway of a round arch; to my thinking the curves would suit Mr Sacheverell Sitwell better.'

The foreword was quoted by 'The Talk of London' in the *Daily Express*, which hurried on to the more important matter of who was at the opening party. They included Lord Ivor Spencer-Churchill, the Duke of Marlborough, Mr Sacheverell Sitwell, the Duchess of Roxburghe, Lord David Cecil, Lord and Lady Weymouth, Mr Beverley Nichols, Mr Serge Lifar and Sir John and Lady Lavery, who bought a picture. As did others. Evelyn Waugh wrote to Patrick Balfour: 'Gerald Berners had an exhibition of pictures and sold them all on the first day which shows what a good thing it is to be a baron.' Actually two were left, but the comment is surely imprecise anyway; even from the most cynical viewpoint, it is a rich acquaintance anxious to please rather than a title that is required, and the acquaintance does not have to be so very rich. The prices ranged between £8 and £35, with the average just under £17.

These successes did not halt Berners' periodic gloom, nor that of his mother. Mrs Bennitt had been growing vague for some time, asking to be reminded of the name of her son, for instance, when he was coming down. It was on 15 February 1931, while in a fit of depression, that she died at Faringdon; five weeks later Berners' step-father followed her. The empty house beckoned.

Chapter X

Heber Percy

Nancy Mitford, who was to become its celebrant, described Faringdon thus:

> It is plain and grey and square and solid and it is as much a part of the rolling Berkshire landscape before it as of the little old market town of Faringdon on which it turns its back and which is hidden from view by the parish church and huge clumps of elm trees. It had been built in the middle of the eighteenth century by the father of the worst poet laureate we have had, Pye, by Mr Wood of Bath.

The Pyes, 'a moſt ancient and honorable family', bought a house that was burned down and replaced in 1770. Sir Walter Scott agreed with Nancy Mitford's assessment and described H.J. Pye as 'eminently respectable in everything but his poetry'.

She continues:

> We must give it to Mr Wood of Bath that he did his bit. He placed the house upon a semi-basement [in which Berners' flat had been] which always makes for warmth and comfort, and to this basement with real eighteenth-century carelessness, he relegated both God and the cook, putting chapel and kitchen there side by side. He introduced a graceful double staircase, pillars, decorated plaster ceilings, classical chimney pieces, as many paltry details, most likely, as the poet laureate was willing to afford; the proportions of all the rooms are excellent . . . To the North, Faringdon has a most beautiful view, enjoyed by all the principal rooms in the house. It extends from a terrace buried in honeysuckle, for many miles over a landscape such as is beloved of all English sporting painters, from Stubbs to Cecil Aldin, that is to say a patchwork of fields and hedges, dotted with elm trees. Not a house or building of any sort can be seen, not a pylon or inch of wire, just green

English grass alternating with brown English arable, mile after mile, until finally they merge into the pale but piercing blue of a far distant horizon.

This was written in 1948 but would have applied in 1931. Indeed, on not too clear a day one can still see twenty-two miles without really noticing the aerodrome, the pylons, the lack of elm trees. The house was, in Peter Quennell's phrase, built for harmony. It was not at all glamorous. Berners set about transforming it and created his master-piece. There was much that did not coincide with his taste. In particular, an oak dresser of his mother's in the drawing-room was reassuring, rather than elegant. That went. Berners was unenthusiastic about flowers out of doors, though inside it was a different matter, which may be why the rosebeds growing before the house, one for each bedroom, survived. (He did enjoy bursting the seed pods of the bladder-nut tree (*Staphylea*) and once asked a gardener to bring steps so that he could pop those out of reach.)

Flowers for the house were grown in the immense and immensely productive kitchen garden. Cyril Connolly was to say that when every sort of luxury had been banned for ever from England, 'Lord Berners will somehow manage to maintain a secret melon house.' There was space in this walled garden for a yew avenue, 400 years old and twenty feet wide, to be almost unnoticeable. The park gave way to a lawn and a gravel sweep before a front door, soon to be decorated with a pretty chandelier hanging outside.

But did he want to be in sole charge of a country house at all? Berners had become, had made himself, urban as well as urbane, a metropolitan figure, who enjoyed driving through, looking at or painting the countryside very much. Indeed, he appreciated its beauty to an exceptional extent, but to live there, for weeks at a time? He was said to be lonely and, if it were true even to a slight extent, might he not be much more so when surrounded by fields and neighbours? And could he afford it? The slump was deepening. Faringdon, though not heavily staffed by the standards of the time, had a butler, a footman, two housemaids, a cook and a kitchenmaid, and five or six gardeners. Nevertheless as early as August 1931, Eddie Marsh, also gloomy about economic trends, recorded in his diary that he 'Went to stay with Gerald Berners thinking I might as well have at least one last weekend of comfort.'

Many were to follow with the same confidence. In particular they

looked forward to their food. Berners was always unashamedly greedy
and thought this 'one of the more amiable vices'. Just as he took a great
interest in cars but never learned to drive, so he employed talented
cooks and inspired them – one was said to have become quite ordinary
once more the moment she left his service – but never learned to boil an
egg himself. He liked rich food. Caviare, foie gras and plovers' eggs had
the advantage that they could not be spoiled by inept preparation. He
allowed occasional bizarre touches. Vera Stravinsky sent a special
powder from Paris to help Berners make a blue mayonnaise. As far as he
was concerned, English cooking was all right as long as it made no
attempt to be French, but it was too conservative. If mushrooms, then
why not toadstools, 'many of which are of far more delicate flavour and
persist into the autumn when mushrooms are no more'? The best
French cooking had fled from Paris and was to be found in the
provinces, while the best cooking in Europe was found in Brussels.
Finally, 'mistrust a man who does not mind what he eats'.

Berners liked to stimulate expectations. He would tell guests over tea
what was planned for dinner. In the same style, Frederick Ashton
remembered Penelope Betjeman demanding as she sat down, 'What's
for pud?' Surprisingly, he hardly concerned himself about wine,
maintaining a decent standard at Faringdon only out of politeness – 'He
liked a good Beaujolais but took no interest in years.'

When a second parent dies, some people feel threatened by death
themselves, some feel overwhelmed with grief or regrets, some feel
liberated and others feel all of these things. Berners felt that he wanted
to start writing an autobiography in September after his mother's death
in February 1931. It is a book that was bound to include much about
her and could not have been published – perhaps not even written –
while she was alive. It is also his literary masterpiece, although a minor
one. Almost as many boring autobiographies appeared then as now, but
they tended to be the recollections of successful men at the end of their
worthy careers. Berners was not yet fifty and had not exactly had a
career; in any case, he recorded only his first thirteen years. He is
defensive about this, quoting in a notebook the doubts of Stendhal: '*J'ai
été découragé par cette effroyable difficulté de "je" et de "moi" qui fera
prendre l'auteur en grippe.*' He continues robustly, however, that there is
no need to apologise, because 'after all it is easier to shut up a book if
you are bored with it than it would be to shut up the author if you were

in his presence' – an uncharacteristic verdict on characteristic misgivings.

In practice he turned out to be not only his best subject but his only satisfactory one. Later, writing fiction simply to amuse, he seems to labour more, perhaps because he laboured less. He sent the manuscript to Rex Whistler, asking if 'sentences might be improved as regards style etc., writing not being my métier'. *First Childhood* was not published until 1934; his later, less felt, books were knocked off in a few weeks.

A modernist in music, unfashionable when he started painting, Berners' taste and style in literature were entirely traditional. Writing about an odd upper-class family, a lonely childhood, unhappy schooldays as an artist among games-playing philistines, his first feeling for music (all subjects that were not fresh then and have become increasingly hackneyed ever since), he is elegant, unsentimental and evocative. To an exceptionally clear memory of what things looked and felt like he unobtrusively adds an adult understanding in words that flow with apparent ease. When the book appeared it was widely and well reviewed. The comparatively young were entertained by it: Compton Mackenzie found it enchanting, L.P. Hartley brilliantly amusing, it made David Garnett laugh a great deal; but Raymond Mortimer was not quite alone in using the word 'cruel'. He probably means much the same as Sir John Squire, a year younger than Berners, who writes of 'audacious honesty'; Hugh Walpole, also fifty, found 'oddity and wisdom'. Mortimer, with irritating coyness, ends a list of Berners' virtues: 'and (dare we add?) a lively imagination'. This is daring only if you are a young snob who hopes to be invited to Faringdon, and Mortimer is guessing – he had no special knowledge.

Nevertheless, Berners does get things wrong and, where facts can be checked, proves fallible; and his view of himself struggling against a philistine world, while fair, is overstated. His emotions do shape his memories, but the whole feel of the book is of someone trying to convey what it was like to be him then, not to improve on stories or amuse contemporaries. Aleister Crowley wrote two years later, 'I have rarely enjoyed a book so much as your Memoirs of Infantile Paralysis. To speak plain truth I do not know another book which even describes the spirit of childhood. In comparison, Alice in Wonderland is shoddy.'

Berners read – all those years alone in Europe – and remembered what he read. Penelope Betjeman said that he could tell you the plots of novels he had not looked at for thirty years. David Cecil referred to him as the best-read man he had ever met and said also that Berners

possessed 'a very sharp critical taste and a very independent one indeed
. . . very cultivated like a person who all their life or for many years had
read the best things or a lot of the best things and knew what was good
about them'. He continued to do so. Cecil's few letters contain literary
chat, recommending Disraeli's *The Young Duke* and asking, 'Did you
know Pater liked to walk about Oxford in a top hat, a bright apple-green
tie and carrying a neat gold-topped umbrella. Was the effect pretty or
ridiculous do you think?' This was meant to amuse and we can assume
it did. A less than sympathetic view of contemporaries is shown in the
verse:

> Take out the muse of W.J. Turner
> And strangle her, shoot her, lynch her or burn her.
> Or give her in marriage to J.B. Priestley
> Or anyone else who is equally beastly.

To Cyril Connolly, Berners wrote when ill, 'I've put in a good deal of
reading: Balzac, Proust, and *Middlemarch*, Old Horse-Face's masterpiece – which I had not read before.' During the war he read the whole
of Dickens. In his last years he confessed to Sibyl Colefax what many
find: 'I can't read new books any more and am confining myself to old
ones', though 'I thought Evelyn Waugh's *Mr Scott King's Modern
Europe* a little too near the knuckle for one who used to love travelling in
Europe. Koestler seems to be the key writer of the day, and my God
how sordid and dreary he is, and one turns with relief to Horace
Walpole.' His last such reference, written to Diane Abdy, is, 'Are you a
reader of Henry James? I read practically nothing else now. One comes
to the conclusion that Americans haven't changed much since 1880.'

Meanwhile, in 1932, a meeting took place that changed his life for ever.
It has been reliably stated that it was exactly as in a *roman à clef* that
Berners was to write three years later, 'down to the smallest particular',
so it seems simple to look up the passage. But there is a slight
complication. The novel, printed for private circulation only, is set in a
boarding school with Berners' homosexual acquaintances as the girls
and himself as the headmistress, Miss Carfax. She is staying in a
cottage-bungalow with her friend in the Lake District during the
holidays, when:

they saw the milk-cart tearing down the road at full gallop. It was being driven by a girl of about fifteen, who looked rather like a gipsy, with bright sparkling eyes, her cheeks flushed with excitement and her dark locks tumbled over her forehead ... When the milk-cart reached the gates of 'Balmoral', the girl who was driving it pulled up the horse violently, threw down the reins and jumped out of the cart. She ran up to Miss Carfax and said: 'Well here I am. I'm Millie.' Millie immediately demands food, 'some buttered eggs and a peach'. The friend suggests a nice cup of coffee and a sandwich. 'Oh, anything for a quiet life,' said Millie and began turning cartwheels round the room.

Millie is certainly Robert Heber Percy, whom the physical description and the exuberance fit well enough, but the meeting did not take place at a cottage-bungalow. It was at a weekend staying at Vaynol with Michael Duff. Heber Percy was not fifteen but twenty, which doubtless seemed very young. The next chapter of the novel begins:

The presence of Millie at 'Balmoral' brought a new interest into Miss Carfax's life. Latterly, though not actually unhappy, she had been suffering from a depressing feeling of listlessness. She had become convinced that there could be nothing more in life that could arouse that wonderful sensation of ecstasy she had so often experienced in her youth.

But now it seemed as though within her breast some strange unreserved chord had been struck that caused her whole being to vibrate ... Millie was wild, unrestrained and a little crazy. You never knew what she was going to do next. Her movements were often violent but, although she was constantly breaking things, there was nothing clumsy about her movements. You felt that if things happened to get in her way and she was obliged to knock them over, it was their fault rather than hers, and everything she did was redeemed by a peculiar gracefulness. She was like a young panther.

Berners was in love. In retrospect at least, he retained a few suspicions:

After a time Miss Carfax noticed that Millie was very fond of telling stories of people making up to her. The stories were all quite innocent and told in a charmingly naïve way, but Miss Carfax thought that it denoted a certain tendency. One day Millie said: 'You know, Miss Carfax, I don't ever allow people to kiss me, but if anyone offered me ten pounds then I should let them kiss me and perhaps even do a great deal more.'

It is impossible to know how literally to take all this (the innocence seems unlikely even then), but it is the closest thing to an account of their courtship that exists.

Who was this figure who had erupted into Berners' life knocking over the furniture? Robert Heber Percy came from an ancient, upper-class country family with 12,000 acres in Shropshire. In this he was not entirely unlike Berners himself, and though he was the youngest of four boys – Algernon was nine, Cyril seven, and Alan five when Robert was born in 1911 – the gap made him a child apart, if by no means an only child. Cyril wrote a book about their boyhood, which paints a vivid, fond but entirely conventional picture:

> Daddy took little part in our amusements as he suffered from asthma . . .
> Mummy did come and say Good-night before the Ball all dressed up.
> She looked beautiful in a long trailing dress with a diamond tiara in her
> hair . . . The hounds arrive. Conversation dies away; excitement is in the
> air . . . We were allowed to watch the drive before lunch, which we could
> do from the terrace . . . Governesses came and went. Sometimes they got
> on with Nanny; more often they did not . . . There was no smoking in
> the dining-room. Cocktails were 'gut-rotting, a pernicious concoction'.

Robert, the afterthought, naturally appears least in the book. His first action is quite in character: though not yet out of the nursery, he pushes his brothers' new tutor into the lake. His next appearance is a disappearance, after several hours of which he is eventually found forcing a bantam back onto her nest so that she will lay an egg. With catapults and then guns his brothers account for a lot of birds. The gamekeeper becomes their best friend, but Robert is less keen on sport. When he first hunts, his inherited bowler hat, though stuffed with paper, comes down to rest on his ears. Still apart, he eventually gets half a page to himself:

> Robert went to Stowe. He was more sensitive than the rest of us and
> Mummy's darling, though she would never show it. Robert was always
> so gentle with her, took her flowers: a thing the rest of us would never
> think of. He liked good books and took an interest in painting. He never
> shot, at least he never bothered about it. Fishing bored him. But he rode
> well and later made young horses with mouths like velvet, so soft that
> few people had the hands to ride them. He went to hounds well, his reins
> held at the buckle on the tips of his fingers, his hands raised (which was
> rather ugly).

By then he had already been the naughtiest boy at his private school, Wixenford. He climbed onto a ledge above a door and managed to pee on the head of the headmaster; he was also unable to tie up his shoe-laces. He was probably the naughtiest boy at Stowe too, but the headmaster, J.F. Roxburgh, became fond of him and saved him from his just deserts. In return he loved the place, the most beautiful public school in England, and used to go back for visits all his life. Algy joined the Grenadiers, Cyril the Welsh Guards ('I whipped in to the Aldershot drag, which hunted two days a week'), Alan 'joined his regiment in Germany' but was killed racing. Then Robert, again forgotten for some time, is once more allowed a passage to himself:

> Robert was commissioned to a cavalry regiment at Tidworth, but his life as a soldier was short. He took off his military cap to the General! Then he arrived back at Tidworth from a party in London in a hired Daimler car in the early hours of the morning, wearing white tie and tailcoat. Finding himself late for stables – a parade attended by all officers except the very senior – he went into the dining-room and ordered himself breakfast. The commanding officer and second-in-command came in. They halted rooted to the ground . . . Robert they realised would never make a soldier. He was asked to send in his papers and did so.

There is another version of the end of his army career, which involves going to Ireland, falling in love and simply not returning. The row grew, a letter was written to George V and all was more or less forgiven, but he was never allowed in the royal enclosure at Ascot. Cyril's narrative continues:

> He went abroad, here, there and everywhere. He worked his passage to America where, among other things, he acted as an extra in Hollywood and had a stand-in part falling off a horse at full gallop. He was a waiter at Lyons Corner House, but was sacked for spilling soup all over a customer. Robert said, 'The man just complained too much.' He also helped run a night club in London.

Cyril's mention of Lyons Corner House fits in with another version of how Heber Percy met Berners, who simply came to tea there. The night-club employer was Kate Meyrick, known as 'London's Night-Club Queen'. She had been the first woman in Ireland to ride a bicycle, but at the end of the 1914–18 war was on her own with eight children to bring up. Throughout the 1920s she opened clubs, which were raided and sometimes closed by the police. The 43, at 43 Gerrard Street, and later the Slip In, which had a reflecting glass dance floor, were the most famous and there the underworld and the aristocracy mingled with prostitutes, film-stars and foreigners for added glamour. In 1924 she went to Holloway for six months, but her daughters went to Roedean and Girton and two of them married peers. In 1928 there was another six-month stretch but worse was the arrest of a friendly policeman, which led to a charge of bribery, for which she got fifteen months. She lost her savings in the Wall Street Crash and her health went, a sad end for a spirited woman. She died in 1933. Heber Percy lived with the family, and always spoke of Kate with warm approval. He was more or less engaged to her daughter Kathleen and gave her away when she married someone else. After handing out novelties at the club every night and tidying up, they would all go home for an enormous breakfast.

When they first met, Heber Percy was not yet twenty-one, Berners was almost fifty. Heber Percy was handsome, although those of Berners' friends who did not approve of him (that is to say most) tended to claim that he looked like a monkey. Michael Duff had it both ways when he wrote a novel, *The Power of a Parasol*, which portrays Heber Percy as Robert Oddman, dressed in 'brown corduroys, a yellow polo shirt, and round his neck, arranged in an untidy mass, was a blue and white spotted scarf; his eyes were hazel and very gentle, and he resembled an attractive ape with his protruding lower lip'. Far more important was his possession of an electrifying wildness, the suggestion of danger, the dash that earned him his nickname of 'the Mad Boy'. He was capable of reckless physical acts, of sudden cruelty or generosity, and of simply climbing over the top of a taxi to get to the other side. 'I used to break things. Gerald would say very sadly, "That was given to me by a very dear friend" to try to make me be more careful. After a bit I thought he had an awful lot of very dear friends.' He did not just do things that Berners, buttoned-up in his dark suits, could never have done, he acted out fantasies Berners did not know he had. No one could liberate Berners himself at this stage, but Heber Percy liberated the air around him.

Nevertheless the romance was not quite the whirlwind it is made to sound. Heber Percy did not go abroad with Berners that year, though he did the next. About sex there is only second-hand evidence. All his life Heber Percy slept with men mostly and women occasionally. When he said to one of the latter, 'I can't think why I bother with boys when I have such a good time with the ladies', he was being polite. He is said to have gone for the weekend to Faringdon, where a night with Berners was not a success. When on Monday he asked, 'Shall I leave?', Berners replied, 'Don't go. You make me laugh. I don't mind about the other.' That fits with Heber Percy saying, towards the end of his life, that they never slept together, except perhaps occasionally if he came home drunk and fell into bed. This was not what Berners wanted but it was what he could have. They never talked about sex.

It was to the borrowed apartment of Victor Cunard, an amusing homosexual who had been *The Times*' correspondent in Venice for ten years, that Heber Percy first accompanied Berners abroad. Berners, as has been noted, knew several artistic young men but now he became part of their world and they part of his.

Cecil Beaton was already an extremely fashionable photographer and journalist, sharp as well as charming, often in the gossip columns, but from Berners' point of view most noticeable as a spectacular social climber, and thus ripe for teasing. When Beaton had published his *Book of Beauty* in 1930, Berners spent time and trouble defacing the photographs of the chic and famous. It is impossible to discern a pattern. He seems to have chosen his victims at random, adding a black tooth or a moustache, elongating a nose, awarding a pendulous lower lip here or a mass of frizzy curls there. Mrs Vernon Castle has a bottle placed in her palm, Tallulah Bankhead is given a glass, but Tilly Losch, Diana Cooper and Emerald Cunard are among those spared. A homosexual expending so much solitary energy mocking or destroying beautiful women might be thought to be full of twisted rage, but it comes across as whimsical rather than sinister. Since then, Berners and Beaton had met in drawing-rooms from Belgrave Square to Rome but remained acquaintances rather than friends. Now when he writes it is in a confiding, almost intimate tone, which never quite makes clear what has been going on:

Dearest Cecil,
It will be the Venetian 'row' (the one that took place in the depths of the night and in the darkness and gloom of Cunard's sinister palazzo) that you will probably find the most intriguing.
My lips are sealed on the subject – but nobody else's are, I'm sure – and why Peter Watson should have thought it necessary to involve Victor Cunard in it I was never able to understand – I suppose it was the

instinct of 'fetching the landlady'. Anyhow Cunard appeared in my bedroom at four in the morning looking like an old aunt in curl papers with his eyes starting out of his head – and my! How his tongue must be wagging now. And Oliver [Messel]'s in Venice too.

Latterly I have taken to adopting homeopathic (not homosexual) methods with the Mad Boy and making 'scenes and situations' myself. Like Lady Colebox and the Americans I succeeded in tiring him out so that he spent the whole day in bed writing poetry (which, unluckily for posterity, has been destroyed) and the rest of the time he was as good as gold.

Then Berners goes on to describe an invigorating scene with Heber Percy:

There was only one terrific fracas in the Hotel Santa Caterina at Amalfi where we went for the night. The Mad Boy woke up in a Neapolitan mood, put on a scarlet shirt, a blue jumper, green trousers and a yellow belt and then suggested that I should go down and have breakfast with him on the crowded terrace. I said No certainly not. Whereupon the creature flew into a rage and hit me over the head with a button-hook; the same button-hook with which Pauly Sudley was struck at Vaynol.

Far from being a strain the incidents of the last month have acted as a tonic and I feel years younger – apart from the fact that the strenuous training I've been through makes me feel as though I could now face almost any odds with equanimity.

I enclose a snapshot of the Roman Madders – l'Après midi d'un faune – Repose in the Campagna after Tischbein's portrait of Goethe.

Write to me again soon.

Love Gerald

'Peter' was Peter Watson, who has been called the love of Cecil Beaton's life; certainly they had a highly emotional, perhaps not physical, relationship between 1930 and 1934, though they were at this moment apart. Watson shared certain characteristics with Berners: an Old Etonian, drawn to Europe, he lived first in Munich and then in Paris, leaving only when war forced him out. He collected pictures and had, according to Cyril Connolly, 'a genius for gracious living', which certainly included good food. He inherited a fortune young (his father made an enormous amount of money out of margarine during the war and left £2 million, to be split between his three children when Peter was twenty-two, so his share made him much richer than Berners). He was gloomy, self-effacing, eager to avoid confrontation, not at all good-looking. 'Somebody asked me yesterday,' Berners wrote years later to Michael Duff, 'if Peter Watson had been very beautiful in his youth. I was able to reply in the words of Lady Desborough (à propos Lady Horner) "My dear, he is just as beautiful today as he has ever been."' Alan Pryce-Jones thought that if he looked like a frog, at least it was 'a frog just as it was on the point of turning into a prince'. Above all, Watson was attracted to Heber Percy and was to give him a car, at which Beaton kicked up such a fuss that he had to be given one too. Watson also gave Heber Percy a golden retriever called Pansy Lamb, but Beaton managed without one of those.

Heber Percy's unacceptably bright clothes echo Michael Duff's description. His lack of familiarity with words and books was already an established joke. Berners' *First Childhood* is dedicated, with heavy irony, 'To Robert Heber Percy whose knowledge of orthography and literary style has proved invaluable' He was quoted as saying, when annoyed, that he had 'taken unction'. Even in his last years he said of Berners' reading, 'That man Nietzsche . . . Have I pronounced it right?' Pauly Sudley, elder brother of 'Boofy', became Earl of Arran having survived the button-hook incident at Vaynol.

Another letter in October tells of even more dramatic events:

Peter will have told you all the news from Munich to Venice: how the Mad Boy nearly killed a woman in the street at Salzburg by hurling down a glass tankard from that restaurant on the cliff; how I got lost on the Schafberg at night and of the awful scenes and situations at Venice culminating in the Mad Boy trying to commit suicide – and being removed next morning by me in a heavily drugged condition. Our arrival at the Hotel Excelsior in Florence was, to say the least of it, sensational, as the Mad Boy had to be carried into the hotel in a semi conscious state still dressed in his Tyrolean costume and with his hair hanging all over his face to the amazement and stupefaction of Bobbie Casa Maury and the entire Dudley Ward family who I found seated in the hall. (It required some explaining away I can assure you!) Anyhow I will send you the complete Mad Boy Chronicle as soon as it is typed out.

This last sounds like a reference to Berners' *roman à clef* but it is early for that and the tone is wrong (possibly it is an early and very different draft); Beaton was most upset about it when it did appear.

By 2 November Berners has finished whatever he was doing and 'my only literary work is writing cheques for the house bills (which are enormous) and letters to you'. After travel plans have been detailed, he continues to Beaton:

> Private and Confidential. I had a letter from Chips [Channon] in which he says 'I am taking my Madboy, Robin Thomas, to America'. I thought at first that it meant that Honor [Channon's wife] had had a baby and it was going to be called Robin Thomas but Diana [Guinness] tells me Robin Thomas is a young man of (what the *Times* Agony column calls) 'good appearance'. I want the fullest information by return of post . . . The Madboy, in spite of his difficulty with the pen, has been an excellent correspondent, indeed a second Madame de Sévigné and writes letters in a peculiarly individual style – and I may say with a peculiarly individual orthography. I have done a most ravishing picture of *L'après midi* – begun from real life and finished from the photograph. The flesh is so exquisitely painted and the ensemble so realistic and lasciviously exciting that I have great hopes, in my forthcoming exhibition, of selling it for a high price to some amateur. It is divine in Rome. I am frightfully happy, but I suppose all that will stop as soon as I get to England.

Heber Percy is the cause of his happiness but Berners expresses it most straightforwardly whenever they are safely apart.

Despite the bumpiness of these early months, Heber Percy was to remain at Faringdon for over fifty years, eighteen while Berners was alive and then until he himself died in 1987. It was understood that he was allowed lovers, though in years to come a wife and child stretched Berners' tolerance almost to breaking point. When asked how Heber Percy's very respectable family felt about this youth being carried off by an ageing homosexual, a friend replied, 'Relieved, I expect'. The Mad Boy was provided for. The Berners family portraits were moved out of the stables, now needed for horses that were actually ridden, and into the hall. Soon Heber Percy was running most things out of doors, though when the lake began to smell of sewage in 1933 it was still Berners who put matters right. Heber Percy was given an allowance and, if he lost money gambling beyond that, he was ticked off and not necessarily paid off. In Berners' travesty, Millie is represented as a calculating gold-digger, but an *un*calculating one might have been fairer. Heber Percy continued to go well to hounds and Berners was proud of the figure he cut, even accompanying him occasionally. Heber Percy presented himself as a philistine as well as illiterate, but said years later, 'It was the first time I met civilised people, people who thought I was funny and did not regard me as an outrageous child. It was wonderful.'

Some civilised people did not take to him. Harold Acton never did; Isaiah Berlin said, 'He was not at all nice but then he never pretended for a moment that he was.' Nor did Heber Percy always take to them, refusing to get a drink for Peter Quennell and Alastair Forbes even when requested by Berners to do so. Often, he would not meet them, simply making himself scarce. Their lives, like their tastes, were naturally separate, though they grew together. Half their friends and neighbours did not understand their relationship, which was in any case less than might have been thought; half did not care. There were rumours of goings-on, of something happening in the basement, perhaps a black mass. Heber Percy enjoyed raising the expectations of his sister-in-law Diana (Bubbles), 'Would you like to see?' But there was nothing: 'I expected at least a crucifix upside down.'

A new friend who did get on with Heber Percy, perhaps because she was only a year older, was Diana Mitford who, deciding who should come to a party, said, 'We must have Berners and Madders.' An invitation was duly sent to 'Lord Berners and Madders'. She was beautiful, with huge, intimidating blue eyes and the elegance that Berners admired. They had been acquaintances, but made friends while staying at Polesden Lacey with Mrs Ronnie Greville, 'an amazing old woman, very ugly and spiteful but excellent company' and the possessor of an outstanding cook. Diana Mitford's marriage to Bryan Guinness (later Lord Moyne) was breaking up and she was given too much advice – 'perhaps worldly people know that it is never taken. Emerald, for example, and Gerald Berners, forbore to cavil.'

She was mentioned in Gerald's letter to Beaton because she was staying with Berners in Rome, as she did for each of the three years before she remarried. They fell into an enjoyable routine: in the morning Berners composed (but what?) or painted, perhaps with Princess Murat. He would interrupt himself to make plans on the telephone: '*Pronto, pronto, e Lord Berners,*' he began in Italian that was fluent, although, making no concessions, 'he pronounced it as if it were English'. So lunch would usually be with Italian friends: 'When one first arrived it took a day or two to get the trend on the scandals of the moment which were discussed in every house and all the time.' In the afternoon they saw the sights and he was revealed as a surprisingly energetic and unsurprisingly well-informed guide. Diana Mitford saw Prince Aldobrandini's villa, motored out to Frascati, ate ices in the Piazza Navona.

That first autumn they drove back as slowly as usual, but visited Max Beerbohm on the way, with a touch of excitement. A Swiss who had made a fortune out of pharmaceuticals had pronounced that there was a wonderdrug, obtainable only in Paris, which cured depression for ever. They were accompanied by a gloomy young man called Desmond Parsons ('I've had a disastrous morning in the Vatican') and he and Berners were hoping that their lives were going to be transformed. They duly arrived in Paris and took some. It did nothing for Diana, and, though the men persevered, they too soon dropped it. Perhaps, however, it accounts for how unusually well dinner with Violet Trefusis went that evening. 'She pointed out that as Gerald had a charming London house, and Faringdon, and Foro Romano, between them they had desirable residences for all seasons and moods, and that if they married and pooled them, how delightful that would be.' Another version makes a pretend engagement a way of getting a mass of presents. In any case such an engagement was reported in a social column in London a few days later. 'Violet telephoned Gerald: "I've had dozens of telegrams of congratulations". "Have you really?" said Gerald, "I haven't had a single one."' Her mother insisted that some denial be made and Berners always claimed that he had sent a message to *The Times* saying: 'Lord Berners has left Lesbos for The Isle of Man.'

The next year, while Diana Guinness was staying, Berners wrote twelve bars of a fascist march, 'because I asked him to'. It appeared in the *Daily Express*. There were no words. She had not yet met Hitler, but was in love with Oswald Mosley; indeed, her divorce was to enable her to be free to see him, though he had no plans to leave his wife and family. Mosley had founded the British Union of Fascists two years before. The BUF was, in A. J. P. Taylor's opinion, 'at first applauded by many respectable Conservatives'. Berners' political naïvety has already been stressed. The fascism with which he was familiar was, naturally, Italian fascism, which had held power in the country he loved for years, was espoused by most of his aristocratic friends and at the time lacked the anti-Semitism that was to become the most abominated part of its thinking. Characteristically, Berners' most memorable dealings with Mussolini were connected with art and ridicule: he took a striking photograph of Il Duce, who was delighted and agreed to send it as his Christmas card. Only when many had been despatched did anyone notice that the colossal nude statue of Hercules just behind was most unfortunately placed and had no fig leaf.

So Berners was an innocent exposed to perhaps the most attractive face of the less virulent strain of fascism; nevertheless, he came close to being a supporter in these years, a fellow-traveller of the right. These were early days, but Hitler was now in power and the Night of the Long Knives of 30 June 1934 had taken place. Nor was Berners exposed only to discreet charm: on 7 June that year he and Heber Percy had dined with Diana Guinness on the night of the fascist meeting at Olympia. She had had a temperature and went to bed, but they went on to the rally with the other guest, Vivian Jackson. William Crack drove them.

It was a huge rally of around 15,000 people, but not all of the same views. With the support of Lord Rothermere's *Daily Mail*, the British Union of Fascists had been doing well enough for communists and anti-fascists of all kinds to decide that they must be opposed: 2,000 such were outside and 500 managed to get in and chant slogans when Mosley spoke. He warned that hecklers would be thrown out. They continued, and he ordered his stewards into action. About fifty were thrown out, some beaten up, but nobody was seriously injured; the police moved in. Jackson was arrested and Berners stood bail. The next day, Jackson was in court, and his twin brother Derek later remembered:

> The magistrate was particularly pedantic: he had taken V's watch and other effects, and V asked for it back – it was a gold watch. This the police insisted on describing as 'a watch made with yellow metal'. Took a disbelieving tone when Gerald (giving evidence) said the police attacked them with sticks. Gerald reciprocated with an equally disbelieving tone, as though he too found it hard to believe – which had the effect of making his statement ring true.

Vivian Jackson was fined a few shillings for obstructing the police. It seems almost certain that Berners went to the meeting out of curiosity rather than commitment, but he was not in doubt as to which side he was on and who his friends were.

Not all his upper-class acquaintances agreed with him. Later that year Lady Diana Cooper was sent on what now seems a batty mission to Italy to inform those in power how strongly England opposed Italian aggression in Abyssinia:

> Just as well send a tramp. What hope had I of harnessing Italy from beneath the hospitable roof of 3 Foro Romano? . . . the only opportunity that offered itself was a luncheon party in my host Lord Berners' house, when several close friends of Ciano, the Italian foreign minister and son-in-law of Il Duce, were present. The burden of my message I must have

spluttered out too vehemently, for the Princess San Faustino made a major exit before the meal was eaten, outragedly banging the door as she left, and the aggrieved Lord Berners found difficulty in forgiving me. I don't blame him, he had the fascist vengeance to face.

Berners' notes contain a few on Hitler. Writing of Corot's ability occasionally to produce towards the end of his life something as fine as his early work, he adds, 'Hitler, a good honest man, but corrupted by the German people's beastliness, their alternately cringeing and arrogant sentimentality, is capable from time to time of delivering speeches full of common sense, even of nobility.' Later: 'It was the banning of Heine that first led me to execrate the Nazis.' And later still:

> But now I find that I can hardly listen to [Wagner's] music. In spite of the fact that art knows no political boundaries, I think I definitely stopped liking Wagner when he was taken up by the Nazis. I still like certain things of Richard Strauss. *Till Eulenspigel*. The incidental music to *The Bourgeois Gentilhomme*. *The Rosenkavalier*. But here I think the literary side protrudes.

During the war Berners dreamed of Hitler:

> Diana [now Mosley] and I go to Germany. We are walking through a field with long grass and a fringe of trees lining a road behind us. We ask to see Hitler. We are standing at the top of a flight of steps in front of a glass door. Hitler comes out and shakes hands with us. Very politely but there is no attempt at conversation. He then goes back. I look through the glass door and see that he is judging five or six people. Two or three of the men are naked to the waist. The place looks like a hospital. I discuss with D. whether H. recognised her.

Next year there was, or possibly was not, a curious incident. Heber Percy has recounted, with a touch of irritation that there should be any doubt, that Berners had lunch with Hitler, 'because he asked him. I was asked in for coffee afterwards. They discussed a composer called . . . Diana will know. Hitler said he was no good and thought of sending him up in an aeroplane. Gerald became furious. He was very upset.' William Crack remembers driving Berners to such a lunch in Munich. Diana Mosley, on the other hand, far from identifying the composer (probably Hindemith), is positive that the meeting never took place. It would have been very odd of Berners not to mention it to her. The only written evidence conflicts with everybody except Crack. A postcard from Munich to Heber Percy at Faringdon in September 1935 ends, 'It was lovely meeting Hitler.' This does not appear to be a joke; on the other hand, Berners does not seem to have been made furious, nor could Heber Percy have had coffee with them. The truth is probably close to what John Betjeman wrote to Penelope: 'Apparently it is all rot about Robert and Gerald lunching with Hitler. They merely happened to be in the same restaurant. We must cross-examine them very thoroughly on what Hitler said to them.'

Chapter XI

The Girls of Radcliff Hall

Meanwhile, Faringdon was steadily being transformed. What happened when is impossible to disentangle; it was a continuous process with some constant characteristics. In many ways the house is modest, though there are touches of grandeur. The core is not large. There are five bedrooms and four bathrooms on the first floor, and Berners and Heber Percy took two of these. (Nevertheless when a young peer, whose own house is justly famed, said to Heber Percy as he looked across at the church, 'I suppose this was the vicarage once', it was not well received.) Nor was the house ever very highly organised. Expected standards of comfort were met but not exceeded, save in the dining-room and perhaps in the fact that it was warm in winter – 'Faringdonheit', Adrian Daintrey called it.

Into the conventional country-house mould Berners poured idiosyncratic charm and humour. He foresaw a certain television programme in his notes: 'It would be an amusing psychological game to be shown a room and to be invited to guess what sort of person lived therein.' No one would have been named with more speed and confidence than Berners himself. One element was the juxtaposition of elegance and junk – a gaudily fake necklace twined round an exquisite little figure, Corots on the wall (also works by Derain, Sisley, Matisse, Dufy and Constable) but a pink Disney pig that squeaked on the table, because it reminded him of Violet Trefusis, and because it amused him. All around were excellent gilded furniture, Aubusson and English carpets from the eighteenth century, stuffed birds of paradise in glass cases from the nineteenth, mechanical toys and, upstairs, a chest of drawers designed by Dali, which leant steeply to one side. The big drawing-room, fifty-four feet long, looked through five French windows, over the fountain, to the view. It had white flock wallpaper, good French and

Italian furniture and a fire at each end. In his novel, Michael Duff adds
a smaller room behind sliding doors:

> the drawing-room had an atmosphere of cosiness and ease with its faded
> green walls. It was too much of a delightful jumble to be of any
> particular period. There were masses of books lying on tables,
> surrounded by butterflies in glass cases, silver-gilt pheasants and pink
> shell-shaped vases from which dangled dirty white ostrich feathers
> interwoven with a necklace of sham pearls ... On the white marble
> mantelpiece was a Regency clock which played a tune instead of striking
> the hour.

Many remember the profusion of flowers, but in a story Berners wrote,
with approval, 'The house looked as if it had long been occupied by
very charming people of taste. Mary always managed to avoid "the
decorator's touch". Nor was she overlavish in her use of flowers. "So
many people," she said, "overdo their flowers and make the place look
like a musical-comedy setting."'

There were joke books (enticingly suggestive titles with blank pages
within). There were joke notices. 'Mangling Done Here' was prominent, and Patrick Leigh Fermor remembers:

> 'No dogs admitted' at the top of the stairs and 'Prepare to meet thy God'
> painted inside a wardrobe. When people complimented him [Berners] on
> his delicious peaches he used to say, 'Yes, they are ham-fed'. And he
> used to put Woolworth pearl necklaces round his dogs' necks [Berners
> had a dalmatian, Heber Percy the retriever, Pansy Lamb] and when a
> guest, rather perturbed, ran up saying, 'Fido has lost his necklace', G
> said, 'Oh dear, I'll have to get another out of the safe'.

Outside, herbaceous borders were held in contempt, although an
explosion of delphiniums was allowed, paper flowers were planted to
deceive, Berners had an unusual enthusiasm for ground elder, and
statues appeared in unexpected places.

The place and stories about the owner are inseparable. Berners used
to walk round the lake every morning, as well as swim in it ('he
considered it the height of vulgarity to have a swimming-bath'). He was
superstitious in general, and in particular held it unlucky to see a white
feather and not pick it up and plant it. Heber Percy once took a sackful
and distributed them along Berners' way so that his stroll was
enormously protracted. There was an anti-dog notice: 'Trespassers will

be prosecuted, dogs shot, cats whipped.' Birds, however, had always been welcome at Faringdon and became its distinguishing feature. There was a plaque sunk into the south lawn which read, 'Fear not to sow because of the birds', a generous point of view. There were flamingos, fed on shrimps to keep them pink; birds of paradise; storks; and a trumpeter bird. They tapped on the windows of the house to gain admittance. 'Odd large-beaked birds,' remembered Sir Francis Rose, the painter and stage designer, 'wandered through the Georgian silver on the Chippendale dining-table, pecked in one's plate or left squarking horribly on some guest's head.'

In *The Pursuit of Love*, Nancy Mitford in a few words described the single creation for which Berners remains best known: '[there was] a flock of multi-coloured pigeons tumbling about like a cloud of confetti in the sky'. The heroine, told that they are dyed each year on Easter Sunday and dried in the linen cupboard, objects, as any such heroine would, but is reassured that they soon learn to keep their eyes shut. In fact they were dyed monthly with harmless vegetable dyes and had masks to put over their heads. Constant Lambert goes further:

> The process which was done in the way you treat a drawing with fixative was entirely harmless and indeed seemed to please the birds considerably . . . Incidentally it may interest scientists and in particular the followers of Pavlov to know that after being dyed the pigeons no longer enjoyed the happy promiscuity for which their race is renowned but mated only with pigeons of the same colour.

(Heber Percy denied this last point.) Simple visitors often asked for eggs, hoping the brilliant hues would be inherited. Heber Percy was generally in charge, but Francis Rose claims that 'it was a common sight to see one's host wearing a huge green apron standing in the drive in front of great basins of magenta, copper green and ultramarine dye, and with the help of men-servants ceremoniously dipping, one after another, his white pigeons and once, I believe, some swans, a duck and a white poodle.'

Delighted with his success, Berners apparently tried to persuade local farmers to dye their horses and cattle purple. His motive was slightly different: colouring the pigeons gave the innocent visitor a sudden unbelievable moment of beauty; colouring the cows would be bizarre and would annoy the neighbours. When the farm needed a telegraphic address, Berners chose 'Neighbourtease' and had it printed on the writing paper. It was not misleading. A new vicar called and said that he was longing to meet Lord Berners and was sure that he would get on with him.

'What makes you think so?'

'I used to be in Chelsea, I knew all the artists, we used to cook eggs on a gas ring. I'm sure we'll get on famously.'

Clearly the vicar was to be teased; when he asked for money for the deserving poor, Berners replied, 'I'm afraid I can't help you much though I'd like to. My parents taught me never to be associated with failure.'

On another occasion some neighbours outstayed their welcome and, though he had escaped to another room, Berners had left his book behind and now wanted to read it. He crawled into the drawing-room on his hands and knees under a bearskin, retrieved the volume and crawled out again. Nobody mentioned it.

Most neighbours were simply ignored. An exception was Lord Faringdon, who lived in splendour four miles away at Buscot. A.L. Rowse recounts a scene at All Souls in Oxford. A fellow, Lionel Curtis, asked:

> 'Why am I mixed up between Lord Faringdon and Lord Berners?'
> Quintin Hailsham, wickedly: 'Ask Leslie [Rowse]: he knows.'
> Lionel: 'But I don't know. Which is which? Why do I confuse the two?'
> Quintin (with a meaning look at me): 'Ask Leslie. He knows.'
> Lionel, thinking this over, raised his voice: 'Do you mean that he is an Enemy of the Family?'
> The butler, appearing round the screen, 'Lord Faringdon to see you, sir.'

Gavin Faringdon was indeed, like Berners, 'an Enemy of the Family', and famously prefaced a speech not with 'My Lords' but 'My dears'. He and Berners also shared many acquaintances and a taste for jokes, though his were rather rougher – in 1927 at the bachelor party the night before his wedding he had, with some friends and a lot of petrol, literally set the Thames on fire. The confusion of Lionel Curtis, however, clearly rested on the title of one being the house of the other.

Guests at Faringdon usually came from further afield. They came to amuse and be amused. Boredom, which might turn to despair, was the enemy. Anyone who failed to amuse, particularly by being too earnest, was known as 'a dry blanket'. At the end of 1933 Berners started a

visitors' book. It does have 'Visitors' on the outside but, far from being
the splendid object you might expect, is a shabby notebook with lines
and headings. Berners put himself first, with Faringdon as his
permanent address, a question mark under date of departure, Rome as
his business address, and, with 'profession' substituted for 'nationality',
'Composer-painter-author. Gourmet. Bird-fancier'. In spite of there
being only room for three or four people to stay in any style, and the
fact that he was away for so much of the year, there were seventy-four
guests during the first year and over a hundred for the next two, before
a gradual decline leading up to the war.

A string of names with their self-descriptions may convey Berners'
milieu: for the Christmas of 1933, Diana Guinness, Gladys Marlborough (commercial traveller) and Edward James (poet) came to stay,
then, in January, Robert Abdy (obelisk fancier) and his tiny wife Diane
(Arcadian). (The Abdys were close and lifelong friends. He was
nicknamed Sir Bertram the Absolute for his uncompromising conversa-
tional style, which extended into his brief career as an art dealer, when
he refused to sell to anyone whose taste he found vulgar.) Heber Percy
relations recur and Kathleen Meyrick (Night Club Hostess) came for
five days. Bryan Guinness (farmer-poet) comes often, but separated
now from Diana. Hubert Duggan (politician) and Harold Nicolson
(critic and author) describe themselves without facetiousness, while
Tom Mitford and John Sutro are respectively Barrister-at-Law and
Barrister-without-Law. Adrian Daintrey is first a painter but then,
obscurely, a cannibal, and later a rotter. Sacheverell and Georgia Sitwell
came for a day with William Walton and Edith, whose profession is
much emended and has 'poetess' pasted on top. Casati returns
(Tempteuse de Serpents), Mario Pansa from Rome, Mark Ogilvie-
Grant, describing himself as a plumber, and Bridget Parsons persists
with 'tug-boat destroyer'.* Sometimes the professions echo one
another. Michael Duff is another obelisk hunter but not on the same
page as Sir Robert Abdy, so probably without knowledge of his entry.
E.M. Murray, an American painter, on the other hand, could see Rex
Whistler's 'peintre de luxe' a few lines above when he wrote 'peintre de
grande luxe', and Beverley Nichols was looking at 'Churchill –
Investigator' when he filled in 'Investigator of affairs of Lord Churchill'.

Anyone who came more than once to these small house parties can be

---

* This obscure phrase perhaps alludes to the fact that the Countess of Rosse, née
Messel, was known as 'Tugboat Annie'.

thought of as a friend. 'Naps' Alington (JP) came twice. Lady Mary Lygon (Sporting Hostess) came several times and her younger sister Lady Dorothy (ADC to Sporting Hostess) came far more often than anyone else, seven visits in one year. They were the daughters of Lord Beauchamp, who had, effectively, been exiled for homosexuality. His brother-in-law, less charming and less popular, had forced the King to pay attention and the police in turn were bound to press charges for what was then, of course, a crime. With only just more sense than Wilde, Beauchamp left while they were knocking at the front door. It is said that the solicitors spent days trying to explain the nature of the disaster to Lady Beauchamp but without success; it was beyond her range.

The girls were left in possession of a fine house, Madresfield, and a freedom most unusual at that time. Phyllis de Janzé had brought Berners to stay there in 1931. Lady Mary (Maimie) was a striking blonde, who was to be engaged many times before she married Prince Vsevolode Joannovitch of Russia in 1939. Lady Dorothy (Coote), only two years younger and so just twenty-two in 1934, was much quieter, as became an ADC. Many years later she and Lady Diana Cooper went to a fancy-dress ball as nuns; 'Diana looked like an actress playing a nun,' said Heber Percy, 'Coote looked like a nun.' What Heber Percy admired in Lady Mary was something of the dash and wildness that Berners liked in him. The sisters became, and remained, constant visitors at Faringdon. At the beginning of the 1930s the sisters had also met Evelyn Waugh and become lifelong friends with him. (The family situation of having a father abroad, the chapel in their house, the looks of their brother, Hugh, all contributed to *Brideshead Revisited*.)

Christopher Sykes, Waugh's friend and biographer, says, 'Berners was a man of deep and genuine talent, and the friendship which grew up between him and Evelyn was more authentic than some others that he [Waugh] formed in upper-class society.' He dates their friendship from the time after the success of Waugh's *Vile Bodies* in 1930, but it seems altogether slighter and later. Waugh's remark at Berners' first exhibition in 1931 ('What a good thing it is to be a baron') is not the remark of a friend – not because it is malicious, but because it is distant. In his diary in 1934 he seems only marginally closer: 'I woke up in time to go to tea with Gerald Berners. When he asked me he said, "It is a tea party you know", with a little giggle. "Don't you think that it is an amusing idea?" I said, "Very amusing."'

Waugh was not amused, but next year, writing to Penelope Betjeman,

he managed the Christian name alone – 'Give my love to Gerald' – and
did stay at Faringdon (profession: 'prospective eunuch', which changes
next year to 'Intact'; he was going to Abyssinia as a war correspondent
but had promised to be true to Laura Herbert, whom he married in
1937). It must have seemed to their many shared friends, Sitwells and
Mitfords as well as those mentioned, that Waugh and Berners were well
suited. Berners had respect for first-rate talent, was a great reader and
above all liked to be amused. It has been continually said of Waugh,
occasionally by himself, that he liked a peer, and he too was easily
bored. Yet they never really went beyond being friendly acquaintances.
Writing did not bring them together. Waugh thought one of Berners'
works 'the dullest book yet seen'. Berners wrote to Waugh defending
Cyril Connolly's *The Unquiet Grave* and does not seem sincere when he
says, 'I suppose you are right to place morality above art and
friendship.' When, in the late 1940s, Diana Mosley told him that
Waugh prayed for her every day, Berners snapped back, 'God doesn't
pay any attention to Evelyn.' None of this would have counted for
anything if they had relished each other's company, but they did not.
Perhaps one seemed too fierce, the other too silly; for different reasons,
neither was an easy friend.

Those who visited Faringdon more than once included several
flamboyant homosexuals of about thirty, that is to say almost ten years
older than Heber Percy and twenty years younger than Berners – his
new set. They were not the centre of Berners' life, nor was he directly
involved in the intrigues, rows, giggling and plots except when Heber
Percy was, though that was often enough. Neither Berners nor Heber
Percy was in the least effeminate or camp – rather the opposite – but
such an atmosphere now became a part of their lives and, as it was not
banished, presumably an agreeable part. It even brought out something
similar in Berners that was not otherwise shown.

   Beverley Nichols ('Shark' in the visitors' book on his second
appearance) was not quite included in this group, thus slightly
undermining the view that Berners wanted only to be amused. For
Nichols, a little older than the others, could certainly be amusing and at
that time seemed to promise much more than he in fact ever delivered.
Instead of becoming Noël Coward or at least Harold Nicolson, he wrote
cosy accounts of his garden. When he gushed about the scyllas and
grape hyacinths at Faringdon, Berners is supposed to have said, 'Oh, I
told the gardener not to plant those nasty little catamites' and to have

trodden on them. Cecil Beaton was very much included, his lasting though interrupted friendship with Berners having been established for a year or two. Ashcombe, the house into which Beaton moved in 1930, was not far.

When Waugh was differentiating between north and south Wiltshire as possible places to live, he wrote, 'I wouldn't mind the Berners Betjeman country. On no account the Juliet [Duff] Beaton Pembroke country. No pine trees.' Pembroke was the Earl of Pembroke, owner of Wilton, which contained his three sons, the second of whom, David Herbert, was another member of this set. He asserted in some memoirs an unlikely piece of gossip, that Berners stipulated in his will that he was to be stuffed and hung in a glass case over the mantelpiece in the drawing-room at Faringdon. The apocrypha that gather round a man reveal at least how he was perceived. Also nearby was the writer Edith Olivier, who was close to Beaton. In her diary for 21 July 1933 she wrote,

> Ottoline [Morrell] and I then lunched at Ashcombe, where Cecil said he was 'alone with Gerald', but no we found them sitting in the courtyard – Gerald painting Lady Castlerosse. Evidently Napier is right. It is a liaison [between Beaton and Lady Castlerosse] and 'we' always includes her. It makes me feel I can never go there again. There is nothing there but a common little demi-mondaine and why should one put oneself out for her.

Edith Olivier had thought Peter Watson 'commonplace', but this was worse. Many would have agreed. Doris Delevingne was a forceful girl from Beckenham. She had once shared rooms with the young Gertrude Lawrence, and Amanda in *Private Lives* is said to owe something to her. The mistress of a duke, when asked at dinner what she did, replied, 'I don't know what you call it exactly, but I think you can say that I am at the height of my profession.' Doris could say the same. In 1928 she married Viscount Castlerosse, a journalist famous for his corpulence and his wit. The marriage lasted five years but did not slow Doris down. She is supposed to have retired upstairs with Beaton at Faringdon and been pursued by eavesdropping guests, who heard him suddenly cry out, 'Oh goody, goody, goody'. Certainly she stayed at Faringdon but she and Beaton did not coincide. Nor was Faringdon quite like that. It was unusual, but not louche. Heber Percy might ride a horse into the house with no clothes on, but nothing more outrageous.

Heber Percy liked Doris Castlerosse; liked her enquiring whether she had slept with him the night before as she simply couldn't remember; liked her saying, when she was short of money and Berners offered to lend her some, that it was sweet of him but anything he could afford would not keep her going for a week. He also liked her being more outrageous than he could manage, and told with approval a story of how in Paris she had bought him a prostitute whom, she said, he could beat to death. Presented with a naked back and a whip, he gave a feeble tap; she snatched the weapon and lashed out a 'welt-raising' blow so that for once the Mad Boy was reduced to saying, 'I say, steady on . . .'

Oliver Messel was travelling with Peter Watson when Watson and Beaton first met in 1933. Beaton begged Messel to relinquish him, which naturally spurred Messel on. They fought 'like bears' at Diana Cooper's fortieth birthday party in Venice and were lifelong rivals as stage designers. It was with undisguised satisfaction that Beaton wrote before the war, 'Oliver has become rather a sad figure particularly in contrast to the brilliant promising and already sensationally successful youth of fifteen years ago . . . a monkey's talent . . . sees only very second-rate people . . . ' (The sensational success had included the commissions from Cochran and Diaghilev for masks for their productions.) Beaton was wrong. Messel continued to flourish and they continued to bicker. ('Well, really, Oliver ought to employ a decorator,' he said, when asked what he thought of Messel's new house.)

In 1933 Messel went with Berners to 'a fashionable health clinic popular with the social set' in Munich, run by 'the famous Doctor Martin', and it was in Munich that summer that Berners and Heber Percy met Beaton and Watson and the trouble-making Alvis car was given to Heber Percy. The feud continued, so that it was generous of Heber Percy to allow 'Ridiculous character. But Cecil did have guts. To wear gold-dust in your hair when and where Cecil wore gold-dust [Wilton] required courage.'

All the same, in January 1934 Berners writes, without any apparent sense of disloyalty, to 'Dearest Cecil' and, after recounting some amateur theatricals at Mount Stewart, goes on to press him to stay at Halkin Street, whether Berners is there or not. To add further complication, when Beaton, Berners and Heber Percy were staying at Madresfield, Beaton asked where Robert's room was and Heber Percy felt that the question did not stem from idle curiosity. He told Berners. Sure enough, later that night there was a tap on the door, a muffled 'Come in' and Beaton tiptoed forward towards the bed. The main bulbs had been removed, so darkness remained. Then the bedside light snapped on, to reveal Berners sitting upright with his nightcap on, saying, 'Oh Cecil, this is so sudden.'

These people, and the atmosphere of gossip, intrigue and giggling that they created, appeared in Berners' next book, indeed they *were* his next book. In 1928, Radclyffe Hall had published, and had been forced to withdraw, a solemn, not to say turgid, novel about lesbian love, *The Well of Loneliness*. Now Berners produced *The Girls of Radcliff Hall*, in which this set appeared as schoolgirls almost exclusively concerned with pashes on one another. The style is based on that of Angela Brazil, as his chosen pseudonym, Adela Quebec, suggests. It was only ever intended for private circulation and the joke was much sharpened by the closeness with which real life, often in small details, was shadowed, so that the better informed the reader, the more amusing it all was.

Berners by now genuinely liked Cecil Beaton, and the heroine is Cecily Seymour, 'one of the most charming and talented girls in the school. She was just as clever with her paint brush as she was with her needle.' And Lizzie Johnson (Peter Watson):

> in spite of her capricious nature . . . was really very fond of Cecily . . .
> Ensconced in the Prefect's sitting-room, Olive Mason [Oliver Messel, described as a mischief-maker, as he described himself in the Faringdon visitors' book] and Daisy Montgomery [David Herbert] were engaged in their favourite occupation, talking about the other girls. 'It's really too preposterous', Daisy was saying, 'that Lizzie should have so many "crushes". She's had more "crushes" than any other girl in the school and how she manages it with that tow-coloured hair and that awful complexion I just can't imagine'.

The plot is set in motion by the arrival of an attractive new girl, May Peabody [Robin Thomas], 'the sweetest little creature you could possibly wish to see, with hair the colour of corn, lovely light grey eyes and a winning smile. In spite of the fact that she had come all the way from America she didn't seem in the least shy.' Lizzie is soon after her, Cecily is jealous, while Daisy stirs up trouble. Now the headmistress (Berners himself) is introduced, with a reverie that gives more information than is allowed about the others.

> Miss Carfax sat alone in her room before a dying fire. Memories grave and gay fluttered like autumn leaves across her brain. In spite of a

superficial gaiety of spirit she often felt unhappy and tormented. She had a deeply romantic nature.

It was true, as Olive had said, that she was rich and that there was no necessity for her to have a profession. It was also true that she was happy in the company of young girls. But not quite in the way Olive had meant it. She had once been passionately in love with a man, but he, alas, had proved himself unworthy of her. He had, in fact, 'let her down'. And this little tragedy in her life had left her with a profound disgust for men.

Is Berners saying that he had only become homosexual because of an unhappy heterosexual affair in his youth? It seems most improbable. He would surely have told Heber Percy, who would surely have passed on such interesting and in no way discreditable information. Why then is it included among so much else that is meant to allude to the truth? As does further description: 'She was a talented woman, she played the violin, had won several prizes for her embroidery, painted charmingly in water-colours and had even written a novel that had not been recommended by the Book Society.' Miss Carfax liked to 'devote herself to some young girl whom she considered to show promise', but 'until now, her ministrations had deliberately ceased, and slander, except on the part of a few morbidly prurient and evil-minded persons, had left her unscathed.' This might be read as claiming a celibate life, or at least a successfully private one.

The only man in the book is the dancing master, Mr Vivian Dorrick (Doris Castlerosse, the only woman model). 'Mr Dorrick was no novice in the art of love-making . . . His personality was veiled, to a certain extent, in mystery.' He takes a fancy to Cecily (as Castlerosse did to Beaton), though Daisy says, 'It's all nonsense. She's only doing it to try and make Lizzie jealous' – as doubtless David Herbert did indeed suggest. Little May is ill, there are blows on the lacrosse pitch, then Lizzie goes off with little May, instead of watching Cecily in the end-of-term play: 'At the performance that night, Cecily, though her heart was breaking, put up a brave show. Never before had she seemed so gay, so brilliant, so fantastic, so delightfully comic . . . But when Miss Carfax went round afterwards to congratulate Cecily she saw that there were tears running down her cheeks.'

In the holidays, things become rather diffuse. Miss Carfax goes to stay with a friend and Millie Roberts (Heber Percy) arrives on her milk-cart. She comes to Radcliff Hall and is very popular: Lizzie (Watson) is 'very much struck with her appearance'. Olive (Messel) explains to Millie that Lizzie is much richer than Miss Carfax. Soon Millie

Berners, Lee Miller
and Gertrude Stein
among the daffodils

Berners and
A Wedding Bouquet

Berners, Frederick Ashton and Constant Lambert

Cecil Beaton at Faringdon

Margot Fonteyn in *A Wedding Bouquet*

Elsa Schiaparelli,
Berners, Moura
Budberg, H.G. Wells,
Robert Heber Percy
and Tom Driberg
at Faringdon

Francis Rose

Berners,
David and Rachel Cecil
and friend

Berners' illustration for the
frontispiece of *Count Omega*

Berners' drawing for
Red Roses and Red Noses

Berners' painting of Faringdon from the south
for the set of *A Wedding Bouquet*

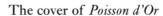
The cover of *Poisson d'Or*

The first page of the
original score of *Poisson d'Or*

Temptation in the Wilderness by Briton Riviere (RA), as revised by Berners

Nancy Mitford, c.1948

Princesse de Polignac, 1936

Clarissa Churchill,
with Berners in the background

Berners, with Jennifer Heber Percy pushing Victoria, and unknown

Berners in 1943

Berners by Gregorio Prieto

'Lord Berners uses
Bromo lavatory paper'

persuades Lizzie to give her a car, a baby Austin: 'I say, what do you think, Lizzie has promised to give me a Baby.' Miss Carfax, interrupted doing her stomach exercises, flushes with annoyance at the news, but that is nothing to how poor Cecily feels and, after a row and a few tears, she gets a cheque for £500 (Beaton got the £1,000 Alvis in real life) and buys one. May returns, drinking too many cocktails and trying to blackmail Lizzie. Any shreds of credibility still clinging to the school story are vanishing.

Millie (Heber Percy) now has the field to herself and is 'overjoyed at the prospect of all the presents she is going to get out of Lizzie'. Miss Carfax notices with considerable annoyance, but thinks she can keep an eye on things. Suddenly, however, she decides to settle down on a poultry farm. 'Oh, Miss Carfax,' Millie cried, 'it has always been my dream to live in the country and keep chickens.' This may be rather closer in spirit than in factual detail to the way Heber Percy moved into Faringdon. There is still more plot (poisoned toothpaste) and even a new character (an American film-star) to come, but things get rather out of hand and further from real life. Cecily, for example, elopes with Mr Dorrick. Lizzie becomes a nun. When Cecily sends a present, there is for the first time a foray into Firbank territory: 'What was her delight, however, in discovering a little velvet ecran, and, inside it, a lovely miniature scourge made of seed pearls and garnished with tiny spikes of blue enamel.' Meanwhile, love blossoms among the chickens, but the last page brings news of a fabulously wealthy neighbour and the book ends with: 'Millie pricked up her ears.'

The Girls of Radcliff Hall is examined here for the light it throws on Berners and his immediate circle, but it would repay study by an expert on the period and milieu, for almost every incident seems to reflect or allude to reality. Above all, the joke must have been unnervingly funny at the time; copies were passed with trembling, apprehensive fingers. Distance lends disenchantment – much of the fizz has gone – but high spirits carry the reader through the hundred pages. The book should be more tightly plotted and should never leave the school, but Berners was not writing for a general reader and needed the liberty to echo gossip and true events. The world he depicted is silly but not sentimental: the young and good-looking are out for what they can get from the old and rich. Heber Percy is depicted as amoral, devious, disloyal and rapacious. He adored the book. Messel seems an amiable mischief-maker; Herbert considerably less so; Watson is unsure of himself and a cause of misery. But it was the heroine, Cecil Beaton, who took most violent exception.

It is said that he went round acquiring copies and destroying them, in an attempt to suppress it and, though there is no direct evidence of this, the book is indeed curiously scarce. He certainly threatened to sue for libel. With neither money nor breeding, his social position was the most vulnerable and meant everything to him.

The story that Berners had presented a copy to Queen Mary and had been congratulated on a conventional but accurate school story was much repeated. Noël Coward wrote, 'I absolutely adored Les Girls. Oh dear! What a beastly little book.' This was generous, as his lover, Jack Wilson (under the name Helena de Troy), had been portrayed as having an affair with Peter Watson. The book is undeniably camp but, even among this set, Berners never really became camp himself. Stephen Tennant wrote, for example, to Cecil Beaton, 'What in life could be more ecstatic an occupation than putting orchids in an ice-box and then taking them out again.' Berners, who had after all ten years before been a close friend of Firbank, had never gone in for that sort of stuff and did not now.

This side of his life was not kept in a compartment. The girls of Radcliff Hall came to Faringdon not in a battalion, but as single spies, mixing with other, older friends; nor did they dominate abroad. A diary of 1934, little more than an appointments book, shows the mix, as well as giving a few unexplained hints: occasionally there is 'Row with Robert', though Berners was notably even-tempered. Lady Dorothy Lygon remembers seeing him angry only once, when Lord Stanley of Alderley, her sister Lady Mary and Fulco, Duc di Verdura, raided the larder, ate the next day's lunch, and put lipstick on a statue. Di Verdura and Stanley left by an early train and Maimie had to face the music, which was loud and discordant. Stanley's entry in the visitors' book ('shit') is bracketed by Berners with the Duke of Verdura's ('recliner on sofas'). The host has added, 'Not to be asked again'; nor were they.

The same year there are surprisingly few musical engagements in the diary, and those that there are do not sound very serious. 'Concert with Emerald', 'ballet with Emerald', the Albert Hall for 'Blackbirds' (the all-black American revue that had been a fashionable success some time before) and the Palladium. 'Disagreeable discovery upon returning home' is not enlarged upon, nor is 'frogface disturbance at 3 o'clock in the morning'. (Watson?) 'Pyjama incident' takes place when Oliver Messel is staying. Some guests were not allotted such volatile companions. Bernard Shaw and his wife ('literary' and 'wife of the above') stayed on their own. Plans for Shaw to visit again failed, his last message eight years later being 'I am most damnably old and deafish, besides being decidedly dotty but I can still keep up a stage effect of being fit for human society.'

The great event at Faringdon in 1935 was the completion and opening of the folly. In retrospect it seems so fitting as to be almost inevitable that it should have been Berners who built the last traditional folly-tower in England. In fact it came about by accident. The site was already called Faringdon Folly, though there was no building, the word being a corruption of the French *feuille*, meaning foliage. There are beech and pine there and, in 1919, a timber merchant wanted to cut them down. Berners outbid him. One day, when he and Heber Percy went to have a look at the place, Berners said something about it being nice to have a tower there. This was overheard and reported. Opposition was voiced, and Berners saw the chance for a major neighbour-tease.

The struggle to achieve his whim was long and fierce and included much comedy. In 1933 a sub-committee of the Town and Country Planning Committee of the Rural District Council of Faringdon met Berners on the proposed site and, though he was willing to reduce the height of the folly to one hundred feet, refused permission. In their report they 'fail to see the object or benefit of the tower, if erected', which is reasonable enough. As Berners himself said, 'The great point of the Tower is that it will be entirely useless.' Kind commentators, unfamiliar with his character, have suggested that it was a twenty-first birthday present for Heber Percy (but that had taken place in 1932), or that Berners wished to create employment during the Depression (he did not; the work was carried out by those already employed on the estate).

It is true, however, that when he found himself thwarted, Berners became committed to the plan. He appealed, and gave an interview in which employment is mentioned, as is a small charge to visitors, which is to be given to the Faringdon Cottage Hospital. This is as far as Berners ever went in playing politics. At a further meeting words such as 'duffers' and sentences like 'I don't want you to be rude, sir. You are quite a young man and a newcomer to this council' were exchanged. There was a letter to the local paper from Vivian Lobb, who lived at Kelmscott with May Morris, daughter of William Morris, saying that Lord Berners planned to install a siren that could be heard from twenty-five miles away and would go off every two hours to waken the sick and dying. Berners, who knew her, replied, 'It would be better if Mr Lobb had ascertained the facts before writing a letter which sounded as though it had emanated from the brain of a crazy spinster.'

The men from the ministry (curiously that of health) came down in October 1934 to hear both sides. Vice-Admiral F. Clifton Brown scored in an early exchange, when he claimed that the tower would mar his view. The architect, who was Berners' old friend Lord Gerald Wellesley, protested: 'But you could not see the tower from your garden without a telescope.' To which the admiral crushingly replied that such was indeed his habit. Wellesley hit back, however, when pointing out to this lover of views how fine would be the vista from the top; he was interrupted with, 'How will you get there?' and was able to reply truthfully, 'By the stairs'. In the end, he undertook that the tower should only peep out three feet above the tallest tree.

There is a detailed correspondence between Wellesley and Berners about the inscription. Wellesley: 'I think *nobile* is all right. You could substitute "*Baro*" for "*Dominus*" if you liked but on the whole I wouldn't . . . I think that the word "*elegantissimus*" might arouse giggles.' The wording of the notice at the entrance was all Berners' own: 'Members of the Public committing suicide from this tower do so at their own risk.' The actual building went smoothly. The tower is square, of brick, and the wooden staircase leads to a belvedere room with three arched windows on each side. Above this is another room, in the shape of an octagonal lantern with elongated oblong windows. Finally there is a viewing platform, surrounded by a stone pinnacled parapet, from which you can see four counties (and on a clear day perhaps five).

Heber Percy remembered a further complication: 'Gerald wanted it Gothic. He chose the only architect who loathed Gothic. Gerald went off to Rome and Gerry built it, classical, up to nearly a hundred feet. Gerald came back and was furious at this and insisted on the top bit being Gothic so the last ten feet are Gothic.' The party for the opening was a great success, with splendid fireworks more than making up for the long walk to and from the house on a cold evening. Guests were allowed up to six effigies of enemies to be burned on the bonfire; this was deemed 'most inadequate'.

Finally, fifteen months later, a poem appeared in the *North Wiltshire Herald*. Berners kept a scrapbook of articles about his music and reviews of his books. In this he also put reports about his folly (thus ranking it as a creation), including the poem. It had been sent in 'almost anonymously' by P.B. of Challow, which was near where John and Penelope Betjeman lived.

Berners' Folly

We came upon it, you and I,
Set on a hill near Faringdon Town,
We came upon it suddenly.
Clouds were drifting across the sky,
Just before the sun went down,
The trees were rustling lazily . . .

The arrival of the Betjemans at Garrards Farm was a huge addition to Berners' life, and to Heber Percy's. John Betjeman, thirty and just three years married, had so far had an unimpressive career, which included leaving Oxford without a degree and – the badge of failure for a middle-class boy – a spell as a master at a preparatory school. His wife was Penelope Chetwode, daughter of Field Marshal Sir Philip (later Lord) Chetwode, Commander-in-Chief of the British Army in India, for which country she had developed a passion. Her family had been established in Staffordshire since at least the fifteenth century and had held a baronetcy since 1700; her parents had not welcomed the match and sometimes it had seemed as if she did not, either. In 1934 they came to live in the village of Uffington for thirteen years and immediately became neighbours to cherish rather than tease. Each was eccentric and amusing in their own way, each brought a warmth that Faringdon occasionally lacked. Betjeman, like Berners, at times held an underlying melancholy at bay by willed high spirits. With more and louder laughter, he would clap his hands and say, 'My word, I am enjoying myself', when perhaps he was not. He had first met Berners at a party given at the Savoy by Heber Percy.

Penelope spoke with uncensored upper-class confidence in a voice that became famous: loud, grating, a touch of Cockney grafted on from somewhere, unceasing but in the end lovable. When H.G. Wells came to lunch at Faringdon, she reduced him to rare and respectful silence by an exhaustive recital of the history and techniques of the Caesarean operation. 'If I were married to that girl,' Wells told Berners, 'I would throw away my encyclopaedia.' She sang, both in the drawing-room and in a quintet ('I was descant') made up largely of the Nortons, who kept the village store. Berners accompanied her in every sense through

'Guide Me O Thou Great Redeemer' and 'Jesu, Lover of My Soul', but resisted her attempts to get him more involved with the church. There were musical evenings with Maurice Bowra, and Osbert Lancaster on the flute. She claimed to have talked Heber Percy into giving a sermon. Her most famous addition to Faringdon was her Arab horse, Moti, which used to come into the drawing-room. 'Gerald loved having him there. He was so domesticated.' Berners had the scene photographed, as indeed was natural, but his eccentricity was one degree more calculated than hers; the photograph found its way into the *Evening News*. He knew the effect he created and enjoyed it; she just did not care.

The Betjemans, particularly Penelope, were an effect themselves – when, for instance, she darned John's underclothes in the Faringdon drawing-room after dinner. 'We loathed smart life,' she said, but Berners included them in his and they enjoyed dipping into it. With the Dalis, for instance: 'Gosh, she was an attractive woman,' Penelope commented. 'Never stopped talking about fur-lined wombs.' Her enthusiasm for horses was a link with Heber Percy and they went riding together. When Betjeman was given a mount at Faringdon, he was chased by some bullocks, came off and shouted, 'You've brought me here to kill me.' Penelope 'laughed so much I almost came off'. Berners did still occasionally ride and painted her galloping on Moti, but from a photograph. And his painting of the folly went on the cover of the Shell Guide to Berkshire, part of the series that Betjeman had helped initiate.

Betjeman reported to Penelope a unique event in Berners' life which happened that year, a speech. It was at the opening of the cinema in Faringdon. He prepared it carefully and recited it, pointing out a 'pause for laughter from the more expensive seats'. In the event, when prompted by the manager, Berners stood to attention and said, 'I declare this cinema open,' and they watched Errol Flynn in *The Lives of a Bengal Lancer*. This brief appearance in the spotlight was photographed for the *Tatler*: Berners laughing, his house party looking rather grim in the drawing-room at Faringdon beforehand.

Berners used to say that publicity helped his work, but it seems clear that he had nothing against it for its own sake. He filled in, for instance, a questionnaire about the requirements for a happy marriage, potentially embarrassing territory for him: 'A short memory, A long purse, Infinite credulity, No sense of humour, A combative nature, The Man should be a Man and the Woman a Woman or Vice Versa.' Not a self-portrait, but perhaps reminiscent of his parents. For fun, not publication, several friends filled in another questionnaire. Diana Mosley kept Berners' self-revelations:

What is your occupation?	Versatility
What occupation would you choose if you had unlimited choice?	Opera bouffe
Do you believe in the equality of the sexes?	–
Which would you rather have, love or money?	Money
What is your favourite pastime?	Doing good to others
What is your besetting sin?	Laziness and gluttony
Do you consider yourself good-looking?	No – but very nice
Do you believe in love at first sight?	Yes and No

Berners suggested another question: 'Would you rather be small, spotty or boring?' but did not answer it. As so often, it is hard to know how much he is joking, if at all. 'Versatility' would be generally agreed; 'Opera bouffe' is in accord with the character he projected; 'Doing good to others' seems to be gentle self-mockery; 'Money' sincere; as is 'Laziness and gluttony', but these are vices of which people are not much ashamed. 'No – but very nice' is the most characteristic reply. That he is equivocal about love at first sight qualifies either the claim that he experienced it or the happiness of what ensued.

Sometimes Berners' own friends threatened to like Heber Percy too much. Betjeman's letter about the cinema-opening continues, 'Gerald is very concerned about Robert and Hanbury [one of John Sparrow's middle names] and hopes Hanbury will not snitch Robert away or always be ringing him up. I said I thought this unlikely.' Penelope had written to Betjeman of their meeting:

John Sparrow staying here last week. On Thursday Robert came to dinner and got on nohow with JS. Robert then repaired to his car and JS said he would stay in his sitting-room and work for an hour or so. The motor left and we found the pink room empty. Next morning JS was very unforthcoming but admitted that Robert was extremely affectionate. JS is penniless and I really believe that, owing to your beneficial influence Robert genuinely prefers the gifts of the intellect to the gifts of the pocket in return for his friendship. Henceforth there will be no more Daimlers with Vauxhall engines and gold cigarette cases but priceless treasures of the mind.

Sparrow, then twenty-eight, was a barrister throughout the 1930s and only became Warden of All Souls in 1952 after Berners' death. Penelope Betjeman is clearly confident that, as long as there are no telephone calls and Heber Percy does not actually leave, Berners would not mind the adventure.

Chapter XII

His Finest Year

The year 1936 was the peak of Berners' life. All his talents were put to work, and with success. His first published fiction was well received, as was his second exhibition of paintings, and he was working on his most ambitious and enduring ballet score. At Faringdon the guests were never more various and elegant, or more numerous. If the reputations of some have slipped a little – Gertrude Stein and Salvador Dali remain famous as personalities but there is a question mark against their work, Aldous Huxley is less well known than he was but is still read, Wallis Simpson never became Queen – others, like Max Beerbohm, remain undiminished, while young Freddie Ashton went on to all that could have been hoped for him, and John Betjeman to rather more than that.

In the middle of January, Berners had a temperature of 105°F and went to bed. Ten days later he was still there, but well enough to start 'a tale'. After less than five weeks, on 1 March, it was completed. *The Camel* concerns a country vicar and his wife who find such a beast on their doorstep one winter morning. 'It's supposed to be based on John and me,' admitted Penelope Betjeman. There is an unpublished and facetious foreword, which says that though the characters are real, they are dead. Although resemblance is not marked or sustained, it certainly exists. The book is dedicated to the Betjemans. The vicar's wife 'as a girl had always been strangely attracted to the Orient'.

There are references to others: an admiral with a double-barrelled surname, not Clifton Brown but Sefton-Porter, who:

> was known to be in the habit of looking out of his window with a telescope . . . although he could not be described as a very intelligent man, he had a very active mind, and he took a prominent part in all local activities. His chief aim in life seemed to be to find out what people

disliked doing and make them do it, or else to find out what they liked
doing and stop them.

The gossipy old verger, 'painfully hard of hearing and inclined to be
impertinent', is called Beaton. He is also inclined to give Antonia sly
looks and 'mutter, with an inscrutable chuckle, "Oi knows what oi
knows"', which may recall Cecil's manner, though scarcely his accent.

Antonia takes to riding the camel. Admiral Sefton-Porter, out for a
ride himself, is so surprised that he falls off. She even inadvertently
joins a hunt. The camel loves her and carries out her slightest whim.
When she mentions how much she would like to have her neighbour
Lady Bugle's fur coat, there is a strange attack:

> As [Lady Bugle] passed the shrubbery she distinctly heard the foliage
> moving, and the sound of heavy breathing. She was terrified and at that
> moment Mopsy [her dog] set up a violent barking. Lady Bugle was
> unable to run, but she hurried with all her might toward the house.
> There was no doubt now that she was being followed. It was like the
> worst kind of nightmare. The sound of breathing was close behind her.
> Just as she reached the doorstep she caught her foot in her dress and fell
> headlong. She uttered a series of piercing screams and swooned away.
> Just before she fainted she had an impression of something tugging at
> her fur coat.

The coat is found on the vicarage doorstep.

Then Antonia, more eccentrically, says she would like to have the
body of her long-deceased dog in the house. Soon afterwards an already
difficult lunch party with Lady Bugle and the Bishop is turned into
disaster when Aloysius, as is his habit, whips off a silver dish cover as
though he were performing a conjuring trick and reveals the little canine
skeleton. Similar incidents proliferate into quite a complex plot.
Aloysius comes to believe that Antonia is in love with a feeble organist
(who, it is explained in some detail, prefers the choir). The climax takes
place at a fête when Antonia says of the organist, who has recently
disappeared, 'How I wish poor Mr Scrimgeour were here now.' The
camel immediately appears carrying something in its mouth. 'Then, all
of a sudden there arose murmurs of amazement and horror, for the
burden that the camel was carrying was seen to be a human body; it
looked as though it had been freshly disinterred and fragments of earth
were still clinging to its clothes.' The vicar hurries off and shoots
himself and Antonia rides off with her faithful steed into the unknown.

This tale of decaying corpses is the cosy, whimsical, allusive surrealism that Berners might have been expected to invent. With three drawings by Berners himself, the book came to 174 pages of rather large type and cost six shillings when it appeared in May. *The Times* gave it a long, friendly review, the *Evening Standard* thought it sagged, the *New Statesman* found it 'sly and extremely entertaining' and was well informed in sensing 'the charm of the scenery as something unspoilt and nondescript, like the few miles of happy poplar land that separate the mansion of the genial author from the home of his grave young dedicatees'. Clive Bell, to whom Berners had written, 'I think it is very funny and I hope you will too', must have been at least civil, as Berners then wrote, 'I am so pleased that you enjoyed *The Camel*. I have squashed the police but not Mr Cecil Beaton who is threatening me with a libel action for having taken his name in vain.' No libel action took place. Stravinsky wrote '*La lecture de votre "The Camel" me ravit*'; the book was eventually translated into French. Admirers continued to identify themselves for years.

At Oxford, Betjeman had been editor of the *Cherwell*, which had run into the usual financial troubles. Someone he later described as 'like an eager terrier scurrying round Oxford in search of culture', Edward James, came to the rescue and succeeded him as editor; they had kept up the relationship of friend and benefactor, James publishing Betjeman's first collection of poems, *Mount Zion*, in 1931. Berners too had known him for many years.

James was uncertain about money, just as he was about the identity of his father, who was almost certainly not Mr James, nor his godfather, Edward VII, as he liked to suggest. Having inherited vast sums, young Edward was capable of great generosity but was also continually, exhaustingly suspicious that people were cheating and sponging off him in some way, as indeed they often were. In the early 1930s, though predominantly homosexual, James married Tilly Losch, a beautiful ballet dancer, very much in Berners' artistic circle. The divorce was contested and sensational; most of their friends sided with her. Berners simply continued their friendship with no change at all, which James thought brave of him. It was probably done without reflection. Berners was loyal and, in this area, confident.

James's name is linked with the surrealists, and the most lasting image of him is the portrait of the back of his head by Magritte. Once, at West Dean, the vicar's wife pointed to a picture and asked belligerently, 'And what is that supposed to be?' In James's words it was:

> in fact, extremely well painted. It had the kind of detail that one finds in
> a seventeenth-century Dutch still life. There was a table in the
> foreground. There were objects on the table and a glass of water that
> caught the light. It was set in a landscape that went away in the distance
> to distant mountains (probably the Pyrenees) and the sea.

Berners replied, 'In Africa, the Hottentots cannot recognise a life-like photograph of a man as representing him. They are confused by the absence of his smell.' James thought this a beautifully clear reply; the vicar's wife was less satisfied and left. A pleasant moment for them, united in defence of the modern.

Though James had an important collection, he did not like to be thought of as a collector or even a patron, but as a creator. For years he built but never completed a fantastic house in Mexico. He wrote enormous amounts and published some bad poems and a novel, *The Gardener Who Saw God*. This last includes Lord Bullborough, an eccentric English peer, 'the Maecenas and protector of all the surrealists in England (of whom there were then only three)', who was 'most soberly and correctly dressed' except for his enamel and platinum tie-pin, which represented a miniature poached egg. James agreed that this character was based on Berners, but fantasy rather than observation was his method here. There are marble pianos in the trees, 2,000 ants and 1,000 grasshoppers neatly made of porcelain and realistically painted, but no insights into Berners' character.

In 1932, James had had a fleeting affair with the Vicomtesse Marie-Laure de Noailles in Paris. The first painting by Salvador Dali that he saw belonged to the Noailles and the next year they introduced him to the man himself. The height of Dali's fame was yet to come, but throughout the 1930s it was growing rapidly. His film with Luis Buñuel, *Un Chien Andalou*, had created a sensation, and he had further success in New York in 1933. He was married to Gala, a woman of great force, a nymphomaniac with a voracious appetite for money. Dali needed a rich patron; James wanted to be attached to a famous genius. But there was more to it than that: James had a genuine feel for painting; and Dali and he, several years later, may have had an affair.

Berners had met the Dalis at the Princesse de Polignac's in 1932, but James reintroduced them in Rome in 1935 and the meeting went very well, the same elements in muted form making for compatibility. Berners was not a potential patron, but still a potential buyer, less involved than James, but sympathetic and knowledgeable about modernity in the arts. He too liked famous geniuses, and Dali's simultaneous timidity and flamboyance appealed to him. Dali always said *The Camel* was one of his favourite books. Berners dedicated 'Surrealist Landscape' to him, of which this is one version:

> On the pale yellow sands
> Where the Unicorn stands
> And the eggs are preparing for Tea.
> Sing Forty
> Sing Thirty
> Sing Three.
>
> On the pale yellow sands
> There's a pair of clasped hands
> And an Eyeball entangled with string
> Sing Fifty
> Sing Forty
> Sing Three.
> And a bicycle seat
> And a Plate of Raw Meat
> And a Thing that is hardly a Thing.
>
> On the pale yellow sands
> There stands
> A Commode
> That has nothing to do with the case.
> Sing Ninety
> Sing Eighty
> Sing Three.
>
> On the pale yellow sands
> There's a Dorian Mode
> And a temple all covered with Lace
> And a Gothic Erection of Urgent Demands
> On the Patience of You and of Me.

The friendship continued. It was during Dali's quite lengthy visits to Berners' house in Rome that he studied Italian painting, much of which was new to him. His effusive letters began 'Très très très cher Gerald'.

Heber Percy thought him 'a sweet man' and Dali gave him a drawing of a horse.

On 11 June 1936 the International Surrealist Exhibition opened and was a great success in terms of attendance and attention. The Dalis arrived on 21 June and came to Ashcombe to stay with Cecil Beaton, as did Berners and James. They dropped in on Faringdon on the way back and Dali had the grand piano placed in the shallow pool on the lawn and chocolate éclairs put on the black notes, before Berners played it to him. Dali undertook to give a lecture on 'Paranoia, The Pre-Raphaelites, Harpo Marx and Phantoms' or 'Authentic Paranoiac Fantasies'. To do this, as he was making a dive into the unconscious, 'plunging down deeply into the human mind', he wore a diving suit, acquired for him by Berners. He held two white Russian wolfhounds with one hand and a billiard cue with the other, had a jewelled dagger in his belt and plasticine hands stuck on to him. This sort of thing was unknown in London and his entrance caused exactly the right sort of sensation. He spoke in French, but soon was seen to be trying to take off the diving helmet. Unfortunately it was bolted on. Dali was now unable to breathe, close to fainting. Berners found a hammer and, though every blow was agonisingly loud for the victim, struggled to save him. Eventually, and not a moment too soon, a workman with a spanner succeeded. The audience meanwhile thought everything was planned and rocked with laughter and enjoyment.

On the same day that the exhibition had opened, Berners had been telephoned by Sibyl Colefax: 'Gerald, I particularly want you to come tonight to meet Arthur.' Berners: 'But I thought Arthur was dead.' (Arthur Colefax had died in February.) Colefax: 'Oh, not my Arthur, Arthur Rubinstein.'

So Berners went round to Argyll House in the King's Road. It was the climax of Sibyl Colefax's dedicated social career. Edward VIII and Mrs Simpson had just dined. As the rest of the guests had arrived, 'the great double doors had stood open, and they could see the garden in the distance, spreading lawns, and what Sibyl called a sea of green trees'. On summer evenings like this one it was lit by Chinese lanterns, 'pale moons of white' floating in the branches. Among the guests were two diplomat/journalists, Robert Bruce Lockhart and Harold Nicolson, who left accounts in their diaries. The King talked to Bruce Lockhart about coming to some square deal with Germany, and to Nicolson about how he had put Anne Lindbergh, wife of the aviator, at her ease 'with my famous charm'.

After dinner there was Chopin. 'Madame de Polignac sat herself down near the piano to listen to Rubinstein. I have seldom seen a woman sit so firmly; there was determination in every line of her bum.' The King, however, looked bored, even talked. When Rubinstein had played three pieces and was preparing to play a fourth, the power of royalty overcame even such cultural force; the King stepped forward and said, 'We enjoyed that very much.' Meanwhile, other guests, the Winston Churchills, Noël Coward, Daisy Fellowes and Berners among them, had arrived and were presented. Heber Percy used to tell a story that must refer to this night. Sibyl Colefax, distraught, her greatest triumph tottering towards disaster, appealed to Berners to play the piano for the King and thus save the evening. When he said that he had come as a guest rather than as a performer, she cried out, 'I'll never ask you here again', and he replied with a confidence bordering on smugness, 'I rather think you will.'

Coward stepped into the breach, the King changed his mind, and 'Mad Dogs and Englishmen' was followed by 'Don't Put Your Daughter on the Stage, Mrs Worthington'. An hour later when the King did leave it had all been a triumph, though Kenneth Clark, embarrassed and angry at the affront, had left earlier with Rubinstein, and Nicolson recorded, 'I much fear that Rubinstein and Madame de Polignac must have thought us a race of barbarians.'

Berners' confidence in further invitations may have been misplaced for, though he and Sibyl Colefax remained friends, the house was soon sold.

Faringdon had never been more visited. Derek Jackson and Pamela Mitford ('shepherdess') came in March 1936 and were married later that year. Randolph Churchill ('Parliamentary candidate') came at the same time as Claire Luce ('Actress??!!!'). The nationalities on one page read French, français, Scotch, British, One of the damned (Kaetchen Kommer), Austrian, Welsh, Plantagenet and British. Evelyn Waugh reported in a letter that he had dropped in to see 'the wicked Lord Berners'. Max and Florence Beerbohm came for a pleasant weekend, with Viola Tree also present. In Rome, John Betjeman, not an enthusiast for foreign travel, borrowed the house.

The most important visit, though, was by Gertrude Stein. Differences in the way society organised itself in England, France and Italy have been minutely scrutinised; nevertheless, Berners managed to inhabit a similar milieu in London, Paris and Rome. Francis Rose, an acquaintance, places him in a set that gathered at the attractive eighteenth-century house of Eric Erickson, 'the most fashionable artist journalist that Vogue employed'. There were 'artists, journalists, great dress-makers, royalty and occasionally a statesman'. Great dress-makers did not exist in England, and even in France the supply was limited: 'Coco Chanel had been forgotten and outshone by the golden papier-mâché and wickerwork mannequins, and leopard skins of Schiap[arel-li].' Otherwise the mix was much the same. Rich young Rose had been taken up by Gertrude Stein and his pictures hung next to Picasso's in the rue de Fleurus.

Gertrude Stein was, like Salvador Dali, a self-proclaimed genius whose work was in the vanguard of the new and incomprehensible. Nearly ten years older than Berners, she had lived for almost thirty years with another American, Alice B. Toklas, and a strange pair they made. It would be generous to call Stein striking, more generous still to remember her, as Hemingway did, as reminiscent of a northern Italian peasant with strong features, beautiful eyes and a mobile face. He admired her hair too, but in 1926 Toklas, cutting inexpertly, had continued to even things up until little was left. Stein liked the result and kept to it. Her local greengrocer's son was Pierre Balmain, another talent she recognised and helped, so he made her loose tweeds and lined them with mauve taffeta.

Less than five foot, Toklas presented herself as subservient, and in photographs 'is always carrying the bags and umbrellas, or sitting in the lesser chair, or walking behind Gertrude, or is scarcely visible at all'. This was misleading. In 1933 *The Autobiography of Alice B. Toklas* had enjoyed great success. This was a calculated career move. Written in a much more accessible style than Stein's early work, it tells of twenty-five years in Paris, with much about the artists they knew but much also about the cook and the dog. Only near the end is the title revealed as a lie, Stein as the author. It made them famous, also fashionable.

How seriously Berners took anyone is hard to judge. He bought from Dali; he was to work with Stein. Penelope Betjeman thought he was impressed by her, Harold Acton was sure he was not. Diana Mosley, while confident that Berners was not for a moment fooled, found the friendship typical of him, of his liking for 'the fashionable life bordering on the artistic life . . . She was a clever old woman. He had to pretend to find Alice Toklas also rather wonderful. She really was the most fearful bore.' Berners' pronouncement as his considered verdict that he had only known one genius in his life – Stravinsky – places a limit on his admiration.

Certainly he allowed himself jokes at the expense of Stein's style and had written parodies of her work before they met. One, 'Portrait of a well-known conversationalist', begins: 'There was one who was wanting to be saying to be saying there was one who was wanting to be wanting to be saying to be saying to be saying. There were many who were wanting who were wanting to be not listening.'

Another, 'Portrait of a Society Hostess', reads in its entirety:

> Give a canary champagne and it spins. Chandelier drops glitter and drops and are conversation. Bohemian glass is cracked in Mayfair. Mayfair-weather friends come and go come and go come and go. The house is always full full full full.
>
> Are you there? Are you there? There! There! Are you not all there? Many are not quite all there but royalty are there and lots and lots and lots. Glitter is more than kind hearts and coronets are more than comfort. She praises and embarrasses she praises and embarrasses she confuses cabinet ministers. Some will not go.
>
> What with one thing and another. What with another and one thing. What with what with what what wit and what not.
>
> Squashed bosh is her favourite meringue.

Parody can be fond, even admiring, and here Berners is mocking the subjects, not the style he has borrowed. Sibyl Colefax had more cause for concern than Gertrude Stein.

In February the odd couple, encouraged by their old friends the Abdys, had made a rare visit to England for Stein to lecture American students at Oxford and Cambridge on 'What Are Masterpieces' and 'An American and France'. Daisy Fellowes told her to stay at Faringdon, as it was the only house in England where the halls and corridors were warm, and they did so ('writer and reader' in the visitors' book, and '100 métiers pas de carrière'). By all accounts, particularly Stein's own, it was a great success, though there were more Hindus and pale yellow-haired men and small men in Oxford than she remembered. Tall, brown-haired, English David Cecil was among her Oxford audience and asked some questions: 'She answered effectively. Not at all annoying but she put one in one's place in a sort of genial, hearty way.' Stein found the Cambridge audience more interesting and went on to stay with the Abdys in Cornwall. Before she left, however, she and Berners must have talked about adding music to one of her plays, *They Must. Be Wedded. To Their Wife*, written in 1931. In March 1936 he writes that he had received the adapted text and that he will do it when he has finished *The Camel*; in July he hopes that she will like what he has written, in August that he will see her in France on the 20th. Once there, he played what he had written on her piano. There is no comment in his ensuing letter of thanks on what she thought, but soon she writes, 'We are happy with the music and everything. Did you know that you left three paint brushes in a long box behind?'

So the summer trip to Bilignin, near Lyons, was if not a working holiday then the continuance of a working relationship. Stein and Toklas had a seventeenth-century manor house on the only street in the village. It was quiet. Berners wrote rather a formal description of the countryside: 'a terraced garden looks out over the valley to the hills beyond. Through the valley meanders a little river. The countryside has a charm that grows upon one. It has none of the luridly dramatic qualities of Annecy, none of the rolling opulence of Burgundy or Beaune. It is intimate and gay.'

The routine was fixed. Toklas got up at five-thirty to gather *fraises de bois* for breakfast, perhaps a bouquet of mauve roses and laurel for a favoured guest. Breakfast for the men was on the terrace, off trays of coloured glass. Stein made a slower start: 'It takes a lot of time to be a genius, you have to sit around so much doing nothing.' That took up most of the morning, but she wrote every day, perhaps for half an hour. Toklas typed it out. The detective stories she devoured were kept in cupboards, because she did not like the sight of books. Food was much discussed, lunch an event, though Berners was disappointed at the decline in culinary standards locally. He described some of the local curiosities:

> Every afternoon Gertrude drove me out in her car to show me things of interest: picturesque and social, for the neighbours are interesting and curious. Gertrude has a knack of dramatising them – and perhaps it is she who makes them interesting and strange.
>
> Close to Bilignin is the Château d'Andosse. A lawyer lived here in the nineteenth century, married a rich wife, tired of her sooner than of her money. Took her for a drive. On the return journey was set upon by bandits (so he said) arrived at the château covered with wounds, the wife and coachman killed. He was arrested, charged and brought to trial. Balzac, a friend of his, came to testify to his good character. The lawyer got off. Balzac wrote a story about it.

We visited another house. The lady who lived there was absent. As we rung the bell, the heads of gigantic, alarming-looking dogs appeared at every window and observed us silently but menacingly . . . I saw a house that attracted my attention. All the more because it was obviously unoccupied. A pretty house has the same effect on me as the sight of a pretty woman on the majority of people. Without any definite hopes or intention of acquisition, I like to have a good look at it.

There was a misunderstanding about seed corn. American friends used to send some to Stein. Berners asked for a little and was given the lot by mistake. Moreover, it was restricted by the donors to anti-fascists, but Stein wrote to them, 'I do not know what he is politically but I do not think he does either so that is alright' and it was.

One last joke for 1936 was the insertion of a message in *The Times* on 21 December: 'Lord Berners wishes to dispose of two elephants and one small rhinoceros (latter house-trained). Would make delightful Christmas presents. – Apply R. Heber Percy, Faringdon House, Berkshire.' The press at least enjoyed it. The *Daily Sketch* invented an answer from Babar, and Berners replied, 'My Dear Babar, I am very distressed at your saying I do not take elephants seriously. I always make a point of respecting people larger than myself . . . they did a great deal of damage in the park and then they got into the town and went about ringing people's doorbells.' The *Manchester Daily Mail*, the *Daily Mirror* and, most fully, the *Evening News* rang up Faringdon and wrote stories. They were told by someone who claimed to be a secretary but sounded like Berners, 'Actually, I haven't seen the rhino myself, sir, but it is often about the house. It's quite gentle I'm told. The weather is getting so cold for the poor things.' So one elephant had gone to Lady Colefax and the other to Harold Nicolson (the rhinoceros was being kept). However, when these two denied all knowledge, this was said to have been an error.

Nicolson said to all enquiries, 'It is just Lord Berners adding to the Christmas merriment. I have known him for twenty-five years but I do not feel too friendly towards him today. I do not want an elephant, have never wanted one, and I have not bought one' – an instance of a contemporary thinking Berners a bit silly, where Berners thought they had grown pompous.

Chapter XIII

A Wedding Bouquet

Frederick Ashton said that the ballet *A Wedding Bouquet* was originally Berners' idea: 'He thought it all out. Constant Lambert and I came in later.' There is nothing to contradict this, but at first glance it does seem a little surprising. Berners had written only bits and pieces since *Luna Park* in 1930. There were two waltzes in 1931, one for the municipal ball in Eastbourne, the other to be played by Jack Hylton at the Savoy on St Valentine's Day, both now lost and possibly the same work. *Opening Fanfare*, also written in 1931, was for the St Cecilia's Day concert for the Musicians' Benevolent Fund, and less than a minute of trumpets, trombones and percussion survives. Berners' music was still sometimes played on the wireless (most frequently a reduced orchestration of *The Triumph of Neptune*) but much less than it had been. As might be expected, there were frequent performances in the early 1920s, fading away until *A Wedding Bouquet* gave his earlier work a boost. In 1934, the eight bars of his Fascist March appeared in William Hickey, and in 1936 his *Fugue* had been encored when Sir Thomas Beecham played it in Paris. These odds and ends, though, could not lead anyone to expect his most ambitious, sustained and lasting piece of music.

People, painting and books seemed to have supplanted composing, in which Berners' interest now appeared at best sporadic. Lambert, still the British composer with whom he was most in sympathy, was probably the questioner himself when he wrote later, 'At one time he gave up composing altogether and when asked when he was going to write again said that as he hadn't started composing until he was thirty-five, he saw no reason why he shouldn't stop for another thirty-five years.' This is a characteristically graceful way of describing, without explanation, Berners' failure to persevere with his major talent.

Lambert was understanding and enjoyed Berners' eccentricities:

A typical example of his desire for solitude combined with his own individual humour was provided by a simple method of keeping a railway carriage to himself. Instead of employing the usual English tactics he would put on dark glasses and slyly beckon in the passers-by. Those isolated figures who stood the risk of entering the carriage became so perturbed by his habit of reading a newspaper upside-down and taking his temperature every few minutes that they invariably changed carriages at the next station.

Lambert, however, was now not only a friend but a champion and had become musical director at Sadler's Wells. He was to be much involved in this production and was to conduct the first performance in April 1937; even if he did not conceive *A Wedding Bouquet*, he was in at the birth.

Gertrude Stein proved the ideal complacent collaborator. She not only wrote, 'Anything you want to do will be what I want you to do', she lived up to it. Her play concerns a French provincial wedding at the turn of the century and she was uncomplaining when Berners used only the beginning and the central situation. The action of the ballet hinges on the embarrassment of the groom at the number of his past loves who appear. When Berners wished to add a new character, Pepe, based on a black-and-white Mexican terrier (though also described as a chihuahua) given to Stein by the painter Francis Picabia, she sent him a photograph. When her words were moved about, altered, sung by a chorus instead of being spoken, she made no demur. Berners continued to be cavalier with the text and was to write to the publisher, 'get the engravers to put a few full stops in!' Indeed, Edward James said that the libretto was really by Berners 'from bits and pieces of Stein', and this is not absurd. She hoped that he would design the sets and clothes himself – 'it would be lovely to have the décor new and fresh' – and was 'awfully happy' when he did. The inclusion of Frederick Ashton delighted her, as he had in 1934 been responsible for the brilliantly successful choreography and staging of the opera *Four Saints in Three Acts* for which she had written the script.

Ashton and Berners were already acquainted through ballet. They had met while working on *Riverside Nights* and, when Ashton wanted to use Berners' *Luna Park* music for a new ballet, he had found him 'most accommodating'. When Ashton took up with Alice Astor, who was married to Raimund von Hofmannsthal, he and Berners became friends;

indeed, the affair was consummated at Faringdon. She proposed to Ashton at this time, but he knew that it would be a mistake and was already interested in Michael Soames, who was to be in the ballet. Constant Lambert was married, but in love with Margot Fonteyn, who was also in it. Berners and Heber Percy, Stein and Toklas came nearest to being happily married couples, but none of them had had a wedding. These were not collaborators likely to be sympathetic to the subject. In fact the only reflection from real life is that Alice Astor's unhappiness was projected by Ashton onto Fonteyn's role as the bride.

Stein had been at Faringdon in February 1936. Lambert came in May and, in June, Ashton ('dancer' still, not yet 'choreographer'); Berners had visited Stein in the summer, played her some music, written more in the autumn. In early March 1937, seven weeks before the first night, Lambert and Ashton came to Faringdon together to work.

Ashton found Berners 'Very professional. If you wanted anything changed he would do it in a very professional way.' Berners had been accused of being unable to write tunes. Here he did so, particularly with the waltz, though Ashton says, 'I used to call them his governess waltzes because it sounded like a frustrated governess pounding away at an upright piano.' It had been Berners' idea to use Stein's words, but when they were changed from being sung by a chorus to being spoken by a narrator he made no objection. Characteristically, he wove in personal references. The backcloth comes from a carpet he saw in Stein's house, which she said everyone admired: 'The pale colours are so American and the house and the river and the simple harmony of it.' Faringdon and the lake appear, as well as Kammer, a house near Salzburg that Alice Astor took each year and that Berners had visited. The clothes he kept simple.

The desired light tone was achieved in the ballet with many jokes and in-jokes, the grandeur of *The Sleeping Beauty* and the charm of *Les Sylphides* being affectionately mocked. The music and choreography were traditional, in contrast to the avant-garde writing, but, if there was a clash, Berners and Ashton won. An idea raised by Ashton, that *A Wedding Bouquet* is a parody of *Les Noces* (a work he himself revered), is hard to accept. Berners would certainly have been familiar with Bronislava Nijinska's masterpiece of the early 1920s (particularly as the music is by Stravinsky); his fondness for parody or at least reference is established; and, as the titles suggest, both deal with the same central event. Even in the face of his expert knowledge, however, it is impossible to see a straightforward connection with Nijinska's humourless, undifferentiated peasants in purposefully drab colours.

Berners, the controlling sensibility, was aiming at a light, sophisticated, occasionally touching entertainment. The narrator (in New York and in a revival in 1941, Constant Lambert) sat in a chair on the edge of the stage or a box. When the curtain rises on the garden of a farmhouse, the maid Webster ('A name that was spoken') is organising the preparations and soon the guests arrive, including poor dotty Julia ('Julia is known as forlorn'), the owner of Pepe ('Little dogs resemble little girls', which is fortunate as Pepe is, naturally, danced by one). Next the bride ('Charming, Charming, Charming') and the groom ('They all talk as if it was alarming, also as if they expected him not to be charming') appear and there is a group photograph. Julia, who has been 'ruined' by the groom, now throws herself at him; Josephine ('Josephine may not attend a wedding'), who is completely devoted to Julia ('not in any other language would this be written differently'), gets drunk. The groom partners his bride in a waltz but then does a tango with his former mistresses. When the bride returns she faints and, as night falls, the guests leave ('Thank you, thank you'), and Julia is alone with her dog.

Berners went out to Bilignin to escort Stein and Toklas to England. They had been depressed by the situation in Europe but now cheered up and liked everything they saw. Stein met Ashton for the first time and decided he was a genius ('being one it is natural that I should think a great deal about that thing in any other one'). She was delighted that the English worried and gossiped only about the parochial matter of the abdication, as she felt this showed a proper feeling for tradition. Constant Lambert also earned approval by using words from her play to introduce the characters in the programme. At a rehearsal, Daisy Fellowes told her that she was the only person not working and Stein agreed with that too. It was wonderful, she later wrote, to hear her words with music. At the first night she was not nervous but excited, for it went so very well, the English danced with freshness and agility:

> and then gradually it was ending and we went out and on to the stage and there where I never had been with everything in front all dark and we bowing and all of them coming and going and bowing, and then again not only bowing but coming again and then as if it was everything, it was all over and we went back to sit down.
>
>   I guess it was a great success.

Edward James, not a friend of Stein's, thought she liked it all too much
and 'as he [Berners] came on stage she bumped him back into the wings
with her big bum'. This does not accord with the memory of Ninette de
Valois, who danced the part of Webster, the maid, and remembers
Lilian Baylis, to whom the ballet was dedicated, and Gertrude Stein
taking a curtain call together – 'A delicious sight that was much to the
liking of the audience.' In any case it would not have needed much of a
bump; without a mask or fancy dress, Berners disliked being the centre
of attention for more than a moment, even when the audience was
applauding.

The reviews had almost no fault to find, but the praise was measured
rather than ecstatic: 'An admirably balanced mixture of ballet realism
and fantasy with a touch of *Crazy Night* by way of spice . . . true wit
that is combined in an enormous and tender sympathy for the period.'
Robert Helpmann as narrator was congratulated on being amusing for
the first time (his mannered delivery of the words reminded some of
Façade) and there was praise for the whole cast except Margot Fonteyn,
who was told that 'Her pathetic idiocy struck a jarring note even in so
cynical a burlesque.' Fonteyn, not yet eighteen but a rising star, had
recently danced *Giselle* and it seems to have been true that at first she
did not vary her 'pathetic idiocy' enough to suit the lighter ballet; later
she did. Stravinsky's verdict, the most important one but delivered
later, was cryptic but not bad: 'I thought his *A Wedding Bouquet* and his
Triumph of Neptune as good as the French works of that kind produced
by Diaghilev, though whether or not this could be construed as a
compliment I cannot say.' There was one dissenting voice. Hannen
Swaffer, who claimed, not entirely ridiculously, that he was the most
widely read journalist in the world, wrote critically and, when they met,
Berners uncharacteristically went for him, provoking 'a splendid row'.

De Valois, Ashton, Helpmann, Fonteyn and Lambert were in the
process of re-creating British ballet, but had not yet done so. It was a
small pool in which Berners had had a medium-sized success, but it was
the only available one and, as always, he was working with talent of the
first class.

After such success it was not surprising that Berners and Stein
planned a further collaboration: an opera about Faust, tentatively
entitled *Doctor Faustus Lights the Lights*. Stein was reported in the
Evening Standard of 19 November 1938 as having dashed off the
libretto in three months, but there are letters from her which show that
Berners was struggling. One begins reassuringly, 'No, no, no, Faust will

not be done to music by anybody but you, that is alright, and perhaps music will come, and perhaps you could come and spend Christmas with us and the mt [mountain] air and the fresh landscape will help.'

The concept was clear in his mind. Berners told a journalist, 'The book is startling and the scenery to be designed by an unidentified Turk is startling but the music will be conventional – straightforward grand opera in three acts.' And he quoted: 'The devil what the devil do I care if the devil is there how do you know if I have a soul who says so nobody says so but you the devil and everybody knows the devil is all lies.' Faust was to be discovered surrounded by light-bulbs, and seen 'from a modern angle', which would present a comedy. The reporter thought that Berners contrived to pronounce Stein's name to sound like Goethe-rude.

Though war was now seen by many to be approaching, Berners took on another project, so it must have been a failure of inspiration, rather than the invasion of Poland, that aborted the most ambitious musical undertaking of his life. A fragment of the libretto that survives consists of thirteen pages and three scenes. Margueritte Ida is bitten (or stung – it is much discussed) by a viper and seeks the aid of Dr Faustus, who at first refuses to see her. There is a dog who says 'thank you' but nothing else.

Meanwhile Berners had continued to pursue his normal gregarious life, with a few unusual extras. He had written to Stein in February 1937 when they were deliberating between *Wedding Bouquet* and *A Wedding Bouquet* as the title. 'I have got a horse running in the Grand National, will you please pray for it on March 19th? Don't forget.' Her prayers, if any, went unanswered. 'Passing Fancy' was a hunter of Robert's and, bearing Berners' colours of green, red sleeves and black cap, fell at the first fence. (Heber Percy got drunk and put his foot through a jewellery display case in the Adelphi Hotel, in order to get a diamond bracelet to cheer up some girl and himself. He was asked to pay; fortunately the jewels were false and he could.) Berners' letter to Stein continues, 'Lady Colefax is in America. I had a row with her about an elephant . . . She was besieged by press photographers asking her if they could photograph her with the elephant. She was very angry. And now I see that she was knocked down by a pig at one of Elsa Maxwell's parties.'

He had also been to Bembridge on the Isle of Wight for long enough to play the King in an ambitious amateur film called *Treason's Bargain*, which had five acts and 106 scenes. Much influenced by the Marx

Brothers, it featured his mildly eccentric hostess Lady Harris in the Margaret Dumont role. Berners apparently fussed, for she wrote reassuringly that:

> Your fevered injunctions shall certainly be obeyed. I have no intention of inviting SC to the film. You ought to know . . . that anyone who can be so cruel to animals as SC was to that poor elephant could never again join the crush beneath my glittering chandeliers. How could she have kept that poor noble beast squeezed in and shut up in that small antique Normandy armoire in the back part of her shop for weeks and weeks never letting it even see what was going on in the front part of the shop and giving it nothing to play with except the old school ties that had belonged to her late husband . . . to go back to that unpleasant personality: how odious it is of her to have romped on the floor with Cecil and the next day to pretend that she had merely watched you dancing the mazurka with Violet, Duchess of Rutland, who when all is done and said, wasn't present.

At Faringdon steady old friends like the Lygons, the Mosleys, Emerald Cunard and the Princesse de Polignac recur; the less steady Sitwells, particularly Osbert, return; and some new faces appear. Berners' relationship with Edith Olivier had taken a physical turn, for she recorded, 'Berners is taking John Sutro's place and I think on the whole I like his lap to sit in better, though they are both frightful to look at.' Ruth Gordon ('actress?') was an amusing and original American in no need of a modest question mark; she wrote in reply to a postcard several years later, 'I am about the only person living who still collects postcards . . . I once said to someone starting out on a journey, "Send me a postcard now and then" and I was spoken of as being quite witty, based on that remark alone.' She continued to recall what seems to have become the standard entertainment, 'Never will forgot the food at your house both in London and in the country and the glass bed [moved from London] and the white horse walking down the front steps when thro' posing.'

Not yet at Compton Beauchamp and so still an occasional guest was an old acquaintance who was to become a close friend. 'Daisy' (for Marguerite) Fellowes described herself in the visitors' book as '2nd least dressy person in the world', in reference to her invariably being described in magazines as the best-dressed woman in the world. She possessed exactly the fashionable elegance that Berners most admired and was bracketed with the Duchess of Windsor and Chanel as streamlined and hard-faced. She also wrote 'neo-French' because, born half-American (Singer, rich) and half-French (Duc Decazes, aristocratic), she had married Prince Jean de Broglie and lived there. He had been killed in the First World War ('On the strength of that she had presented herself at the English Court all in black, train, plumes and all, a striking figure in the midst of débutantes all in white') and though her second husband was Reggie Fellowes, a cousin of Winston Churchill, she remained in France. In 1924 she had been taking ballet lessons. Her teacher, Sokolova, had complained of a headache and Daisy gave her a white powder. It worked wonders, but Diaghilev had noticed and diagnosed cocaine. The lessons came to an end.

Her only book, a novel called *Cats in the Isle of Man*, which appeared in 1927, tells of an elopement with a weary sophistication that lends it an intermittent sardonic charm – 'The first time an illicit couple arrive at an hotel together it is very trying for both of them' – as well as authoritative notes on fashion: 'That year extreme thinness was the thing and black dresses were being worn in the evening next to the skin.' Cocteau had recently said in *Vogue* that presence was the new thing and that Daisy was the person who had it. Schiaparelli had created a black hat in the form of an upside-down shoe with a velvet heel sticking up like a small column, which only she and Schiaparelli herself had the courage to wear.

In a letter to Nancy Mitford a few years later, Berners is restrained in his praise:

> I am glad to hear Daisy's party was lovely – I thought it would be. She is so socially competent. Except when she deliberately intends not to be. Did you hear of that pre-war party when all the most deadly enemies in Paris were locked into a boiling room placed next to one another at table and given deliberately heating food to eat; outside they could see cool gardens and fountains but the windows were locked.

Berners was not cruel, selfish or ruthless himself but he sometimes relished these qualities in others. A.L. Rowse thought Berners glamorised by Daisy, and himself immune, but she bamboozled him into allowing her to take a book out of the Codrington Library in All Souls, a thing forbidden to non-members of the college. Francis Rose described her as 'the beautiful Madame de Pompadour of the period, dangerous as an albatross' (and Billa Harrod, later a firm friend of Berners, as 'a wicked woman with much to offer') and she did indeed appear glittering and heartless, like the black swan in *Swan Lake*. Nevertheless, Berners was not only enchanted but became fond of her, and there came a time when Diana Mosley 'sometimes thought he almost resented the presence of Hugh Sherwood, even though her name for Hugh was H.L., which stood for Hated Lover'.

The smart young Kenneth Clarks went everywhere and so naturally came to Faringdon. They found there Schiaparelli ('Hopeless job') and H.G. Wells ('lighting and hot water expert') who was allowed to bring his mistress, Moura Budberg, and had been forgiven *The War of the Worlds*, which at school Berners had found 'rather silly, so horribly scientific'. Also present, making a large party for Faringdon, was Tom Driberg, a regular. A successful gossip columnist, the first and best 'William Hickey' in the *Daily Express*, he had, admittedly in one of her more mistaken enthusiasms, been described by Edith Sitwell as the hope of English poetry and was shortly to become an MP on the left of the Labour Party. As Hickey, he had reported on a game called 'Bulgy', 'invented by Lord Berners as a substitute for the word "Snap" in the card game. Instead of saying "Snap" when your card is the same as your opponent's, you bulge out your face, and the one who laughs first loses his cards.' Worldly, sophisticated, homosexual, Driberg thought Berners 'one of the wittiest men I have ever known', but all this would have availed him nought if he had not been amusing himself. As he was, they remained friends.

On the Saturday of that weekend, the vicar's wife said to Schiaparelli, 'Oh, what a pity you weren't here yesterday, you could have helped us sort the jumble,' which she took well. An entertaining mixture, but how did the picture of them lined up on the steps get into the *Tatler*?

Towards the end of the 1930s the visitors' book does not always reveal 'professions'; the Clarks, for instance, do not go in for such facetiousness. Nor did Derek Jackson, identical twin of Vivian who was at the violent Mosley meeting of 1934, or his wife, Pamela Mitford. When it was said that she lacked the 'Mitford shriek', Berners said no, she had it, but hers was 'a tenor shriek'. She could remember whole meals eaten years before in minute detail, a suitable accomplishment for Faringdon. Though Jackson married six times, this one lasted fifteen years, with, said Pamela, 'never a dull moment'. He was a brilliant physicist, a fanatical rider, whether hunting or racing, capable of great arrogance and rudeness but with, in James Lees-Milne's phrase, the charm of a chameleon. What he and Berners shared was a fondness for disconcerting the pompous, though Jackson's was a more explosive technique. He once told a hunt official that he must know who he was. The man, put out, asked why on earth he should and was told 'Because I am so pretty'. Berners enjoyed that.

Halkin Street had by now been transformed into a miniature, metropolitan Faringdon, as described by Constant Lambert:

> In the hall busts of generals and statesmen were notably improved by the addition of pantomime masks representing negroes and cats. Half-way up the stairs was a large cage [later a glass wall] housing a rare and exquisite tropical bird [later there were many birds]. In the drawing-room the piano was littered with an extraordinary heterogeneous collection of objects ranging from a fish in copper dating from the renaissance to a beer mug representing the Duke of Windsor which played the National Anthem when lifted. But on the piano desk itself might easily be the latest work of Stravinsky with a dedication by the composer and after tearing one's eyes away from the more facetious objects on the mantelpiece one would be entranced by an exceptionally fine early Corot, flanked by a Sisley and a Matisse.

The original bird was 'John Knox', whom Berners, when in bed with lumbago, taught to turn somersaults. When it died, Berners placed a notice in the personal column of *The Times*: 'Died of jealousy, aged fifteen, John Knox, emerald bird of paradise belonging to Lord Berners. His guests are asked to wear half-mourning.'

What must have been an exciting interlude that autumn was Berners' only trip to America. George Gershwin and Bernard Herrmann, who was tactfully referred to as 'confrontational', were among the Americans he had run into in England. Herrmann, who had met Orson Welles but had not yet written the score for *Citizen Kane*, let alone *Psycho* and other Hitchcock films, was already established with William Paley and the Columbia Broadcasting System and, a great anglophile, became an effective champion in New York. Sadly, little is recorded of Berners' visit. All that is known is that he had 'a typical Jewish dinner' with Herrmann on Second Avenue and 'a wonderful time'.

It was natural for the team of friends that had collaborated on *A Wedding Bouquet* to collaborate again, though who chose the next subject is unclear. A letter from Berners to Robert Helpmann presents him with a 'topping idea for a ballet . . . A. Bliss could write Powerful Music for it.' In December 1938, Constant Lambert was at Faringdon and in February the following year he was there again, this time with

Ashton. By now they had selected the tale of Cupid and Psyche to be told in three scenes, corresponding to the plot: god meets girl, god loses girl, god gets girl. Berners asked Francis Rose to design the sets and costumes this time and he stayed in Halkin Street. They went to the British Museum together to study Greek sculpture. Then, at Faringdon, Rose recounts that 'we worked hard on music, painting and dancing in a world without time, except for dressing for dinner and the formal meals of a peer with liveried footmen, who spent most of their time hunting for tins of Fribourg & Treyer snuffs which Gerald had mislaid or put into the wrong eighteenth-century snuff-boxes.'

Industrious harmony did not continue, however: 'It was difficult for Gerald to conform to the hard work of the theatre, and as the ballet progressed, Constant Lambert, the great conductor, became more difficult. There were quarrels,' and Berners almost conducted the first night. Lambert had been ill, drink was taking its toll, his marriage had broken up, his workload was heavy. Rehearsals were chaotic, 'tights without slips, wings that fell off, wings that did not fit, and at the dress rehearsal the costumes were only half there; in fact on the first night they arrived act by act'.

Rose managed a lyrical description of his own work: 'The curtain rose on the grey and white and pale blue landscape of Greece. Tanagras in violent purple, scarlet, crimson, and pale lilac moved through the crowd in grey and white. The God Pan in lime green tights danced and piped until shimmering Venus appeared.' Everyone else concerned with *Cupid and Psyche* rather skims over it in their accounts and there is no reason to differ here. Psyche is a Greek princess, so beautiful as to provoke the jealousy of Venus, who sends her son Cupid to humble her. He too falls in love and carries Psyche off. In Scene Two, Psyche is happy in Cupid's palace but has never actually seen him. He visits her only at night and is invisible to her in the day. Her visiting sisters suggest that he is a monster. Oddly, it is not until Scene Three that she creeps up on his sleeping form, unfortunately wakes him and he flies off. She wanders after him, Venus punishes both of them, then Pan turns up and persuades the other gods to befriend the sad young couple and they in turn persuade Venus to relent. There is a wedding feast and they live happily ever after – literally, because Psyche has been made immortal. Berners in a rather formal note explained, 'The subject is not treated in a strictly classical style, but more in the manner of Offenbach's *La Belle Hélène* and *Orpheus aux enfers*. The music is straightforward ballet-music and does not lend itself to unduly serious treatment.'

Tosh, then – but perhaps charming, inventive, amusing tosh. On 27 April 1939, with Ashton riding a string of successes, it appeared with Michael Soames as Pan, Julia Farron as Psyche and Margot Fonteyn stepping into a small part at short notice. The convincing verdict in the history of Sadler's Wells is:

> *Cupid and Psyche* was an attempt to treat a rather sad little story in an ultra-smart and witty fashion. The music by Lord Berners was light enough and Sir Francis Rose designed shiny, bright sets and costumes, but Ashton seemed quite unable to weld his ingredients into an interesting choreographic design. It was as if someone had said, 'Wouldn't it be fun to show Venus as a rather shop-soiled floozy, to have Cupid fly away on a wire at the end, and to have two figures placed at the head of the steps on each side of the stage declaiming the story before each scene' – and then the joke went rather stale before it even got onto the stage. As in *Le Roi Nu*, the story posed one insoluble difficulty and no one was ever able to think of a way of indicating that Cupid was in fact invisible to Psyche . . . The usual way of a Wells audience with an indifferent ballet was to cheer it loudly on the opening night and then gradually lose interest, but the gallery openly disapproved of *Cupid and Psyche* at its first performance and booed it loudly.

This last point is disputed: the *Daily Telegraph* thought 'the audience appreciated it to the full', *The Times* that 'the ayes had it', the *Liverpool Post* that it was a success, with 'a few dissentients somewhere'. The *Chesterian* said that the music did not steal the ballet 'but was content to support it which it does very well', but then it also reported that it received an enthusiastic reception. Berners' contribution was by no means discreditable, but for the first time he had had a total flop. The ballet lasted just three performances.

Chapter XIV

War and Collapse

Many had foreseen the coming struggle with Germany, indeed so felt its inevitability that Chamberlain's triumphant return from Munich at the end of September 1938 seemed just another shameful and mistaken postponement. Not Berners. Though children were being evacuated from the cities during August 1939, he had booked rooms and was poised to set off for his usual trip to Rome, when Britain and France declared war in early September. Several of his friends, such as Derek Jackson, thought Berners' trip unwise. But he had houses in England and Italy, and they, with France and Germany, combined not just to form his world but to mould everything he thought and felt, everything he was. Now the four countries were locked in a struggle that, whatever the outcome, must destroy any such combination for the rest of his life. Berners felt despair as he looked forward and saw not just the eclipse of an attractive way of living, but a world in which the things he revered and admired simply did not exist. It was not only that everything would be difficult and drab – though there was that, too, and he felt that he would not be suited to coping with it – it was that his sort, his style, would be pointless, too marginal to be noticed and then gone altogether, like the Russian aristocrats living in Paris after the revolution.

It seemed unbearable. He could not bear it and had a breakdown. Both he and his friends saw the war as the cause and he left such notes as 'The war – myself – the ultimate corner'. It is reasonable to remember, however, that his grandfather could be fairly described as a gibbering lunatic, that his mother was given to bouts of gloom, and that Berners had since youth lived a life of planned repression, devoted to surface gaiety, but subject to recurring melancholy. Nor did the collapse take place immediately, though it is a little difficult to disentangle cause and effect. He shut the house in London, confessing later that he was not afraid of being killed but that he had nightmares in which he was

horribly wounded and unable to reach a doctor. He retreated not to
Faringdon but to Oxford, where he stayed with Maurice Bowra at
Wadham. A.L. Rowse suggests that this was a contributory factor:
'That did not work out. I expect Maurice's boisterous ebullience was
too much for Gerald's nerves. At any rate he got one of his attacks of
depression, which used to take the odd form, for a rich man, of thinking
he was reduced to poverty.' Berners wrote to Cecil Beaton about Oxford
and the job that Bowra had secured for him in the Taylorian Institute:

> The war has set me back mentally a bit and cataloguing books is about all
> I'm good for at the present moment. One must have something to do
> every minute of the day. Otherwise it's hell . . . The general atmosphere
> is serious and intellectual – but life is hard what with world worries and
> personal worries. If I could find God I think it might help – but he
> seems to be very far off just now. I go to Pusey House every morning at
> eight o'clock in search of him and Penelope has had a mass said for me at
> Uffington. This is serious. I wish I could find Him.

In Heber Percy's words 'He sent for all the Oxford people, the rabbis
and the Catholics and they all came traipsing out here [Faringdon, so
later] terribly excited about getting a new convert. "They keep telling
me that God loves us," he said after one session, "but I say, 'Is that any
reason to love God?'"'

Rowse describes wartime Oxford, full of the unfit and of refugees,
'Czechs, Austrians, Germans crowded the pavements. We used to say
that on the buses to North Oxford one needed to speak German.'
Berners moved to lodgings in 'an old house that looked out on St
Giles's, number 22'. His landlady, Miss Alden, tall and bony and with
hair that 'simply wouldn't grow grey', was a character, and she or
Berners decreed that few friends were allowed to cross the threshold.
'Miss Alden wouldn't like that,' he would say, and there was no
knowing whose wish it really was. Heber Percy, she decided, 'in her
knowing way', was an illegitimate son and so an exception.

In November Berners dined out a few times with a small circle of
dons, though it was noticed that he was even more silent than usual. He
went to Faringdon at weekends to start with, and a letter to Violet
Trefusis sounds sane and in at least momentary high spirits. 'NO
TRUFFLES FOR MRS TREFUSIS' is printed across the top:

> Dearest Violet
>   The stories you have been spreading about having been raped by

blacks while at Faringdon have done me a great disservice. Nearly every female of my acquaintance is now clamouring to come here in the hopes of meeting with similar experience. *J'ai beau dire* that the whole thing was a figment of your imagination but still they press . . .

My work in Oxford is not, I regret to say, War Work as I was unable to find anything satisfactory and I can't afford to live in London now my house is closed down. But it is of great assistance to culture – for which I believe we are fighting. I am working in the Taylorian Institute which is a library and am employed in cataloguing and classifying Foreign Books. It is quite hard work – hours 10–12 and 2–5 or six – and it keeps one occupied. I didn't apply for an F.O. job in a Foreign Embassy as, again, I don't think I could afford it and it would be impossible to get a paid job of this sort. I think if the war goes on for a long time, I shall come here and assist Morris [presumably Maurice Bowra] in growing edible matter in the garden. I told you all this in one of the letters you haven't got. I was cut to the quick by your insinuation that the 'gay life' of Oxford had hindered my letter-writing activities. In the first place God knows there is not much 'gay life' in Oxford as far as I am concerned. One is always being urged to 'Dig for victory'. So when you return you may find me an expert market-gardener.

You will never guess where I am going for Xmas. To Sachie and Georgia. We have buried the hatchet and are now great friends . . .

Love from

Gerald

In fact Berners was wrong; there was no need to worry about money and it was indeed a part of his depression, but it was not completely insane to be apprehensive. His income from the Berners Estate Company fell from £5,000 at the beginning of the war to £2,000 at the end of it, then almost doubled, then collapsed for three years, recovering a little before his death. In the same way his working hours, though a little shorter than most, were not negligible and must be seen as coming after more than twenty years without such employment. His only other war work was to be on a panel organised by Paul Nash with John Betjeman, David Cecil and John Piper, to list painters who might be useful, but soon the War Artists Advisory Committee superseded them.

There were no dramatic scenes but Berners' depression was severe and prolonged. At first he had had nothing to do, which

left me a certain amount of time on my hands for introspection. And this introspection has not proved very flattering. At moments I have come to the conclusion that my character is utterly contemptible. This conviction reached such a pitch that I resolved to have recourse to psycho-analysis to discover the reason why. Four times a week I visited an amiable Viennese Jewess, a pupil of Freud, and lay on a sofa in a small room in the Woodstock Road and was invited to say anything that came into my head (free association), evoke any early memories and recount my dreams. (The first discovery was that I had a dead bird inside me – walking with my nurse in the fields at an early age I came upon a dead swallow. It was my first sight of death.) It transpired that most of the delinquencies of my character were due to the rather abnormal conditions of my early home life. My father who was far more intelligent than my mother was in the navy.

Though he had seen a psychiatrist briefly in his youth, this was an admission of failure and distress for someone of his age and class, and so entailed a certain amount of humiliation. Some treated it as a guilty secret; Berners did not, but his references to it are light, even facetious – 'they have found a fish in my subconscious' – his normal way of evading an issue. Writing to Betjeman, who had been packed off to a psychoanalyst by his wife to rid him of his persecution mania, he returned to his 'dead bird'.

Presumably because he was told to, he began to record his dreams. They are less dull than most, often nicely written little scenes, but the aimless, pointless quality is inescapable, which is not to say they are insignificant. Friends appear: 'I suddenly see Daisy Fellowes in the water, at least my friend says it is she. I am pleased at being able to tell the lady I am a friend of hers and call out to Daisy. She comes across the river, which has suddenly got very wide – and the scene changes. We are in Paris.' Some dreams are suggestive: a room full of people gathered round a table, gambling. There is a scrap screen.

I notice a rather pretty adolescent face: the face suddenly materialises into a real adolescent standing next to me. I lay my face against his and find that it is smooth and cool. We go out of the room together ... A question arises in a group of friends as to whether the coffee is good or not. I am appealed to as a specialist and in drinking it, some is spilled on my white flannel trousers. Michael Duff appears. The youth I met in the gambling room is there. Michael knows him and disparages him. There is some question of walking to the Foreign Office.

When Berners sees his house in Rome, now unreachable, 'I burst into tears in an ecstasy of self-pity. The friend was sympathetic and pretended not to notice that I was crying. A little boy in the street jeered.'

Some dreams are rather sinister: 'Dark courtyard in the snow. I slip and fall. Near me what I take to be two large birds fighting. One of the combatants is a raven, the other an evil-looking little man. The raven is getting the worst of it. The little man says it will make a good stew.' Others are sad: 'On the Riviera – brilliant sunshine – a reality dream. I regret that I shall not be able to travel any more. I talk to a woman – an officer's wife – am slightly ashamed but feel that it is nice for her to be seen talking to me. Am reminded of the Casati and think of what she was and what she is now.' Even such a random handful conveys something of his state of mind.

The hatchet mentioned to Violet Trefusis had been out for Georgia, not Sachie, Sitwell. He did go to them for Christmas; John Sparrow was there and it was a success. A friend of theirs remembers Berners' manner as having 'a kind of sparkling diffidence. I was struck by how frequently he blinked his eyelids when talking.' And he was up to his old tricks: *Education, Intellectual, Moral and Physical* had a frontispiece of the author, Herbert Spencer, which soon gained 'the trace of a glint in the eye, a knowing lift of the eyebrow, the hint of a missing tooth and a leer, till the smug, sanctimonious eminent Victorian became a mask of crookedness and louche connivance with a subtle overall air of tipsiness.'

During the phoney war Berners wrote a novel about Oxford at this time, *Far From the Madding War*, which forms another fallible guide to his thoughts and feelings. The plot is slender, indeed inadequate, more a series of incidents that give rise to conversation, and in this perhaps reminiscent of Firbank. Emmeline Pocock, the daughter of a don, shares some of Berners' own attitudes, though more calmly:

> The war had come upon her as a very unpleasant surprise. The twenty years of her life had been spent in the company of eminently sensible people ... Being neither a keen nor a very conscientious student of politics, she had put her trust a little too implicitly in the words that fell from the lips of some of the eminent statesmen who occasionally came to her father's house ... she was deluded into rather too optimistic an outlook.

She wonders what sort of war work to adopt and decides to unpick, stitch by stitch, a very fine, rare and valuable piece of embroidery, of which, as it happens, she is not fond. It will be 'tedious, laborious and heartrending' – above all not in the least enjoyable – and it will place her with 'The Great Destroyers and so be suitable for the times . . . It was a pity of course that what she was doing could not possibly help to win the war, but then the same could be said of a great deal of war work that was very much applauded.' And of Berners in his library.

Berners described the book as a *roman à clef*. An old school friend, Lady Caroline Paltry, is Penelope Betjeman, with 'great vitality and overwhelming persistence' as well as an unmistakable voice. Berners denied this to Penelope Betjeman herself but confirmed it to her mother: 'In fact she and I were the only real characters in the book.' This was not true either. For the most part it describes the new milieu in which he has placed himself. Emmeline is struck by a curious sense of sterility in the dons' conversations, which never seem to lead anywhere. Traces of analysis creep in. A particular bore is Professor Trumper, who is not prey to social inhibitions, 'indeed, one often wished that he were; that he could be psycho-analysed in an inverse sense and given a few'. Berners has picked up other phrases: Emmeline finds her work a cure for 'neurosis and introspection', while a friend's baby is 'already beginning to show signs of phobias and repressions'.

As in Berners' life, some dons are amusing and become friends. Mr Jericho is based on Isaiah Berlin, though A.J.P. Taylor detected a resemblance to himself, and Jericho's appearance – blond and rather Flemish-looking, 'he wore very large steel-rimmed spectacles, through which his eyes focused you with an alarming intensity' – is that of Robert Zaehner, an equally distinguished expert on Iran. Berlin was then thirty, unmarried, soon to join the Ministry of Information in America. Though far more intellectually brilliant, he appreciated Berners' light touch and found him 'a delightful, whimsical and, on artistic matters, intelligent man'. He came to the house in St Giles's and heard Berners and Zaehner playing an orchestral work by Berlioz, transcribed by Liszt for four hands. 'He played with immense spirit, so did Zaehner, who on the whole won.' Berners, his senior by over twenty years, naturally describes Berlin without the respect, almost reverence, that settled round him later:

> It was characteristic of this ebullient personality that you rarely heard or saw him coming. He appeared quite suddenly, like a pantomime demon or a cuckoo out of a cuckoo clock . . . You felt there was nothing his eyes

missed, and, indeed, that they often saw a good many things that weren't
there. He was a tutor of Modern History at All Saints [Berlin had been
at All Souls, but went to New College in 1938] and was said to be one of
the most brilliant exponents of that equivocal science, the philosophy of
history. His interests centred also in the less serious weaknesses of
mankind and particularly in those of his colleagues . . . The most trivial,
the most anodyne item of personal news was transformed by his
exquisite artistry into a little masterpiece of psychological literature.

A talented gossip, in fact, but the barb in the tail applies more to
Zaehner: 'If Mr Jericho suffered from any social defect, it was rather
from excess of tact than its absence.'

Berners' recent host Maurice Bowra also appears, as the Provost of
Unity (instead of Wadham) and aged well over seventy (instead of
scarcely middle-aged):

> He spent most of his time in his vaulted neo-Gothic study, surrounded
> by early editions and fragments of Greek archaic sculpture, writing his
> memoirs in a large volume bound in vellum. It was unlikely that these
> could be published until after his death, and when they were, they would
> undoubtedly cause a certain amount of surprise and annoyance to a great
> many grandchildren.

Later on the Provost becomes gloomy, but the dangers of looking into
fiction to see reality increase as the exigencies of plot and the
imagination of the author take hold. Mr Jericho thinks he has
discovered the cause of his despondency. The Provost is said to regret
not being a man of action. He has tailored himself for the role of
eccentric and now he dislikes it:

> But it is too late. The eccentricity that is growing on him is not the case
> of a fictitious reputation becoming real. It arises from a repressed sense
> of dissatisfaction and vain regret. Had he been a statesman, a man of
> business, or a military leader, we should no doubt have lost an agreeable
> friend – however we must not think only of ourselves.

This, surely, is not Bowra, who was not particularly eccentric, but the
newly psychoanalysed (note 'repressed'), more self-conscious Berners.

Emmeline may voice some of her author's opinions and other
characters touch on his view of himself, but there is a full-scale,
conscious self-portrait as well. Almost halfway through there comes a

reference to the 'versatile peer', working in the Blood Transfusion Service, as Berners had when he first arrived in Oxford. 'Don't you remember, Mama?' says Lady Caroline. 'He came to our wedding wearing a mask.' Then he goes unmentioned for almost fifty pages before popping up in All Saints garden, and named as Lord Fitzcricket. He falls into conversation with Emmeline, who does remember him – as 'agreeable, if slightly absurd' – but when he says that he is unusually lonely this afternoon, she 'felt sorry for him. He looked so unlike the grinning photograph she had once seen in the *Tatler*.' There is then the longest description of a character in any of his novels:

> Lord Fitzcricket was a stocky little man with a countenance that varied rather considerably with the mobility of his features. Quiescent, they appeared saturnine, but when animated they took on an air of benevolence. He had now become completely bald, and when he was annoyed he looked like a diabolical egg. He possessed, however, no inherently satanic characteristics, and the impression was merely due to a peculiar slant of the eyebrows . . .
>
> He was always referred to by gossip-writers as 'the versatile peer' and indeed there was hardly a branch of art in which he had not at one time or another dabbled . . . he did a great number of things with a certain facile talent. He was astute enough to realise that, in Anglo-Saxon countries, art is more highly appreciated if accompanied by a certain measure of eccentric publicity. This fitted in well with his natural inclinations . . . When travelling on the Continent he had a small piano in his car, and on the strength of this he was likened in the popular press to Chopin and Mozart. Someone had even suggested a resemblance to Lord Byron, but for this he had neither the qualifications of being a poet nor a great lover.

Over tea, Lord Fitzcricket tells Emmeline about himself:

> For a time the war knocked me out. I felt as if I had been pole-axed. I was unable to do anything at all . . . It all seemed to have become so pointless. I believed it was the end of everything and certainly of people like me. You see I'm all the things that are no use in war. My character is essentially pacific and hedonistic . . . I've never been any good at anything practical. I'm an amateur and fundamentally superficial . . . I have never been able to summon up any great enthusiasm for the human race, and I am indifferent as to its future. I have always led a self-centred sheltered life and my little world consists of my hobbies and my personal relationships . . . I realise that what I am is a grasshopper, and it's now

the turn of the ants. The world has no use at present for middle-aged
grasshoppers.

The trouble with charming self-deprecation is that it tends to be
believed, particularly if it is as close to the truth as this. That his world
consists of his 'hobbies' may seem noticeably hard; he had put 'none'
under recreations in *Who's Who* just before the war and this is fair –
painting, writing and composing were more than hobbies. To dispel the
impression that he was busy or serious, he wrote an article explaining
that he had thought it priggish to say his whole life was a series of
recreations and mentioned the Old Man of Thermopylae, who never
did anything properly. The reference to the fable of the grasshopper
and the ant is precise, or so an entry in his notes – 'Decidedly the ants
are better off in the war than the grasshoppers' – suggests. Hence his
chosen name, 'Fitzcricket'.

Emmeline suggests psychoanalysis and he says, 'That's an idea'
(rather than 'I've tried that'). He disappears again for a bit, Emmeline
thinking him 'an absurd little man and frightfully futile'. On his return
he talks of suicide, admits to a nervous breakdown and to taking a rest-
cure.

The character and the book seem rather at a loss and though a
proposal, a concert and a murder, as well as the suicide, provoke
discussion, gloomy inertia creeps over both. When asked about death
Lord Fitzcricket replies, 'I'd really rather not think about it today, if
you don't mind. I'm a mental coward and I can't face theories.'
Emmeline is more determined, but the last words are hers and much the
same: 'If only one didn't have to think.'

There were other dons whom he had met who did not squeeze into the
book. John Sparrow soon returned to the army, but David Cecil was a
fellow of New College and he and his wife Rachel had met Berners
while staying with Naps Alington not long before; *Far From the
Madding War* is dedicated to them. Cecil describes Oxford at that time
as 'an odd little enclave, people with very similar tastes and interests',
and names Berners, Berlin, Bowra and Roy and Billa Harrod. '[Berners]
began writing those various books there and we used to read aloud to
each other . . . he felt that nothing he cared about counted for anything.
Well, when he found that it could count for a little in Oxford, then he
pepped up again.' Unbattered by air-raids even when the phoney war
was over and the real war had begun, the Oxford theatre remained open

and there were occasional concerts to which Berners would sometimes go with Cecil.

Billa Harrod had already met Berners through the Betjemans (she had been briefly engaged to John), and Roy Harrod, the economist, was now at Christ Church. She went to *Gone With the Wind* with Berners who, as they walked to supper, said in a fatigued voice, 'And the next thing they are going to do will be the Bible and it will last for two days.' They became firm friends. A.J.P. Taylor, who had come to Magdalen in 1938, was also a close friend, writing twice in his autobiography that Berners was one of the few people he missed. They had met through Frank Pakenham and dined together once a week, often at the George Restaurant, 'where he was greeted obsequiously as "My Lord", while the Duke of Leeds at a neighbouring table was ignored'. He was once seen there hooking a waiter round the neck with his umbrella to get his attention. Taylor's wife, Maggie, who has been described as 'a middle-class Ottoline Morrell', was enthusiastic about music, ballet and Berners – rather too enthusiastic, he felt, and so to be mocked. Some gold ornaments, including chickens, had been brought over from Faringdon and after she had lunched in St Giles's and had just left, Berners pursued her down the street, crying, 'Maggie, Maggie! Wait a moment! I do so want to show you my cock.'

All these were younger couples, but a contemporary, Sir John Beazley, professor of classical archaeology and a great scholar, found a shared interest in improper French novels, and his wife, an Armenian called Marie, was an excellent cook. For a time they saw each other. Berners found Marie comic but endearing, and she was fond enough to knit him skullcaps to keep his bald head warm, in which, it must be admitted, he cut a ridiculous figure. Harold Acton, who might have become a much closer friend had he not been in China for seven years, returned and lunched with him. He found Berners 'Very down . . . desperate in fact', but also blowing soap bubbles about the restaurant to delight, or perhaps disconcert, the other customers.

Churchill became Prime Minister in May 1940 and it was soon afterwards that Berners played a variation on one of his old tricks on Sibyl Colefax. He sent a note:

Dear Sibyl,
    I wonder if by any chance you are free to dine tomorrow night? It is only a tiny party for Winston and GBS. I think it important they should get together at this moment. There will be nobody else except for

Toscanini and myself. Do please try and forgive this terribly short notice.

Yours ever

Eight o'clock here and – of course – any old clothes.

Beverley Nichols takes up the story:

There was only one thing wrong about this heaven-sent epistle, which was written in longhand; the address and the signature were totally illegible. The address looked faintly like Berkeley Square, but it might equally have been Belgrave Square and the number might have been anything from 11 to 101. As for the signature she could not tell whether it was male or female.

Lady Colefax did not quite dare approach Downing Street, but she rang everyone else with increasing desperation: 'There is something almost heroic in the thought of her small, thin determined figure, sitting in her drawing-room in a hail of bombs, reaching out so desperately for the next rung of the social ladder that, for her, reached to heaven.'

So Berners was not continually depressed after his first months in Oxford; there were ups as well as downs. After a bit, he began to go to Faringdon for weekends, but only had ten guests during the year, one at a time except for the Cecils.

Clarissa Churchill was the exception – she stayed four times. The niece of the Prime Minister, she was nineteen and at Oxford. She remembers becoming aware of Berners at the Cecils, 'There was this quiet little man in the corner, looking down at his knees. I was told he was having a nervous breakdown. I had no idea who he was.' Occasionally they left at the same time, and acquaintance grew. 'He said, "I've got this house in the country I'm thinking of opening up." We went for a weekend.' One day she glimpsed a figure in khaki. 'I asked "Who was that?" and he said, "Oh he looks after things, he's the agent."' In fact it was Heber Percy. 'I'd never heard of him either. Eventually I worked it out.' One day she opened a drawer and 'photographs came tumbling out – Sitwells, Diaghilev, everyone. It was a revelation.'

David Cecil insists that the appearance and position of Emmeline in *Far From the Madding War* were taken from Jane Gordon, the daughter of the President of Magdalen, but Berners himself named Clarissa Churchill. Of Emmeline, he wrote:

The first impression was one of gentleness and modesty. Then you began to realise that she was extremely pretty ... She was of rather diminutive stature, but her body was so well proportioned that she appeared taller than she really was. Her hair, as a poetical undergraduate once said, was reminiscent of a cornfield at daybreak. Her complexion was of that fairness that invites freckles, but as she never exposed herself to the sun this was not a serious defect. Her type was more suggestive of the eighteenth century than of the present day. She looked like a nymph in one of the less licentious pictures of Fragonard.

The friendship continued after Clarissa had worked things out. They went to Oscar Wilde's *Salomé*, and she pleaded with him to come to the health farm at Tring, 'Aunt Clemmie, who has done it often, says that it's a week or two after one's left the place that the full effects begin to show, and then one feels as if one's walking on air.' She thought his psychoanalysis a complete failure because of its humourlessness: 'He was very funny about it.' Billa Harrod 'almost thought in a dotty sort of way that he might marry her', and she was not the only one. Betjeman wrote to John Piper as late as September 1942, 'They tell me Gerald B. is still in love with Clarissa Churchill.' When Harrod mentioned the idea to a younger sister, she was met with laughter and 'Goodness, how extraordinary, how could anyone marry him. He's exactly like Groucho Marx.' That was how he now struck the young.

In *Far From the Madding War* Lord Fitzcricket proposes to Emmeline and is gently refused. Clarissa Churchill, who married Anthony Eden in 1952, says that she had no idea of any such feeling and, if Berners had proposed, would have been 'very surprised'.

Robert Heber Percy was hostile, as he had been to begin with towards Diana Mosley, possibly because he sensed a threat. A report of his driving, however, shows nothing out of the ordinary:

> Robert nearly killed a dog on the way to the station – the train was gone. Our journey to Didcot hell-for-leather in Mr Webb's Rover was a sort of *Destry Rides Again* – the car made a noise like the first aeroplane, only chance remarks were possible – I remember screaming 'not another dog' as we nearly killed a second one. We caught that train by a fraction of a second. Mr Webb was sweating and shaking.

Heber Percy had been away for some time. Because of having more or less deserted before, he could not get a commission and had begun the war by joining something he described as not a regiment but a kind of chicken, The Light Sussex. This led to his guarding the coast of Kent as a private. Laura, Duchess of Marlborough, wrote later that he spent some time 'under lock and key for a very minor motoring offence'. His car was also used for the getaway after raids on Woolworths, from which he is said to have run with armfuls of cheap goods; perhaps these are versions of the same story. Drabness was suddenly transformed into glamour, if not into comfort, however, when he got some intelligence work in the Balkans and later in the Middle East. He returned in the summer of 1941 and Berners wrote to Penelope Betjeman, 'Robert on account of his continuous headaches and the peculiar conformation of his brain has been granted unlimited leave and is now at Faringdon where he is busily engaged in bringing in the hay and giving moral lectures.'

In May 1940, Sir Oswald Mosley had been arrested and interned as a fascist. Diana had just had their son Max and was living at Denham. Though Oxford friends tried to persuade him that it was unwise, Berners arranged to go to visit her by bus, a new experience for him. They spent 'a delightful day' trying to persuade each other that their fears were exaggerated – hers that the government would go much further in persecuting her husband, his that civilised life would never return – and they 'laughed a lot'. Soon afterwards, to her surprise, she too was interned and he wrote immediately and often, though at first his letters did not reach her. 'What can I send you?' one asked. 'Would you like a little file concealed in a peach?' When he sent *Far From the Madding War*, she reported, 'the walls of my cell echoed with my laughing'. She also discovered later that he had promptly been to take her son Jonathan out from his private school: 'Oxford was full of posters about my arrest, Gerald tried to divert his attention and they spent the afternoon in a tea-shop.' Later Berners was allowed to visit her in prison.

Lady Aberconway remembered 'an evening with Gerald when he remarked "Couldn't one make a poem about 'noses' and 'roses'?" I said "Let's." We were all given pencils and paper, and Gerald, concentrating for only a moment or two, produced a memorable poem, which later he polished.'

> Some people praise red roses
> But I beg leave to say

That I prefer red noses –
Red noses* are so gay.

A Kempis says we must not cling
To things that pass away.
Red noses last a lifetime
Red roses but a day.

Red roses blow but thrice a year,
In June, July and May.
But those who have† red noses
Can blow them every day.

This sounds as though it took place before the war, but in 1940 Edith Sitwell wrote Berners a letter which, after characteristically congratulating him on attacking Clive Bell and suggesting that he turn his attention to Raymond Mortimer, asks permission to include 'Red Noses' in an anthology. 'I think it is a little dream of a poem: Sachie [says] it has a Horatian quality; I admire its mingled suavity and firmness.' Perhaps spurred on by this, he set it to music.

One day he was showing the Princesse de Polignac over Oxford. When they went into Christ Church Cathedral they found the organist, Thomas Armstrong, later principal of the Royal College of Music, practising. On request, he played them some Bach; they became friends. Later Berners called and said, 'Since the war I can't compose anymore, but I don't want to lose touch with music. So I want to ask whether you could put aside an hour a week to explain to me the technique of Palestrina?' Armstrong recalled that he came for

> a number of weeks . . . his was the most alert and far seeing brain that I have ever had to do with music. You only had to mention one of the rules that guided Palestrina and Berners at once knew why the rule had arisen and what was its musical purpose. I was absolutely fascinated by his insight into the processes that led to Palestrina's style.

Although the future seemed to hold nothing but war, Berners was recovering from the first onslaught.

---

* 'They' in some versions.
† 'owners of' in some versions.

Chapter XV

The Novelist

In 1941, Berners was involved in the publication of no fewer than four novels. This was a remarkable feat, particularly for someone who had published only one before. He wrote to Penelope Betjeman's mother, 'I don't know whether it is the war or Blood Transfusions that has made me so prolific.' The first, in July, was *Far From the Madding War*, but it had already been written. His psychoanalyst may have suggested that he write it, though the style is light and not overtly confessional; or perhaps he needed an occupation to while away the hours of his comparatively solitary existence.

It was well received. Many friends commented on how refreshing it was to talk to Berners, during the war, because his style and content seemed to be, as in the title, far from it. The reviewers recorded variations on this theme: the *Sunday Times* found 'a little nonsense . . . and how welcome just now'; *Time and Tide* 'chuckled all night long', but 'Frankly, I do not feel quite sure if this is really the best moment for this story (as my uncle said at the funeral) but there you are'; the *Manchester Guardian* also found it 'a chuckling tale' but approved that Berners 'does not turn his back upon the war but accepts it in the spirit of "So what?"'; *The Times Literary Supplement* was charmed; the *New Statesman*, though thinking it 'a delightful fantasia', went wildly wrong when it found the theme to be Woman as the frustrater and destroyer of Man and all his works. No one thought the author in distress.

Berners was pleasurably surprised by the praise. John Lehmann immediately asked him to write an article about Blenheim for *Penguin New Writing*, but he replied that he could not manage anything but fiction. 'I could write a story about its inmates but that, I think, would be as unacceptable to your magazine as it would be to them . . . The idea of having to be accurate and critical always appals me.' It was of *Far From the Madding War*, however, that Evelyn Waugh, when he caught up with it in September, wrote to Randolph Churchill, 'Berners has written the dullest book yet seen', though he had admittedly written in a thank-you letter of 'the delight of reading *The Camel*'. There was also some social murmuring that this was an odd book to have written in wartime.

The strongest reaction came, not unreasonably, from Harold Nicolson. He began his diary for 10 December, 'An unhappy day. I begin by glancing at Berners' new novel *Far From the Madding War*, and am horrified to feel that Mr Lollipop Jenkins must be a portrait of myself. Ben [his son] sees no resemblance but I do.' Nicolson is right, Ben wrong, as Berners explicitly states in a letter, and it is not a kind portrait. Mr Jenkins had enjoyed a brilliant youth and is a successful author, journalist and MP:

> In the eyes of the world he was a success. Yet as he approached middle age his more thoughtful friends began to suspect that something was going a little wrong. Although outwardly the rose retained its rubicund exterior intact, they scented the presence of an invisible worm . . . people began to feel that there was something really rather terrible about an enfant terrible who was growing middle-aged and slightly pompous.

Bits and pieces of the ensuing correspondence survive. Nicolson wrote protesting, Berners denied all, and Nicolson wrote again in a moderate tone, listing clues to the identity of Jenkins. Berners replied that they could fit others, Nicolson denied it and added:

> My grievance is that many people who have never known me will believe that Mr Lollipop Jenkins is meant to be me, that they will then assume that I possess the character which you have ascribed to Mr Jenkins . . . [but] I am not in the least the sort of person to force my books upon my friends or to be jealous of other people's success or to tour round bookshops asking them to display my wares. You know that as well as I do.

Berners underlined 'my' in 'my books' and noted, 'It wasn't Mr Lollipop's book.' He was still working up the case for the defence and we have a draft. In it he finds that the identification is not proved, that Nicolson has 'developed an almost Sitwellian sensitiveness that is positively narcissistic'. He quibbles skilfully, perhaps woundingly:

> You are well known as a biographer but not as a novelist . . . nor do I

consider you predominantly fat and pink . . . When I saw you at a dinner party in the George, the book had already been written for over a year. Neither did I notice that it was a party of undergraduates. In fact the only person I saw was Father D'Arcy who can hardly be described as an undergraduate.

Berners adroitly mentions *Some People*, in which Nicolson drew portraits of contemporaries: 'Can it be the ghosts of Ronald Firbank and Hope Vere have risen to fill you with an inverted sense of guilt?' The tone is not conciliatory and he ends by saying it is Nicolson's own fault if he is saddled with the portrait, because he has been talking about it.

Whatever the merits of the arguments employed in this debate, the verdict remains guilty. Berners did base Lollipop Jenkins on Nicolson and added a few details. It was generous then of Nicolson in his next letter to say that when he first came across the portrait, he had just seen the news that the *Prince of Wales* had been sunk, and was glum. 'If I had read it in a better mood I should only have been amused.' He promised never to mention the subject again; but he was wounded.

Another model for *Far From the Madding War* protested, but without rancour. Berners again denied the charge in his reply to Penelope Betjeman, and went on to describe his recovering, if gentler, social life:

> I can't imagine how you can have supposed that you in any way figured in my recent work on Oxford in wartime. Your mother wrote to me about it and, reading between the lines, I think I detected a slightly malicious pleasure at the idea of her daughter being held up to obloquy. I assured her of course that she had been mistaken [untrue] quoting lines from the well-known poem 'Can a mother's tender care cease towards the child she-bear?'
>
> Robert says 'conquer your sloth at once and send us some [cream?]'. That is his contribution to this letter. I fear his God is in his Belly. So unlike me.
>
> I have just been staying with the equestrian poet Siegfried Sassoon. I saw Rex Whistler there and Daphne Weymouth who lives in the neighbourhood. She explained to me that she was 'keeping up the morale of others by letting down her own morals' which seems to me a very amiable form of war-work . . . I am sending you two little stories in lieu of a long letter – but that need not deter you from writing me a very long letter.

He had asked himself to stay with Sassoon and enjoyed his visit:

My dear Siegfried,

I was staying the other day in the neighbourhood of your residence and felt a great longing to come and batter at the gates of your ivory tower but was prevented from doing so by the usual lack of petrol. Perhaps if I had you might not have taken it kindly – one never knows how people may be feeling in wartime. Personally, after many months of depression, cured by psycho-analysis, I am feeling fine and ready for anything. All the same it is sad that I never see you now considering what chums we used to be. Would nothing persuade you to visit this city of decaying dons or Faringdon where I go every Saturday to Tuesday? It would be awfully jolly to see you again.

Poor Cecil Beaton is having trouble with 'Les S.' on account of *Time Trouble* and I understand that I am in some way involved. Really they are too difficult and sensitive. If one speaks about them, one is liable to be sued, and if one doesn't, so also is one liable to offend. So what is one to do?

Byebye, cheerio and toodle-oo,
Gerald

Beaton and Peter Quennell had collaborated on a book about their circle. Osbert Sitwell wrote a seven-page letter of eccentric complaints, which included the positioning of photographs and a denial that the three siblings were responsible for the war. Beaton wrote to Sitwell at equal length; and to Sassoon, 'Your anxiety is needless . . . Osbert's fuss is nonsense.' Berners struck a characteristic note from Faringdon:

My attention has been drawn to a photograph of myself appearing in your recently published *Time Exposure* in which I am represented standing half in and half out of a door way.

This would seem to imply that my position in the world of art is not fully assured and that I am merely poised on the threshold of the Hall of Fame.

I have no doubt that the publication of this malicious photograph will do incalculable harm to my reputation as a composer, an author and a painter. It may even prejudice my social standing . . .

P.S. To say nothing of you having placed dear Anita Loos's picture on the same page as that dreadful Siegfried Sassoon – and why include the Sitwells?

He does indeed seem to have recovered, feeling ready for anything. He remained on good terms with all, but Beaton and the Sitwells were not reconciled for over five years. Though Faringdon is once more in use and Sassoon invited, the book records no visitors in 1941. It seems more likely that his friends did not think it worth resuming the custom of signing until the next year, than that no one stayed a single night.

The two 'little stories' that Berners had sent Penelope Betjeman were 'Percy Wallingford' and 'Mr Pidger', published in one volume. 'Mr Pidger' is the slightest work among Berners' slight fictions. Forty-six pages long, it starts with a disclaimer: 'No reference is intended to any living dog.' This is untrue. Mr Pidger was based on Teresa Jungman's dog Wincey (short for Winston), a King Charles spaniel that accompanied her everywhere, including visits to Faringdon. Walter and Millicent, an elegant young couple, are going to visit her rich Uncle Willy, of whom she has expectations. Millicent insists on bringing her eponymous Pomeranian, although Uncle Willy is famous for his hatred of dogs. So Mr Pidger is smuggled in but discovered, and the couple are asked to leave in disgrace. Uncle Willy makes a new will, but when he dies a month later it cannot be found. Walter and Millicent inherit, until Mr Pidger digs up a tin box in the garden that contains the new will. On the train that, for a second time, takes them away from the beautiful house that might have been theirs, the one surprise of the story occurs: Walter picks Mr Pidger up and throws him out of the window. The corpse is retrieved, but not the marriage. John Sparrow, a dog-hater, said that the end of 'Pidger' was one of the best moments in all literature; he was too kind.

Phrases about the house suggest Faringdon, and there are touches of Berners in Uncle Willy:

> He did not believe in the Perfectibility of Man and in any case it was not likely to occur within his lifetime, so what was the good of bothering about it. During his long life he had done his best to ignore the follies and wickedness of the human race. To be enabled to do so, he said, was one of the chief advantages of being rich.

Berners himself was fond of dogs, but not of this one; the diatribe against them and their owners, as well as the defenestration of Mr Pidger, seems to have had real emotion behind it: 'Why are these loathsome beasts known as the friends of man? It is because they flatter his foolish self-esteem in a way that no other animals do. Their subservience gives the weakest character a sense of domination.' There is a teasing-the-clergyman passage. Berners exercises his gift of being pleasantly readable but, even for those interested in the author, this short work might with advantage be shorter still.

'Percy Wallingford' is more interesting. It too is set just before a great European war, this time in 1914, and there is a house party in the country. Evelyn Waugh, with a similar feeling that civilised life would never be the same again, was shortly to write in *Brideshead Revisited* an evocation of the glamour and luxury of such a place. Berners feels no such nostalgia: 'The bedrooms were, for the most part, small and uncomfortable . . . the bathrooms were situated in a distant wing, and the bath water was apt to be tepid . . . even in the coldest weather there was never a fire in the bedroom.'

A narrator tells us of Percy Wallingford, the perfect specimen of a certain type of Englishman. He had hero-worshipped Wallingford at Eton, but 'manhood had improved his looks. With his wavy golden hair and his pink and white complexion he might easily have given an impression of effeminacy or flashiness. But nobody could have accused him of either of these defects.' He was never assertive, but always right in argument, about books, about food. 'He would among several restaurants whose exteriors were identical, invariably select the best.' Wallingford soars through the diplomatic examination, but the narrator, 'having failed twice . . . applied for an honorary attachéship as the next best thing, and was sent to the embassy in Rome'.

Now they meet again, Wallingford with a new wife. He had said in a rare moment of comparative intimacy, 'A rather ordinary sort of girl would suit me best, the sort of girl who would fit in with my way of living whatever it is going to be' and, of course, he has found her precisely: 'In the way of ordinariness she was without flaw . . . her outlook on life seemed to be that of a bewildered housemaid. But at the same time a conscientious housemaid.' Wallingford now seems less self-assured and all the better for it. Later the narrator makes progress with the new wife, Vera, but there is a peculiar look in her eyes and later a peculiar incident. He discovers her putting a book away in the library in the pitch dark.

At this stage, a little more than halfway through, Berners has succeeded in blending mystery and social observation in a most intriguing way. The reader wants to know what will happen to the marriage (probably something bad), and what is inside Percy Wallingford (possibly something good). The answers are disappointing as far as the story is concerned, but suggestive, if baffling, about Berners himself.

The narrator hears from others that Wallingford has had a nervous breakdown and resigned. He had 'lost all his buoyancy and self-assurance', 'mooned about looking miserable' and had now returned to England, but seeing no one. Then he reads in the papers that Vera 'has met her death by asphyxiation in a hotel room in France'. Society is ruthlessly flippant and cynical, the attitude summed up by a beauty: 'She was such a frightful bore. I am not in the least surprised at his doing her in.'

Time passes and then the narrator, staying in a hotel at Avignon, recognises Wallingford, 'not exactly aged but his features had shrunk and his body was unnaturally thin' and his look had become shifty and evasive. He is coaxed into confession:

> On the first night of my marriage I was a little awkward and embarrassed. Although I had had one or two flirtations I was never much of a womanizer. In fact I had never had an affair with a woman of my own class. I felt it would make matters easier if I turned out the light. Well, I won't go into any more details. Suddenly Vera began to giggle hysterically. I was a little taken aback and Vera explained why she was laughing. 'You can't think how funny you look,' she said, 'with your hair sticking up like that.' At first I couldn't understand what she meant because, as I have told you, there was no light in the room and it was pitch black.

Vera can see in the dark. This revelation does not just amaze him, as it would anyone; it obsesses and discomforts him:

> The nights became a torment to me. I was unable to sleep for fear she might be awake and looking at me . . . I began to wonder if other people had some strange hidden superiority of which I was unaware and, talking to some quite humble individual, I would be suddenly seized with the idea that he too might possess some secret gift, telepathy for instance, and be able to read my thoughts . . . in the train when we went through a tunnel I used to make faces at the people in my carriage in case one of them might be able to see in the dark.

He begins to hate Vera. He recounts how a charcoal brazier had been put in her room, with instructions that it was not to be left there overnight. He was in another room, she apparently forgot and was found dead. He reacts so strongly to the word 'remorse', however, that the narrator is left with the impression that he did indeed kill her. Just as war breaks out, he hears that Wallingford, still in the hotel where it all happened, has shot himself.

If a man who has recently had a breakdown writes about a man having a breakdown, it is natural at least to consider whether he is using his own experience. Berners' writing comes alive when he is drawing on emotion, if not quite expressing it, and bits of this are startlingly vivid (other bits contrived and repetitive). Yet it does not correspond in any direct way. Berners is not just unlike Percy Wallingford. Wallingford stands for all that Berners has been acutely aware all his life of *not* being. No one is as naturally assured as this character, but to Berners it seemed that others were and he was not. The idea of someone seeing you in the dark, seeing through you, reading your thoughts, is unbearable and leads to hatred. The murder is perfunctory and unconvincing, the sense of inadequacy – or of defences that have proved inadequate – intense. No one 'saw' Berners in that way except perhaps Robert Heber Percy, and if some past memories or feelings had been called up during Berners' analysis, nothing else in the story suggests him. The revelation on the wedding night and the curious choice of it being his hair that is mocked, when Berners had no hair and was sensitive about the lack, suggests emotional incoherence, but also that the sense of frenzy comes from the physical, the sexual.

The reviewers, fewer than before, were friendly, though one thought 'Mr Pidger' silly, another almost farcical. The *Spectator* gave 'Percy Wallingford' twenty lines and found it 'A tragic story told with dry control and from the long view, and with the author's sceptical manner very deftly adjusted to vitalise a sad and puzzling little tale.'

In the preliminary pages of *Far From the Madding War* there had been an announcement: 'A new story by Lord Berners is in active preparation: *The Last Trump, the tale of a Symphony and its Composer*, with illustrations by the author.' There was a corrected title in *Percy Wallingford and Mr Pidger*: 'in preparation: *Count Omega* [and] *The Romance of a Nose*'. Curiously, Berners did not sign his contract with Constable, on which the title was corrected from *The Last Trump* to *Count Omega*, until 3 June 1942: he must have kept it unsigned for months. *Count Omega* duly appeared a month after 'Mr Pidger'. It is more substantial, at over 200 pages, and interesting in that the hero is a composer. Emanuel Smith is not, however, like Berners; he is twenty-three, fair-haired and slender and has a profound contempt for opera and ballet. He is searching for a sensational climax to his symphony when at a party he hears an enormous trombonist called Gloria who can hold a note without apparent effort while it swells to a volume that is almost physically painful before diminishing to silence. He pursues her, breaks a tepid engagement for his new passion but then discovers she is false, a trick, she was merely miming to hidden players. Nevertheless, the symphony is played and when Gloria puts down her instrument and the note continues, chaos erupts. Emanuel goes to live quietly in the country and marries his old fiancée.

Without altering his relaxed style, Berners mixes observation of the musical world, fantasy, fairy story, realistic romance, wish-fulfilment and, most dangerously, farce. The ingredients blend into a whole that is his own; the plot, which he had not really tried before, is managed adroitly. There is scarcely a dull page. Subjects that interest or disturb him are, however, only glanced at: a cause of breakdown being sex starvation or, interestingly, inappropriate occupation; suicide attempted but this time failing; a marriage of sublimated convenience, which this time takes place and indeed provides the happy ending.

There is also something approaching a theme: Gloria, in spite of her penchant for cake, is almost Emanuel's muse, but she is fake and capricious, leaving for ever without warning or compunction. While she is near she exerts an attraction so strong that he has no choice but to pursue her at whatever cost to his friends and ordinary life; when she is gone he tells himself and others without fuss that he is all right without her.

The book is more skilful than any fiction Berners had written before and touches on things that were important to him, and it is readable and original; nevertheless it is too mild to make a lasting impression. The reviews, more numerous again, mentioned a tradition of fantasy, told with elegance and wit, which was traced from Wilde through Beerbohm. One claimed that the book was really a satire on publicity stunts, another on the methods of composers; only the *Spectator*, hitherto friendly, found it a 'shade laborious in prankishness'.

One other person was displeased. Long ago, Berners had known William Walton well and in 1931 *Belshazzar's Feast* had been dedicated to Berners, in return for a badly needed fifty pounds. Walton remembered this cash transaction with gratitude and did the same himself for Elisabeth Lutyens. Since then they had drifted amiably apart, though David Cecil remembered meeting Walton through Berners at Oxford and going to a concert that contained a work of his. This was probably Walton's violin concerto, which Berners applauded but also awarded faint criticism: 'I'm afraid Beethoven's better.' Now Berners sparked off a row. In a letter, he had written:

> If you read *Far From the Madding War* you may have imagined that the musician Francis Paltry was meant to be you. But it wasn't. I am reserving you for a forthcoming novel *Count Omega*, which I will send you as soon as it appears. I thought it only fair that the funniest English composer should be immortalised by my pen. I must inform you that, should you, in Sitwellian fashion, propose to take action for libel, the book has been gone through by a lawyer and that I have insured myself against possible damages for libel. Anyhow send me a line to say how you're getting on.

Walton took this seriously, consulted his solicitor and asked to see a copy before publication: an excessive reaction perhaps, but had he written back to Berners, he would have been acquiescing to he knew not what.

Berners prepared four drafts in reply. One was sniffy: 'Something seems to have destroyed your sense of proportion. You surely do not imagine that your personality is sufficiently interesting to appeal to me as a literary theme. If you persist in trying to thrust yourself into my novels in this fashion I shall apply for an injunction to restrain you from doing so.' A similar one imagined Walton 'feverishly searching its pages for any hint of similarity between yourself and the charming hero of my story'. A third said that he had been told at a dinner-party that Walton was taking the letter seriously, before reverting to much the same text; a fourth, friendlier in tone, said that of course he (Berners) thought the lawyer's letter was a joke, that he was not 'offended – only a little surprised' – and that the publishers were annoyed at the prospect of an injunction delaying the book beyond Christmas. A note that was actually written on Faringdon paper simply said, 'I'm afraid you may have some difficulty in proving libel as the novel in question is in the nature of a fairy story and is about an over-life-size female trombone player.' This is disingenuous, because libel would concern Emanuel and perhaps his use of fraud.

Also Francis Paltry from the earlier book is described as 'the great white hope of English music', as Walton had been, and Walton's First Symphony did have a different ending after its opening performance. Berners meant to tease. He also wrote to Walton's solicitor, 'I am shortly bringing out a book, called "Ridiculous Composers I have known". If your client Mr William Walton should consider it necessary to see a copy before publication, will you kindly tell him to apply.' And he wrote to Osbert Sitwell, explaining the story with the comment, 'Curious, isn't it?' He adds a PS: 'There may be something in what dear old Mrs Hunter used to say about it being a mistake to be playful with someone who is not quite a gentleman.' Actually it is Berners who seems to have kept things going; in a friendly reply Walton wrote that he only approached his solicitor 'to give you something to gossip about' and that since then he has read and enjoyed *Count Omega*, though 'the composer is too like Edmund Rubbra* for my liking'. When asked about the incident in 1974, Walton wrote that he remembered nothing about it, but mentioned the fifty pounds for *Belshazzar's Feast* with gratitude. There is irony here. *Belshazzar's Feast*, dedication or not, was just the sort of work that made Berners think Walton was taking himself too seriously, perhaps seeing himself as the successor to Elgar. Constant Lambert wrote, 'What a fool Willie made of himself.' Solicitors are not approached and encouraged to write aggressive letters so lightly. Walton's decision to treat it all as a joke between friends may have come rather late.

Having got into mild trouble by using others as models for his works, Berners was now selected as a model himself. Denton Welch, primarily a writer, not yet twenty-five or established, was to achieve a certain durable fame when his posthumous book, *A Voice through the Cloud*, was published in 1950. Evelyn Waugh wrote then to Diana Cooper that he was:

> reading and am fascinated by D. Welch, a little dying pansy describing pathetic picnics in the rain – rye-vita and milk chocolate – and tiny two-bob antiques and then when he meets the great Eddie Sackville-West, Mrs Nicolson, Herbert Read, Sickert, Osbert Sitwell etc. the most frightening penetration. He met only one woman he thought perfect – Sibyl Colefax.

In 1940, Welch painted a picture from a photograph of Berners, aged eight, got up for a fancy-dress party. He was inspired perhaps more by the wish to interest a rich patron than to create a work of art. To discover the true colours he wrote to Berners, who replied, 'I am very much flattered that you should think my youthful portrait as Robinson Crusoe worthy of being made a conversation piece of. My hair in those days was brown and my eyes also. Latter are still brown but my hair has

---

* A prolific English composer (1901–86), in the mould of Vaughan Williams.

more or less flown!' He describes from his excellent visual memory the crimson and blue macaw on his shoulder, the humming bird in his fur hat (rather indistinct), the fox's mask and the skins of small animals of the weasel type round his waist, but admits, 'The shoes I fear were rather a let-down as they were ordinary dancing pumps.'

The picture was begun, courageously rescued from a burning house, and a meeting to view the work-in-progress at the Randolph Hotel in Oxford arranged. Welch wrote it up. Berners

came in with a bounding step and sank down on the bed in front of the conversation piece I had made. I thought as he sat there that he bore a very faint resemblance to Humpty Dumpty. He immediately produced a little gold box and began furiously to take snuff. I was not offered any, and I cannot decide whether this was rudeness or true politeness.

'It's perfectly charming,' he said in a sort of amused indulgent voice.

Berners made suggestions, but after forty-five minutes instead of offering to buy it, only said, 'You'll let me have a photograph when you've finished, won't you?'

'Oh, yes, of course,' I said gaily, feeling rather miserable.

Lord Berners' eye roved round the room. He looked at my ivory-topped bottles and brushes and then at my squalid little face flannel. It was ringed round with roses . . . I had purposely hidden his *Far From the Madding War* under an old volume of Pope's pastorals which I had bought for twopence. It had seemed too fulsome to leave his books about bare and uncovered . . .

'What did you think of that?' he asked urgently.

'I enjoyed it awfully,' I said quite untruthfully. I thought it a trivial little book.

'I'm so glad.' He seemed to relax after my answer. I felt rather ashamed for giving him pleasure.

'I've got more coming out before Christmas,' he added with busy pride. And I understood for I knew how easy it was to appear childish in one's enthusiasm.

'Will you write in your book for me?' I asked.

'Yes,' he said eagerly, 'but I haven't got a pen.'

I lent him my stylo. He held it too slantingly and could not make it write well. He began in big letters 'Denton Welch, with good wishes from Berners. Oxford 1941.'

The 'Berners' was extra large, much larger than the 'Denton Welch'.

He looked at the spidery lines and shaking his head said: 'It's not my writing.'

Berners then insisted on showing Welch some closed rooms, saying:

> 'Isn't it an extraordinary hotel? John Betjeman loves it.' They shook
> hands on the steps. 'Goodbye,' he said. He put on his black hat which
> accentuated the fact that he was wearing a shirt of tiny black and white
> checks. I watched him trotting down the pavement. He looked like a
> busy, useful Easter egg setting out on its daily round. And I felt lonely.

Betjeman approved of this account enough to publish it in *Time and
Tide* after Berners' death, with the comment, 'Had they met more often
Mr Welch would have understood the shyness of Lord Berners. He was
so shy that he could hardly bring himself to speak to someone when he
first met them.'

Welch and Berners did try to meet again. The exchange of insincere
compliments, which each may have believed, continued. Welch went on
trying to sell the picture. Berners replied that he simply had not the
space. Welch, apparently unaware of the walls of Faringdon, was
understanding but not entirely resigned: 'I saw at Oxford how little
room you had and it is quite a large picture. Perhaps one day.' At last it
was offered for sale at the Leicester Galleries for forty pounds, found no
takers and was given to a friend. Welch sent a collection of his stories
when they came out and Berners' praise for these is apparently sincere;
indeed he asked him to stay, but Welch died the very week he was
expected.

Chapter XVI

War and Recovery

In the new year of 1942 Berners was unable to leave Faringdon: 'the front door blocked, two feet of snow on every bough and all the robins snowed under. We have only food for two days so if it goes on we shall have to kill and eat a soldier. I am rather tempted (should it come to this) to try the major, who is impregnated with whiskey and might make an excellent haggis.' This was an American major, for as Berners wrote to Ruth Gordon:

> We have American soldiers in the house and they are not only charming but helpful. One of them, a wireless expert, helped me to mend my radio; another who had worked at Antoines in N.Y. insisted on doing the hair of my female guests and a third, a Southerner who ran a mortician's business in his home town said to me when he left, 'If ever you feel like dying just send me a cable and wherever I happen to be I'll come along and fix you.' One can't say fairer than that, can one?

Faringdon had become an American Army hospital.

According to the visitors' book, kept once more, Clarissa Churchill was the first as well as the most frequent visitor. One, two or three people came about every other weekend, with a strong Oxford contingent: the Beazleys, A.L. Rowse, David Cecil and the Harrods. Familiar names recur: Margot Fonteyn and Constant Lambert twice, Cecil Beaton, Dorothy Lygon and, for Easter, Peter Quennell and Cyril Connolly. It is generally assumed that Berners was far removed from the mainstream of literary life during the war, but Quennell and Connolly made a link. Two poems by Berners appeared in Connolly's *Horizon* in July: 'Surrealist Landscape', dedicated to Dali and already quoted, and 'The Performing Mushroom', dedicated to a famous

Cambridge classicist, Professor Jebb. The title is not misleading and it ends:

> To rest upon one's laurels late in life
> To settle down with children and a wife,
> Enjoying wealth amassed by honest toil
> And then when life has ceased to ebb,
> To die at home and fertilise the soil,
> While other mushrooms fry in boiling oil
>   For You, Professor Jebb

In the same issue of *Horizon* there is a lament for Pilot Officer Frederick Ashton being unavailable to create ballets. Connolly's aim was 'to make our culture into something worth fighting for', so contributions did not have to concern the issues of the day or even be serious; his editorial spoke of the magazine being an oasis of beauty and clarity of thought. Faringdon, the great appeal of which lay precisely in being so very far from the madding war, could just about claim that it too was carrying on traditions of civilisation and culture. Not everyone, however, was at ease with the idea of comfort, even luxury, at this point in the war. Connolly himself wrote in mock protest:

> It must be awful to be as wicked as you are – you must have very sleepless nights, with the load of pleasure – I can hardly bring myself to write the word – such vile names do vile things have – weighing upon your conscience and the God-proof mackintosh of art wrapped round you! I shall say a prayer for you to Kirshnamurti. What about making a start and pulling up this year's strawberry bed? The ground would be so pleased.

The mention of strawberries goes straight to the heart of the matter. In these years the whole country, and in particular, it seems, Cyril Connolly, was underfed and so seems to have thought of little else. Originality was used to replace unavailable ingredients. Anne Scott-James in *Picture Post*, for instance, recommended dandelion and wood-sorrel salad, elderflower fritters, purée of Good King Henry, rosehip jam, herb sandwich spread and stinging nettles on toast. Whalemeat, rook pie and spam became familiar. Dehydrated eggs and potatoes (to save shipping space) now appeared. 'In fact, I doubt if you can cook,' Scott-James comments, 'until you have made an omelette with margarine, dried egg and chopped chickweed.'

It was not quite like that at Faringdon, though Billa Harrod remembers a delicious consommé made with Marmite and grated carrot. Somehow, high standards were maintained and much appreciated. There was the home farm. Game was not rationed. Heber Percy, in a rare letter, had asked for news of the ducks on the lake and commanded that the water-hen trap be set again. Berners, in the preface to a cookery book, admits that at this moment 'it must be pitched in a minor key. There can be no inspiring visions of pints of cream, pyramids of eggs and dishes rubbed with truffles.' Nevertheless, he nursed hopes and wrote sadly that his pigs still seemed to have no instinct for nosing out the latter; he came out strongly for toadstools; lobsters could also be acquired. Enough cream was found to go with caramelised carrots, which apparently made the mouth water. Over tea on Saturday he would still hold forth about the delights of dinner, but things faltered a little during the week.

A curious little row in May cast all the characters in unfamiliar roles: Berners as aggressor, Nancy Astor as victim, George Bernard Shaw as peacemaker. Someone had sent Berners a book on Christian Science. He assumed it to be Lady Astor and resented the implied bossiness. He was wrong. She was understandably put out to receive a complaining letter and told the Shaws. Shaw wrote, 'We have known Berners for years and years . . . this row must not be, as you two are to my knowledge deserving persons in spite of your unfortunate rank.' He also wrote to Berners, 'she is a genuinely good sort' and Berners in turn wrote to Lady Astor apologising, and asking her to imagine Margot Asquith sending her a Roman Catholic pamphlet. He received a forgiving reply ('Certainly the hatchets will disappear').

The squabble shows Berners still touchy about religion, though he gave up enquiries into Roman Catholicism easily. Soon Heber Percy and he mocked the suggestion of converting and, in particular, Penelope Betjeman, who after her own conversion tried to bring them over with her to Rome. But the subject recurs with Berners, as if he felt the lack, but then could not believe in even the minimum required. David Cecil was surprised to come on Berners in Christ Church Cathedral and thought him 'bewildered' – somehow religion 'didn't take' with Berners. His phrase about religion requiring a talent he lacked was echoed years later by John Betjeman writing to Tom Driberg's wife, 'I think Faith is rather like an ear for music, a gift kindly supplied by the Management.'

Shaw gracefully refused an invitation to Faringdon:

We both liked Faringdon House and have such pleasant recollections of
the day we spent there, that your invitation tantalised us; for alas! your
next story must be about a man with an ideal house who invites a couple
whom he liked when they were, say, middle-aged, forgetting that in the
intervening years they must have become old crocks who ought to have
had the good manners to die.

They arrive, the man a dotard, the woman an invalid whose utmost
power of locomotion takes her barely ten steps, mostly bedridden and
having to be nursed, both dotty and unable to remember people's names
or get up and downstairs beyond the first floor, and not then safe without
attendance.

The servants all give notice; and the host curses the day on which he
first met them. Fortunately he has built in his garden a replica of the
Venice campanile. He persuades them that they must see the view of the
White Horse from the top, and has them carried up by his outdoor staff,
assisted by himself. While they are looking for the White Horse, he
descends and leaves the country. Their skeletons are still in the tower.

An alternative ending would be that as he leaves the tower his senile
guest overbalances and falls on him from the top. The old lady, with a
superhuman effort, just manages to throw herself after her husband, and
they all die happily ever after.

There is a slight mystery about the appearance of Berners' next and last
novel, *The Romance of a Nose*. Michael Sadleir of Constable had written
in September, hoping to have it out in time for the Christmas market,
and indeed the first edition says 1941. Nevertheless, the reviews and a
rather silly picture in the *Tatler* comparing Berners' own profile with
that of Cleopatra appeared in May 1942. Perhaps the printed copies
were not ready by Christmas and were then held for the following
spring.

The model for Berners' protagonist this time is Daisy Fellowes, and
the conceit indeed concerns Cleopatra's nose and is explained in the first
sentence: 'In my opinion it can hardly grow any longer.' The princess is
grotesque, though talented. She squabbles with her brother, with whom
she shares the throne and whom she should marry. There is much
plotting, but she is at a disadvantage because so open to ridicule. She
hears of a plastic surgeon in Thebes and flies to him (finding the
pyramids vulgar on the way). The new nose is a triumph ('She had the
same instinct as she had about clothes'). History would have been
changed, had her nose not been. With her new one, she finds she can
gull a Roman governor sent to bring her home, but this is mere

rehearsal for Caesar. Supported by him, she defeats her enemies and at the end is poised to go to Rome, pregnant with his son.

The tale is elegantly told, the modern language in a classical setting sometimes amusing, but the whole thing appears trifling. Daisy Fellowes, it seems, had not touched any deep feelings. 'Witty' is the word most used by the reviewers, though 'prankish' recurs and *The Times* thought 'The feminist tract ripples delightfully along, frequent in gleams of surprise and twists of mirth, and always lightly in touch with history.' The novel did, however, appear in France as *Le Nez de Cléopâtre*.

Constable were extraordinarily relaxed about all aspects of publishing *The Romance of a Nose* and a letter from Michael Sadleir returning the signed agreement is dated 3 June 1942. The same letter expresses regret that he cannot come to Berners' new play in Oxford. This was called *The Furies* and is, curiously, little remembered. Harold Acton, David Cecil and Billa Harrod are among friends with no recollection of it. The designer, Tanya Moiseiwitch, knowing that Berners had designed *A Wedding Bouquet* himself, was 'very much in awe when I went round to show him my scribbly sketches. He didn't look at them for a while, but said, "Shall I play you a piece I have just composed?" and did so. It calmed my nerves.' A.L. Rowse lent his first name, Alfred, to the hero and was observed watching him. 'Footling plot about Man pursued by women. The author [Berners] and A.L. Rowse immediately in front of us. V. amusing. Rowse coldly receiving some of the jokes. Every one was acknowledged with furious eyebrow action from Berners.' This is from the diary of Oscar Wood, who was to teach philosophy and linguistic precision at Christ Church and later commented on his own style, 'I think "Every one" means every joke – not everybody. There is a small gap between the two words in the original. My recollection is of a lot of in-jokes which I did not understand and of Berners turning to Rowse to make sure that he saw there was a joke.'

Berners could not have been unfamiliar with *The Family Reunion*, with which T.S. Eliot had scored a great success in London in 1939. In that play, the Eumenides, or Furies, of Greek myth pursue a twentieth-century figure. It is odd of Berners to draw attention to the similarity with his own title, particularly when it is not integral to the play, more a reference; perhaps when he has a character say 'Because I do not hope to turn again,' a line from 'Ash Wednesday', he is acknowledging the loan.

Alfred Eversley is a middle-aged writer who longs to be left alone to get on with his work. He has fled to Cornwall and dropped one of his oldest friends, an amiable duchess, to achieve this, but society ladies pursue him. He decides to marry an adventuress whom they describe as a tart and will not receive. This holds them at bay for a little but soon they make friends with her and are back. Alfred flees to Haiti with his male secretary and the play could end there, with a misogynistic happy ending. In the third act, however, the women recapture both of them, though only after Alfred has confessed to having become rather bored living in paradise with a black mistress and nothing to do but work.

The plot is told in the conventional style of the time, opening in front of french windows with two engaging young people explaining the situation to each other. Characters are discussed before they appear, even the yacht that is to rescue Alfred in Act III being carefully alluded to in Act II. Throughout, the men are feeble and boring and do nothing but flee, while the women, sometimes ridiculous, provide the energy and the jokes. Some of the origins of the play are discernible, but the young secretary is hopelessly priggish and cannot be seen as in any way based on Heber Percy. The most pushy of the women is Adelaide Pyrex, who says, 'Houses are my passion', and keeps suggesting alterations to those belonging to other people, which brings the interior decorating of Sibyl Colefax to mind. Berners wrote in a letter, 'I have just written a play about Doris Castlerosse', who could only be the socially unacceptable wife, exclaiming, 'Gosh', 'Cripes' and 'It's swell', while in search of a gin fizz. In the end she realises that Alfred will vacillate about leaving, so she drugs and kidnaps him for his own good – ruthless but with a heart of gold. Berners had not fled society in order to write, but he had done the two things in that order, and after initial relief, found that he too missed his old life. For himself, he had come up with the rather less drastic solution of leading a solitary existence in Oxford during the week and seeing friends at Faringdon at the weekend.

In spite of many of those friends' failure to notice it, the play's run of a week at the Oxford Playhouse went so well that Berners, optimistic now in every way, hoped that its transfer to London might coincide with victory, 'when the public will wish for frivolous escapist entertainment'. This was not to be. The reviews were acceptable, even encouraging. One reviewer, a friend of John Sparrow, was not hostile but 'he did call me an amateur and judging by the context I would say it was designed to tease. I don't in the least mind being called an amateur, any more than Beckford, Horace Walpole or Congreve would have minded.' The *Guardian* thought the story and production poor but that Berners had 'the trick of the play-writing craft already, and since his dialogue keeps the ears alert, and often tickled, it is obvious that he will write a good play.'

In the same letter that mentions Doris Castlerosse, Berners wrote:

> There is a scorched earth policy going on in the Faringdon cellar too. The less wine there is the more people seem to drink. Demand is galloping ahead of supply. It is an economic phenomenon about which I shall have to consult Roy Harrod . . . Robert has been removed from the army for being loopy. And is now at Faringdon driving tractors – and employing himself generally in agricultural pursuits.

Heber Percy was not loopy, but still prone to migraine and being paid £500 a year by the Berners Estate; he ferried furniture from Faringdon to the Oxford Playhouse to spruce up the set for *The Furies* (Rowse suggests that Daisy Fellowes, a neighbour since the fall of France, supplied the curtains) and had done rather more than that. He had got engaged.

Jennifer Fry was young, pretty, rich, pregnant and loved him. She had visited Faringdon more than once before the war, but this was a bombshell. Friends familiar with the outcome have tended to assume that Berners accepted the situation easily. This was not so. For a week he pondered in silence about what was to happen, whether he was in effect to separate and reshape his future. If Heber Percy had thought Clarissa Churchill a threat, now the tables were turned. The first verdict is given very mildly in the fragment of the draft of a letter:

> J. and R. are in the house at this very moment. I have found them a very nice nest . . . I wish I could accommodate them here but alas it is impossible. The military are in half the house and there isn't room. However, I expect I shall see a good deal of them as it's only 5 miles distant . . . I am glad to find that I can write for the theatre. It will be a great comfort to me in my old age.

In practice even half of Faringdon could shelter more than one man, and it did so.

The marriage took place on 11 July 1942. Jennifer was twenty-six, the daughter of Alethea and Geoffrey Fry, who had been private secretary to Stanley Baldwin until 1937 and was a member of the chocolate-making family. If she had little idea what she was letting herself in for, nor had Berners. 'He was suddenly landed with me, oh dear,' is how she described the event, and indeed for Berners it was less like losing a lover, more like gaining a daughter-in-law. Marriage often introduces people into new and not necessarily congenial milieux, but these usually belong to the husband or wife. Jennifer found herself among Berners' as well as Heber Percy's friends. Some were less difficult than expected, but not all: 'Daisy Fellowes was nice to me – I can't think why, dim I was . . . Gavin Faringdon was a bit difficult.' Later, when the Mosleys came over, Jennifer locked herself in the bathroom and refused to come downstairs.

Some people she knew a little already. Her aunt, Evelyn Gardner, briefly married to Evelyn Waugh, had been a friend of Nancy Mitford, who now came to stay with increasing frequency and perhaps contributed more to Berners' posthumous fame than he did himself. Nancy was six years older than her sister Diana Mosley and so six years nearer to Berners in age, but he had not known her in the 1920s or early 1930s. In 1935, in a letter to her sister, she refers to him as Gerald, but they are still not close in 1941 when she goes to stay in Oxford with the Harrods and reports, 'Gerald has taken up his residence there. Apparently he has a mania for tea-shop life & Billa says it is a kind of task, undertaken in turns to face Gerald across rather grubby check tablecloths at mealtimes.'

When he was further recovered and they did become firm friends, it seemed entirely natural for they had much in common. For each the word 'tease' covered a lot of amusement and a touch of cruelty. She personified his ideal of elegant women, constantly buying Dior models whether she could afford them or not. Her description of herself as a water-beetle, 'gliding on the water's face with ease, celerity and grace', recalls his desire to avoid murky depths, a deliberate decision to enjoy the surface of life. In an essay Nancy was to describe staying at Faringdon during the war as 'a paradise to people working in London since there they found a double relief from discomfort and boredom'. And in a letter to Heber Percy after Berners' death she wrote, 'Nobody knows what he meant to me, I can still say that. Really in the war Faringdon was more like my home than anywhere.'

Berners would visit Heywood Hill, the bookshop that Nancy had turned by her presence into a centre of gaiety and gossip. He also made suggestions about her novels before their publication, as did Evelyn Waugh and Raymond Mortimer, and it was in a novel that she painted a full-length, truthful but wholly affectionate portrait. Lord Merlin in *The Pursuit of Love*, published in 1945, owns, as well as Merlinford, houses in London and Rome, his telegraphic address is 'Neighbour-tease', his whippets wear diamond necklaces. A famous practical joker, from whose house modern music pours, he comes of hunting stock and has built a folly on a hill nearby. In the guest rooms are inappropriate notices, including MANGLING DONE HERE and his pigeons are, of course, dyed.

Nor is his name a chance invention. In an essay Nancy wrote, 'There is something magic about all of Faringdon and Lord Berners himself, in his skull cap, looks not unlike a magician.' There is much detail, more of it accurate than an unknowing reader would guess, but there is embroidery too: Merlin's folly, for example, outdid Berners'. It 'was topped with a gold angel which blew a trumpet every evening at the hour of Lord Merlin's birth' and 'glittered by day with semi-precious stones, by night a powerful blue beam was trained upon it'. The nearest to criticism comes when the narrator, Fanny, is left alone with Merlin: 'I was by no means on such intimate terms with him as Linda was. To tell the real truth he frightened me. I felt that, in my company, boredom was for him only just round the corner . . .' Many felt that, and even those who had got to know Berners felt at the next meeting that they had to start all over again. Berners endorsed the book and the portrait of himself, but 'I must take you to task for Lord Merlin's only lapse which occurs on the last occasion of his appearance in the book. I should never dream of attempting to snaffle anyone else's cook — that is a form of wickedness in which I should never indulge.'

The Pursuit of Love was nearly dedicated to Berners. Nancy Mitford was in love with Gaston Palewski, head of de Gaulle's Cabinet, and dedicated the book to him. He was delighted but, just before publication, had a momentary loss of nerve; perhaps the communist opposition would make something of the connection with Unity Mitford. Telegrams were sent: 'DELETE DEDICATION SUBSTITUTE LORD BERNERS', then 'LEAVE GASTON IGNORE INSERTION PRINT AWAY'. 'Please never let Gerald know,' she begged her publisher Hamish Hamilton and he did not. When an edition came out in France, Palewski's qualms were justified. 'HITLER'S MISTRESS'S SISTER DEDI-CATES DARING BOOK TO M. PALEWSKI' read the headline and the row was bad enough to force Nancy Mitford to leave Paris for a time.

If Faringdon was a paradise for others during the second half of the war, it was a pleasant enough limbo for its owner. His equilibrium returned to its never entirely certain previous level, though his domestic arrangements continued to be unusual. Not everyone agrees that Berners ever fully recovered, but Diana Mosley thought he had and that such a recovery was established by 1943. She and Sir Oswald were allowed out of prison that year and lived for a time in a dirty and uncomfortable inn at Shipton-under-Wychwood, twenty-five miles away. 'I warned him about the horrible food, chill rooms and that my four sons all had whooping cough, but he bravely came' and cheered them up. Berners told them a story about a prince who built a palace in the eighteenth century and placed an ornamental lake next to it, in the shape of an S, because his princess was called Sophie. In the war the lake was a landmark for enemy pilots, one of whom casually demolished the palace on his way home. The story was never written but perhaps reflects Berners' unease about Faringdon. He had begun visiting London again. Harold Acton remembered meeting him in Chapel Street, where their friend Phyllis de Janzé lived. She used to cheer Berners up, but Acton 'could not help being aware that underneath his gallant façade he was deeply depressed'.

Berners told A.L. Rowse at about this time, when he was approaching sixty, that sex was over for him, 'and a good thing, nothing but a nuisance', although it is not clear that there was very much before. For the rest of his life his health remained uncertain. The first mishap he described to Michael Duff: 'It seems frightfully silly to rupture oneself coughing. I thought one only did it lifting heavy weights, helping lame dogs over stiles and that sort of thing. But however one does it, it's a very tiresome thing to do and I've been in bed three weeks.' To Violet Trefusis he referred to it as 'Careless Rupture', and was in high spirits to all, begging for details about Dorothy Wellesley and The Poetry Reading.

This was a grand affair, organised by Edith and Osbert Sitwell at the Aeolian Hall in the presence of the Queen and the two princesses, to raise money for the Free French Movement. T.S. Eliot read from *The Waste Land*; Walter de la Mare, John Masefield and the Sitwells themselves were among those who performed, in alphabetical order. At the interval it was discovered that Dorothy Wellesley was drunk, but luckily she came last and the royal family had left before she realised that she had been omitted. Then she found Edith Sitwell and shouted, 'You beast! You brute! You have humiliated me. I have never been so insulted in my life.' Edith Sitwell burst into tears. Harold Nicolson was hit by her umbrella, Beatrice Lillie restrained her. Somehow she was got to the pavement outside where she sat and banged away until a taxi arrived.

Berners was entranced by the incident. By chance he had been asked to get Dorothy Wellesley to recite at an Oxford festival and had approached Harold Nicolson. Now he wrote:

> I must thank you for the friendly and helpful spirit in which you have taken my request. I was unaware at the time of writing that you had been whacked on the head and Vita bitten and I feared that you might regard my letter as an example of bad taste. So many strange reports come to me as I lie on my bed of sickness: that D. had a rough and tumble with Beatrice Lillie, that a young poet knocked her down in the vestibule and tried to sit on her head, that Raymond was given a black eye, etc. etc.
>
> I am sure that the whole episode must have been very unpleasant and not as funny as it sounds from afar . . . It is all the fault of that silly old Yeats who in his dotage seems to have had a deplorable effect on ladies.*

In a later letter, Edith Sitwell is thanked for a 'vivid and prompt reply to my enquiries' and is subsequently sent a couple of poems, with a note saying that Berners hears 'Dorothy Wellesley is suing Harold for saying she was drunk – whereas it was merely a Dionysiac Frenzy. I am mad at having missed it all.' Finally there is the draft of a letter intended for Dorothy Wellesley herself:

> Dear Madam
>
> I have been reading such daring accounts of your trying to break up a poetry reading at the Aeolian Hall.
>
> Please allow me to congratulate you. I, too, hate poetry and think it ought to be stopped. What use is poetry nowadays, especially in war-time? [Crossed out: 'and anyhow my great great great-uncle was the last decent poet. I should like to meet you, Yours with admiration and sympathy Mabel Longfellow']

---

* Yeats, a friend, had put several of Dorothy Wellesley's poems in his 1936 edition of *The Oxford Book of Modern Verse* (1892–1935) and had referred to hers as 'the noblest style I have met of later years'. He was accused of showing partiality to friends of the moment.

I should like to meet you. I think we should get on top-hole. Ring me
up at the M.O.I. when you are next in town.
                                        Yours,
                                        Mabel Pope

In the summer of 1943 *A Wedding Bouquet* was successfully revived,
with Margot Fonteyn, Robert Helpmann and Leslie Edwards among
those repeating their roles. Constant Lambert narrated and his
'imperturbable delivery gives the nonsense an extra nonsensicality by
making it sound like sense'. Ann O'Neill (later Rothermere, later still
Fleming) had the company to dinner just before they embarked for
New York: 'Freddy [Ashton] was already doped for the ordeal, he had
discovered a splendid drug given to dogs to prevent their barking
during air raids, it is called "Calm Doggie".' Constant Lambert
reported to Berners their 'crashing success' and how he as narrator had
been able to 'steal the picture from Bobbie [Helpmann] much to his
annoyance . . . Incidentally several of the orchestral players asked me if
you were actually a "Lord". Most of them seemed to think it was a
name like Duke Ellington.'
    The genuine peer was now at work on a new volume of
autobiography, which would deal with his time at Eton. He was also
making a new departure by writing for the cinema, having been asked to
provide the music for a faintly creepy melodrama, *The Halfway House*,
directed by Basil Dearden and featuring Glynis Johns and Guy
Middleton. This apparently surprising development was brought about
by Ernest Irving, musical director of Ealing Studios. Four years older
than Berners, a composer himself with a passion for Mozart, he had
conducted in every theatre in London except the Windmill. On behalf
of Ealing he approached practically all the interesting composers of the
time, and obtained film scores from, among others, William Walton,
Vaughan Williams, John Ireland, Alan Rawsthorne, Richard Addinsell
and the Frenchman Georges Auric. So he was not worried by
inexperience. He also made up crosswords for the *Daily Telegraph* and
set chess problems for the *Manchester Guardian*. Asked to arrange the
music at a memorial service, he declined, because 'They told me,
Heraclitus, they told me you were dead' was to be read – a homosexual's
lament for his friend – and 'We don't want anything to do with fellows
like that at Ealing Studios.' This suggests that he was not personally
acquainted with Berners.
    Halfway House is a remote hotel in Wales. The guests each have a

problem, which in the course of one day is solved through an advance in self-knowledge; crooks reform, sweethearts are reconciled. This contrived formula is made more interesting by the audience knowing all along that the building was bombed the year before and the proprietor and his daughter killed. A quietly creepy atmosphere is established, the daughter throws no shadow, the newspapers are of the wrong date. Finally the hotel burns once more and the unconvincingly improved guests disperse.

Atmosphere can clearly be enhanced by music and Berners, with his strong dramatic sense, rose to the occasion. His experience of writing ballet music, with its need to produce brief, precisely timed supporting passages, was also helpful. Aware of his audience, Berners was at his most accessible and so, sometimes doing things again that he had done more idiosyncratically before, was less interesting to his more sophisticated admirers. The music over the opening credits, for instance, leads into a concert where a piece reminiscent of *The Triumph of Neptune* is being played. The new version does not stand up as well by itself, but then it was not meant to. The next year he supplied 'Come on Algernon' and a polka (originally written in 1941 for a pantomime, *Cinderella, or There's Many a Slipper*) for *Champagne Charlie*, a tale of rival music halls set in 1860. 'Come on Algernon' is a jolly, energetic pastiche and could easily have been a popular hit if the film had been more successful. Berners watched it being made, was given a deck chair and enjoyed himself.

Life on the home front had not been so satisfactory. Heber Percy's marriage was never a success. Billa Harrod remembers him striking the steering wheel of his car with sudden passion and exclaiming, 'I hate it! I hate it!' only a few weeks after the wedding service. A daughter, Victoria Gala (after Gala Dali, surprisingly), was born on 28 February 1943. When a known homosexual marries a pregnant woman there will always be some who say the child is not his. Jennifer Fry had had another admirer who was killed in the war. It would not have been unlike Heber Percy to have stepped quixotically into the breach. It would, however, in some opinions, have been unlike him to remain discreet about it, even among his closest friends, over the next forty years. In any case, the daughter, Victoria, was beautiful almost from the day she was born and remained so. Heber Percy was never suited to domestic life and tended to turn on those who were too close; Berners, however, took to it. There are stories of his impatience with children, but babies were different – or anyway this one was, a sort of surrogate grandchild. He composed the music for her christening and played it on the organ himself. He pushed her, gurgling and well behaved, in her pram and devised a ramp so that he could negotiate the steps. When Cecil Beaton came to take photographs of domestic life at Faringdon for publication in the *Sketch* that October, Berners threw himself into the event and is to be seen centre stage in the drawing-room holding the baby, and centre again in a striking pose with a book before a tapestry, while Robert and Jennifer sit or stand in unconvincing dutiful postures beside him. Soon little Victoria was toddling about the house and in time used to collect mushrooms with Berners. To a casual onlooker, all seemed fine.

In April the following year, James Lees-Milne came to Faringdon with Billa Harrod:

> Jennifer Heber Percy was sitting in the sun, on a swing seat, against the curved retaining wall. There were small chickens running around. This frightened Billa for she hates birds. We talked until 1.45 when we lunched off chicken (she doesn't mind eating them) and rice. Lord Berners, wearing a green knitted skull cap and yellow bow tie, was positively cordial. He is a considerate host. Robert came in to lunch from driving a tractor on the farm. He was wearing a pair of battle-dress trousers and a yellow aertex shirt open at the neck. Very bronzed by the sun, youthful and handsome. He is the *enfant terrible*, all right. What a curious family they were, sitting around this large round table. But they know how to live. I thought how enviable their *ménage* ... Much confusion and comfort combined. Jennifer's baby Victoria playing on the floor like a kitten.

Soon after this scene, Heber Percy had Jennifer's belongings put in a removal van and sent to Oare, her parents' house, which was conveniently empty. After this decisive action he became kinder: 'Robert came to see me ... he was very affectionate, as if nothing had happened ... Billa was rather rough and said, "Do stop bursting into tears".' It was over. Victoria continued to visit Faringdon with a nanny and, in 1949, Jennifer married the poet, writer and editor of the *London Magazine*, Alan Ross.

During these upheavals, Berners continued to cope with the inconveniences of the war as best he could. He was in constant touch with both Diana Mosley and Nancy Mitford, who had been on less than cordial terms. The Mosleys were now under house arrest at their newly bought home of Crux Easton, so Berners had to visit them. He was delighted with himself for finding a train from Swindon to Newbury, which had 'grand drawing-room-like carriages with armchairs upholstered in crimson velvet and no corridor'. An invitation sent by Berners to Nancy may be over-modest but does not entirely support the tales of sustained high living: 'Would you join us for an orgy of tinned loaf, twice-cooked meat and an egg – "boiled of course".'

In December 1944, he was ill once more. Elizabeth Longford wrote to Billa Harrod, 'Gerald is in the Acland with another rupture, looking very smart in dark green crêpe de chine pyjamas and a green skull cap to match. Lady Beveridge is his chief visitor and she (and Bev) is graduating as a Great Liberal Hostess and has already persuaded Gerald he is a Liberal and is putting it about that Frank is but doesn't know it.' (The Earl of Longford converted from the Conservative to the Labour Party in the 1930s and did not move again.) Berners' political thinking remained anecdotal: he reported to Violet Trefusis, now in Somerset:

> Some people were complaining in the presence of Coalbox that not enough had been done for General de Gaulle when first he came over.
> 'Nonsense,' said the Coalbox, 'A tremendous lot was done for him.'
> 'Well, what?'
> 'Harold asked him to lunch.'

In March 1945, Nancy wrote to Diana, 'Gerald's latest fantasy is he has to wear dark glasses because he has such kind eyes that beggars etc. swarm round him asking favours. He is a fool.' But this was making a joke of affliction, very much in her own style. He had been to 'the eye hospital' in January and his eyes were weak and grew weaker. Nancy was staying at Faringdon when her brother Tom was killed in Burma. Berners answered the telephone and broke the news, suggesting that she stay in her room, but she insisted on coming down to dinner as if nothing had happened. In fact it was a terrible blow, particularly cruel when the end of the war was clearly coming. Berners too had been fond of Tom, playing piano duets with him with more gusto than accuracy.

Elizabeth Bowen was staying when peace finally arrived in May. She described in a letter how the fountain in the middle of the lawn, which had been turned off when war broke out, was started once more:

> After lunch we all went out and stood on the terrace; Robert did

something to the fountain; there was a breathless pause, then a jet of water, at first a little rusty, hesitated up into the air, wobbled then separated into four curved feathers of water. It was so beautiful and so sublimely symbolic – with the long view, the miles of England, stretching away behind it, that I found myself weeping. I think a fountain is much nicer than a bonfire; if less democratic.

Chapter XVII

Peace

The war had realised many of Berners' worst fears. And a Labour government elected in July seemed dedicated to completing the task. European travel, which was not a pleasant addition to his life but part of its inherent pattern, had been impossible for over five years and remained difficult. The house in Rome was let and the house in London soon sold.

Friends who had seen little or nothing of Berners since his breakdown noted the change and felt that he never recovered. Certainly with his health now unreliable, he had become an old man at sixty-two. David Cecil, accurate as well as courteous, felt that 'He looked . . . or rather one imagined that he had done himself very well but I don't think he did. I suppose he just had hardening of the arteries. He had a rather reddish face. He never drank much but he did take snuff.' (This is perhaps the truth of James Lees-Milne's diary entry the year before: 'At 5.30 to tea with Emerald. Lord Berners gave us a white powder to sniff, which he said was cocaine. It smelled of menthol, and I liked it, but Emerald did not, complaining that it burned the membrane of her nose'; though Waugh wrote later, 'Daisy Fellowes is said to have taught Gerald B. to take cocaine.')

Peter Quennell found Berners:

> Short and . . . bald. He had a thin moustache, a tremulous eye-lid, an eye-glass, and usually wore a spotted bow-tic. His alert yet hesitant attitude at once reminded me of Lewis Carroll's White Rabbit; but the resemblance, I soon discovered, was entirely superficial. He might hesitate with an expression of wild surmise, his hands fluttering and his eye-glass flashing; but his pretended bewilderment was merely a part of the persona he had adopted many years ago.

This was a new acquaintance charmed; Osbert Sitwell, now a friend of twenty-five years' standing, had written wearily from Renishaw, 'Dear Gerald is here, God he is a bore now, bless him, with all his little diableries. But I am very fond of the old boy, very sweet and pathetic, but those stories of his are like flies circling round one on a summer day.'

Peace brought its own disturbances. Heber Percy surprisingly enjoyed army reunions in London. At one he met Hugh Cruddas, who had been wounded in the leg and a prisoner-of-war. A pleasant pink-and-white young man, he came to visit Faringdon and stayed almost indefinitely, outlasting Berners himself by a long way. Charming with Victoria when she visited, skilled in flower arrangement, adept at mixing Bloody Marys, endlessly agreeable, with an imitation of the Queen Mother said to surpass even that of Freddie Ashton, Cruddas gradually took over the running of the place. Berners had no objection; indeed, it has been suggested that he too took to the young man to such an extent that for a time Heber Percy had him banished. ('Of course, one was rather pretty,' was Cruddas' comment in later years.)

Certainly he went to Tripoli in the Lebanon for a while. Berners wrote him a friendly letter:

> Is it very Oriental or just sordid and suburban? Beverley Nichols was here last weekend. He taught Robert backgammon which is maddening as Robert is trying to teach me and I think it is the most boring game in the world and anyway I can't count. Robert misses you very much and whines as poor Shine [a dog] did when Robert was out of the room.

Cruddas returned to the same role and Faringdon became the centre of his world, though he was granted few rights there. Opinion is divided as to whether Heber Percy was unnecessarily cruel to him or angelic to put up with him for so long. In the end, many years after Berners' death, he was expelled.

In July 1945 came Berners' second volume of autobiography, *A Distant Prospect*. A slight volume, it deals with his time at Eton, the title neatly taken from Gray's *Elegy*, which Etonians are given as a leaving book. It received the most widespread and laudatory reviews of anything he ever achieved, many admittedly written by friends. John Betjeman found it 'at once simple and profound, short and full'; Peter Quennell 'an unassuming but unusually enjoyable book. The portraiture is neat and vivid: its criticism of people and systems shrewd and lively:

the author's satirical humour is of a pleasantly sub-acid type.' E.S.P.
Haynes also thought it the best of his books and Berners' observation of
human nature, both adult and adolescent, extremely shrewd. Elizabeth
Bowen, writing at length in the *Tatler*, examined memory and
concluded, 'It is the manner – the style, the shape, the mood – of the
memory that gives *A Distant Prospect* its human value and high aesthetic
claim.' The *Daily Despatch* was a rare complainer, thinking eight
shillings and sixpence a lot for 120 pages, but admitted that 'what there
is of it is good'. Desmond MacCarthy agreed that the reader came to the
end all too soon: 'one longs for more'. Rosamond Lehmann wished it
five times longer and reported Beaton as being 'enchanted'. The chorus
is one of praise, some a little faint, with 'slight', 'detached' and 'ironic'
the favourite adjectives. Graham Greene raised a dissenting voice and
Berners drafted a reply to 'your catty little review', saying that he
understood that it would not appeal to 'a writer of thrillers that so
happily combine the styles of Edgar Wallace and Charles Morgan'; the
review had got to him. The book was among those 'most in demand'
that year and reprinted the next.

July also found him back in Richmond, having seen Dr Gottfried
(whom Harold Acton considered a dangerous charlatan, and Cecil
Beaton thought a masterly physician, modelling Professor Higgins'
study on his own in *My Fair Lady*). Again, in October, Nancy Mitford
wrote to her mother, 'Just off to see Gerald. His heart is too high and
they are lowering it in a nursing home, so they come in every five
minutes and say things like Lady Juliet Duff is outside to make it sink,
or so we suppose.'

Cyril Connolly had turned his depression into an anthology, *The
Unquiet Grave*, and sent Berners a copy, which impressed him. Evelyn
Waugh and Connolly had long had an uncertain relationship: something
less than friends, each had respect for the literary judgement of the
other, so it came as a blow to Connolly when Waugh gave the book a
blistering review. Berners said that to attack Connolly was like shooting
a sitting robin and wrote Waugh a letter of protest. This was said not to
have arrived ('Something happens to letters sent to White's. I suppose
they must be stolen by that autograph-hunting hall porter'), and when
Berners heard this he wrote another, this time conciliatory in tone:

> The Lord himself, I think, must have taken the matter in hand and
> caused my letter to disappear. It's just as well. I regretted afterwards
> having written it and felt that it had been an unnecessary interference

for, after all, Cyril is quite capable of taking care of himself. But he seemed so downcast by your review that I wrote under the influence of a momentary compassion. It is not the first time that my kind heart has involved me in indiscretion. However as you didn't get my letter all is well and if it does eventually reach you, please burn it unread. I suppose you are right in placing morality above art and friendship.

He supposed no such thing. A few years later Connolly and Clarissa Churchill were staying at Faringdon and Connolly took his own *Enemies of Promise* off the shelf, only to find 'Or Why I Can't Write a Book' written in Berners' hand on the title page. But: 'Wasn't it fearful,' Diana Mosley wrote to Nancy Mitford, 'G has not been told.' And this was right. Berners would not have wanted even his mild mockery to reach the sensitive author. Berners also wrote on page 4, 'Pleasure is like a butterfly that settles on a flower. She can't control it. To speak of the Pursuit of Pleasure is nonsense. The highest pleasure is creative work.' A conventional thought, but at odds with what many expected from Berners. Heber Percy said, 'There were periods of his life when he did nothing. I tried to get him to do occupational therapy, which I'd heard about. A nice lady came to teach him knitting . . . she just gave up.'

Berners reported *The Unquiet Grave* to be 'very sad and full of original sin'. In the same letter he wrote, 'People here are growing unpredictable and sometimes quite ferocious. Cecil B. and Mr Rattigan [already author of *French Without Tears*] took poor Lady Colefax out for a walk here [Faringdon] last Sunday and pushed her through a barbed wire fence so that she was nearly torn to pieces.' Terence Rattigan claimed innocence but agreed that the deed had been done on purpose: 'Sibyl, of course, was pushed. There is no doubt of it whatever, and should her hand grow gangrenous and she die, I shall feel it my duty to pass a spirit message to her telling her who was responsible, and providing her with proof of guilt.' Delighted with the incident, Berners wrote of it again in a letter that also reports:

> Robert is getting awfully dotty. He had a slight temperature yesterday and went to bed in the drawing-room and said that he had got consumption and that the red damask from [illegible] would make a very pretty death-bed scene and asked the gardener to send in some lilies. He also wanted a Roman Catholic priest as he thought a death bed conversion would be very effective. However, he seems better today and is going out hunting.

When a less sympathetic outsider describes Berners and Faringdon, they appear in a rather different light. A.J.P. Taylor arranged to visit Kelmscott, the home of William Morris, and brought with him an immensely distinguished medieval historian, K.B. McFarlane, who reported that Berners met them 'dressed in a grey suit, tartan socks and black-and-white shoes; he is stoutish, ugly, bald and sixty-three. He wears dark glasses always.' Their entry was opposed by a tenant but:

> Berners merely slipped past her into the house and we followed. It was an absurd and very embarrassing adventure. We marched through the house to a stream of protests and 'no, you can't go in there's' ludicrously mingled with guide's patter . . . we emerged on the road in less than ten minutes battered and giggling; only Berners was unperturbed; even the brassy Alan was shaken and unhappy.

So here is Berners the unstoppable leader and man of action, not giggling, unembarrassed to the point of insensitivity.

The party lunched at Faringdon. 'There are signs even outside of Berners' Victorian tastes: huge urns of geraniums, lobelias and daisies. Inside richly but rather incongruously furnished. Masses of pictures including some of B's own rather messy efforts.' So much for the conscious modernist and rebel against the Victorians. Heber Percy was like 'some pleasant kind of animal; on the whole a pony or a stag . . . Berners wears queer little hats indoors and during lunch had a grey woolly jockey's cap on his bald head . . . A butler was the only servant visible and we helped ourselves to an excellent lunch – roast chicken, green peas, marrow and small potatoes, all obviously home-grown.' That is familiar, particularly if it is remembered that chicken was not then the ubiquitous fare it was to become. 'The conversation was general and what would be called "amusing". We had had excellent iced cocktails in the sitting-room to help us chatter.' Faringdon talk was not used to those derisive quotation marks. Gavin Faringdon was present and McFarlane liked him, but sums up:

> I don't feel the same about Berners. His music and pictures repel and most of his books are silly. His autobiography (*First Childhood* and *Distant Prospect*) I do like. Both volumes are charmingly written, entertaining, and while superficial and not strikingly original, nevertheless attractive. I have them both. But his selfishness and silliness are too much in evidence in real life. He may have a kind heart and he is independent to the point of an amusing eccentricity, but there is no –

how shall I put it – chime between us. He is too much of a dabbler. He
has little in common with his ancestor, the translator of Froissart; at least
he has no interest in the fourteenth century.

The great event of 1946 should have been Berners' triumphant return
to ballet. Frederick Ashton had planned to collaborate with Berners and
Beaton while he was a depressed and incompetent airman in 1942. He
was an admirer of the novels of Ouida, and *Moths* was chosen, although
in the end not a lot of the 400-page melodrama was used. The story is
set on the beach at Trouville in 1904, much the same date as *A Wedding
Bouquet* but too early for Berners to be familiar with the sophisticated
world with which it dealt.

Things seem to have happened slowly. As early as June 1945, Berners
wrote that he could not manage an essay on 'Prejudice' because 'I have
had a rather strenuous musical task imposed and have got to finish a
ballet for Sadler's Wells sooner than I had expected.' In November he
turned down another commission because 'I am busy orchestrating a
ballet I have written and when I'm on music I'm afraid I'm off
literature.' This accords with an otherwise jarring letter from Roy
Douglas, who says that in September he had been asked to orchestrate
Sirens and Seagulls and in October he came to do so and soon found that
he was to do the bulk of the work:

> [Berners] played the music to me on the piano during this visit (and
> during three later visits, as he finished composing the various sections)
> giving certain broad indications of the scoring he envisaged (can one
> envisage scoring?), such as: 'this is an oboe, or horn, or flute solo; this
> should be strings only; bring in the brass here' and so forth. But the final
> result was that the full score of 1600-odd bars consisted almost entirely
> of my own orchestration, that is the choice of notes to be given to all the
> instruments, and the balance between them – in short (apart from the
> indications I have mentioned) the decisions as to who plays what were all
> mine. The score was finished on 15 July 1946.

Douglas was ill-paid (£160), sworn to secrecy, not mentioned in the
programme – in a word, disgruntled. In his opinion, Berners' own
scoring of a few brief sections at the end was so amateurish and
ineffective that 'I had to revise most of it, or do it again from scratch'.
Berners was capable of doing such work efficiently, for there are no
other such complaints. Whatever the truth, the music was as allusive as
ever, and the choreography was to be full of references and jokes. A

character called Adelino Canberra reminds the initiated of Berners' pseudonym Adela Quebec; there is Italian opera, plus a Spanish dance similar to Berners' own *Fantaisie Espagnol*.

Fonteyn, Lambert and Ashton had been to stay in November and Beaton came in the New Year. In May 1946, Ashton sent a telegram to Beaton in New York asking him to return immediately and, that summer, Beaton wrote:

> While Gerald Berners worked at his piano in the drawing-room at Faringdon I laboured, with more detailed love and care than usual, upon the designs in an upstairs bedroom. Lunch was not only a pleasant interlude but a gastronomic treat. At the end of the day I would show Gerald my progress, he would play his score, while Freddies imagination was fired to further frivolities. After dinner, upstairs again to paint another filigree row of struts in the Trouville pier or more ducks'-eggs pearls on Otero's costume.

Berners wrote thanking him for an American food-parcel – 'I am obliged to live entirely on "luxury" food. Hothouse peaches: forced strawberries and potatoes. Foie gras people bring from France' – so the gastronomic treats obviously continued. He also reported that he was going back into his 'lovely nursing home'.

He was out of it for the first night of what was now *Les Sirènes* in November. The curtain rose on a beach, deserted save for a pair of seagulls watching two mermaids comb their hair. Soon some children with attendant nannies arrived, then Countess Kitty and her fashionable friends. A huge yellow motor-car drove on and La Bolero (Margot Fonteyn), a famous dancer, emerged to captivate the gentlemen and discountenance the ladies. Next an Eastern king (Frederick Ashton, with a suggestion of King Farouk) was carried in by slaves, and a third spectacular entrance had an Australian opera singer (Robert Helpmann) alighting from a balloon. Each is entranced by La Bolero, jealousy leads to violence, and La Bolero leaves in her car with yet another admirer, an Englishman, but not before everyone has had the chance to change into Edwardian swimming-costumes. The beach is once more left to the seagulls.

All this was extremely lavish, colourful and complicated to stage. It is easy to imagine it being received as a charming and amusing trifle, but it was not. Beaton had returned to New York, 'confident that I had left behind me a delightful legacy', and describes the 'lukewarm reports':

Yes, it was faintly amusing; Margot, with eyes rolling, tongue in cheek and rose behind the ear, was alluring in her black jet and flounces; some of Freddie's choreography for his oriental entourage and the bathers was witty; but my designs were considered too fashionable, and Helpmann, bursting into song, embarrasses the Covent Garden audience. Gerald was beginning to suffer from the illness from which he died, and was, no longer, at the height of his powers. His perverse and comic muse did not carry an evening; it was not in the serious mood of the moment when post-war ballet enthusiasts were looking for something more significant. The ballet soon faded from memory.

Beaton was not quite fair to Berners. The music only had to carry one-third of an evening and was perfectly efficient, if predictably in the style that was now expected of him. The trouble was more that this form of frivolity now looked dated and silly to all but a few; Roland Petit and Balanchine scored the successes in London that year.

By December, Berners could write calmly to Alan Dent, 'It seems to have offended the more solemn addicts of ballet and I hear Adrian Stokes is so disgusted that he has decided to write no more books about the ballet – which is a pity as they were so funny.' But it was his last theatrical work and a great disappointment. Luckily, he was already at work on the music for the film of *Nicholas Nickleby*. Unluckily, *Nicholas Nickleby* was not to be a success, either. When it came out in November 1947 it was called anaemic and stilted, and was compared unfavourably with David Lean's *Great Expectations*. Berners' last music was again highly efficient, but again there was nothing to startle, nothing that he had not already achieved elsewhere.

Berners kept in touch with old friends and, probably through John Lehmann, made a new one, William Plomer. Plomer was a novelist, poet, and homosexual, neatly and formally dressed like Berners (he said himself that he looked like a dentist), and, like Heber Percy, capable of wildness. He and Berners wrote to one another about books and friends, Elizabeth Bowen, the Sitwells and, particularly, about Mrs Belloc Lowndes. She was the sister of Hilaire Belloc, and as fertile a writer, with many thrillers and novels to her credit, bearing names such as *Duchess Laura* and *Love is a Flame*. A warm gossipy creature, she was known to Berners for fifteen years. He exchanged characteristic remarks of hers with Plomer: 'When I used to say I always considered Margot [Asquith] to be sexless people said "You're kind". I replied no I'm not kind but I'm passionately interested in human nature,' and 'I know it's true because he told me in the strictest confidence.'

Berners had not seen E.M. Forster for fifteen years but, encouraged by Plomer, asked him to stay. When Eddie Sackville-West was added to the party, Berners was delighted and wrote, 'I should think he is rather Forster's "cup of tea". He is certainly mine . . . I have been "dipping into" *Finnegans Wake*. It is the only thing to do with it.' Forster came and made the now almost obligatory polite comments about the food, 'It improves one's health permanently', but there were only twenty-four other guests that year and no greater number subsequently. Max and Florence Beerbohm had come just before Christmas to meet Desmond MacCarthy and a couple whom David Cecil modestly describes as 'his daughter and son-in-law' (Rachel and Cecil himself).

> Lord Berners mentioned Lady Cunard, with whom Max had spent an unhappy weekend long ago in Edwardian days. 'I haven't seen her for years,' he said, with an innocent air. 'Has she changed at all?' 'No,' answered Lord Berners warmly. 'It's wonderful, she's exactly the same.' Max did not answer for a moment: then, still looking innocent, 'I am very sorry to hear that.'

Cecil commented later that it had been the best-timed remark he had ever heard.

John Betjeman remembered Beerbohm at Faringdon answering questions about forgotten poets of the 1890s: 'He knew about them all, delicious, revealing, personal details which subsequent research proved to be quite correct. "Let me see – didn't he take drugs in order to shine at Aubrey Beardsley's parties? I think that was after he had been rediscovered by Henry Harland and put in the Yellow Book".' The Beerbohms were delighted with the goose they took away, 'a fully worthy descendant of those ancestors of his who saved the Capitol'.

An old acquaintance rather than an old friend was Leslie Hartley. Berners wrote to congratulate him on the publication of *Eustace and Hilda* and Hartley replied warmly, including a memory: 'As I was rowing along the back of the Giudecca I suddenly had a startlingly clear vision of you sitting in your gondola painting the canal which is bordered by Mrs Eden's garden and ends with a view of the Salute – I wonder if you have the picture still', to which Berners replied, 'All the time I was reading the Venetian part of your book, I had a very clear remembrance of that occasion. In fact it obtruded itself upon all other views of Venice . . . I don't know what happened to the picture. It was not a success.'

A new friend was Hugh Dalton, the Chancellor of the Exchequer (and so the enemy, for Berners was again depressed about money, as were many of his class). Dalton came to tea: 'Robert said he was very silly and didn't know anything about economics. Perhaps he is right, I mean, Robert. But one thing Mr Dalton does do. He laughs at one's jokes. And mine are pretty poor nowadays.'

News of people sped back and forth around his familiar circle. Nancy Mitford wrote from Paris, 'Violet came to see me dressed like Marie Stuart in darkest black and glittering like an Xmas tree with all Mrs K[eppel, her mother]'s wonderful jewels. She seems to have been left everything. You must give Cecil the photograph for his next book of beauty.' Berners wrote to her of his health:

> Please excuse this enormous handwriting. My eyes are, alas!, still bad. I have horrible fears they may not get well . . . Poor Daisy seems also to have had a disagreeable accident – she was hit in the eye by a jitterbug (they seem as dangerous as doodlebugs) at a dance given by Elsa Maxwell in London . . . How curious and uncourteous is Derek Hill's behaviour . . . and Evelyn's visit! It can't be merely Catholicism that makes him so pugnacious.

Edward James was a loyal friend, having Berners for Christmas at West Dean in the last years when he was not well. Berners thanked him in his usual style: 'Nancy writes from Paris that she went to a fancy-dress ball as a Polish king in long black tights and a small beard and that she was mistaken by everyone for YOU – and that as the night wore on her laugh grew more and more diabolical.' James replied, at great length and in minute detail, entirely about himself. Beaton visited both Faringdon and the Richmond nursing home, to which Berners returned from time to time in the following year, and wrote too, sometimes from New York: 'Edward James relayed some of your letter to me . . . Is it not extraordinary how little he has changed with the years? Most people have sobered up a bit but he behaves just as outrageously as ever and his life is one long lawsuit and folly.' Nancy Mitford wrote to her sister Diana, 'What is this about Gerald leaving it in his will that he is to be stuffed and sit in the hall at Faringdon? Poor Robert will never keep a servant if he does,' and received later: 'Gerald nearly ate his nurse's hand, stuck a fork in it, I said did you think it was chicken and he said No, ham.'

By now Daisy Fellowes had moved to a house called Donnington Grove near Newbury, so she was only twenty miles from Faringdon. She placed before the house a statue of St Joseph, whom she referred to as the patron saint of cuckolds, and devoted her social talents to brightening the drabness of rural England. Even in those difficult days she managed a constant flow of chic Europeans, which would have been enough to make her an irresistible neighbour for Berners, but he had always loved her for her own sake and for her renowned elegance. With her worldly values, her tendency to be rude to servants, her reputation for malice rather than wit, it might gratify a low wish to report ill of her. In fact Daisy's only surviving letter to Berners, from Mexico, is mildly amusing – 'I'm writing in the garden and there is a small typhoon. Hibiscus blossoms and oleander are behaving as if they were going into training for a battle of flowers at Nice' – and full of gratitude to Edward James for fixing up her house. She remained a loyal friend and worried about Berners' health. 'We must get Gerald into espadrilles,' she said; but he would not go to her villa at Cap Martin.

The general tone may seem to suggest frivolity and fun, that the carousel was once more spinning as merrily as ever, and one incident was indeed like the old days. In October 1947, André Gide came to Oxford to receive an honorary degree and Dr Enid Starkie, an expert in French literature and an admirer, was in charge of him. The vice-chancellor was so nervous of Gide's sexual reputation that he dared not have him to dinner, ringing up Dr Starkie and saying, 'You know this fellow Gide, I don't know what to do about him. I hear he's a very queer fellow', to which she replied in her Irish accent, 'Do you mean queer in the modern, technical sense?', to which he had to say yes. So she had Gide to dinner at Somerville and brought him and Dorothy Bussy to Faringdon on the Sunday, with the Cecils at lunch and Cyril and Lys Connolly also staying the night. Berners thought him 'the best writer in Europe and the most delightful of men' and wrote two careful drafts of a reply to Gide's letter: '*J'ai beaucoup lu dans ce nursing home –* Isabelle, Palides, Le Père Goriot, Faust *dans l'admirable traduction de Gérard de Nerval dont Goethe lui-même parlait si bien à Eckerman.*'

Berners was entranced with the whole event – but back in the nursing home. From there he also wrote, 'When I was young I used to love resting. Now that I am getting old and ill and have to rest, I hate it.

Such is life.' Rallying, he wrote, again to Nancy Mitford, 'Did you know that one's status in the nursing home depends entirely on one's flowers? Robert brings me enormous chrysanthemums looking like poodles from les serres de Faringdon and I stand very high.' He loved Richmond and wrote an essay in praise of its charms: 'Walking by the river on a hot summer's afternoon one is transported back to the early nineteenth-century atmosphere of Turner's pictures.'

With the possible exception of Edward James, his friends were slowing down. Berners went to the cinema with Diana Cooper and was less than polite to her. Heber Percy asked why and got the reply, 'She's been going on too long' (she was to go on for another forty years). In certain moods Berners felt they all had. Peace had not brought back ease and luxury, even if the strictures on his life – guests had to have a car sent to an arranged rendezvous, where they could change vehicles because of the shortage of petrol – were less severe than most. Some of the letters he received were written expressly to cheer up an old man, while others were frank. Osbert Sitwell wrote, 'I am permanently depressed. The Government, I loathe. Even more than Winston.' Letters by Berners himself were often in the same tone. He wrote to Plomer in 1948 that he had been ill for two years. At the end of the war he had written in high spirits to reawaken his friendship with Siegfried Sassoon. Now the mood had changed:

You ask how I am – Alas! not at all well. Since I last saw you I have suffered a general breakdown in health. Heart trouble, high blood pressure with the result that I can hardly walk and scarcely think, and am unable to pursue my little hobbies, writing, painting and music, which is very depressing (to me). I'm afraid this letter will be a wail – a wail of a letter if you'll pardon the pun ... Between 7 and 8 in the morning when formerly I felt delight in life and the prospect of another day, is now the time when I chiefly long for death. I have had these periods of gloom before and have got over them, but this time (as one likes to associate oneself with greatness) I fear it is the last, as with Cowper and Ruskin.

He cheered up to add a postscript, 'Do you know the little poem:

Mrs Belloc Lowndes
Would not ride to hounds
Except once – as a boon
To Siegfried Sassoon.'

He did recover, and in 1949 was writing a further instalment of his autobiography, left uncompleted. He read bits of it aloud to David Cecil, as they had read work in progress to each other in the war. That same year, Plomer hoped that Berners would soon complete *The Ibsen Room*, a new version of the story from his youth, and there was a plan for a play about Saul. As a whole new departure, Berners also planned to create a scent, but heard that it was possible to make such a stink that the house had to be vacated, so decided not to risk it. He made up riddles: if the clocks were to feel that they had no one to talk to or keep them going, what publisher would they refer to? Answer: we have no one to Chatto and Windus.

But gloom kept breaking in. In a notebook he wrote:

> In 1947 I seemed suddenly to grow old and ill: to break down physically and mentally. This coincided with a similar breakdown in the conditions of Europe and in particular of England. All my life and in particular during the last thirty years of it, I have given myself up to hedonism and self-indulgence. (To anyone who reads this stuff, it is to prove to myself that I can at any rate formulate sentences. I feel day to day as if my brain were giving way, dissolving and it is a slight relief to me to find that I can still write sentences that make sense.)

In another letter he wrote: '*Je reste ici à Faringdon. Je ne vais jamais à Londres. C'est encore quelque chose d'être à la campagne. Robert est encore ici – nous avons une petite ferme.*'

Unfortunately Beaton met Berners in a low mood and wrote it up in his diary:

> Gerald is fading fast . . . [He] comes blinking into my room, 'Oh well it's not worth getting upset about, but I might as well take a month off for, after all, health is everything, isn't it?' And it's never quiet at Faringdon with Robert about. I've been very worried there lately . . . Pathetic Gerald! When he returned to Faringdon life was made no easier for him. He was not even allowed his breakfast in bed. It was not long before, in desperation, he turned his face to the wall.

This Beaton places before October 1947, though the conclusion seems later. It was to cause trouble.

Berners thought of death and what came after, and here too his mood veered. Penelope Betjeman had converted to Catholicism in 1947 and battered him with information that might lead him to follow. Notes on

St Augustine and the way to approach prayer end with: 'All I can tell you is that the HOLY, CATHOLIC CHURCH IS THE CAT'S WHISKERS.' Even Heber Percy was approached: 'Darling, here is a book to start on, it will be jolly funny if you make it before Gerald.' Berners gave her grounds for hope – though when ill and saying who might visit, he stipulated, 'I don't mind Penelope as long as we don't have any of that God nonsense.' Most recorded, however, is his constant atheism. He repeated in his notebooks that religion was a talent he did not possess; to James Lees-Milne he said in 1948 that he would like to become a Catholic, if only he could believe. Peter Quennell found their last meeting impressive:

> He seemed old and tired and bowed by pain and I suspect that he had given up hope. Our talk was desultory. Then he began to speak of certain friends – cultured warm-hearted Catholics – who had set about converting him. They went on and on he said and never left him alone. It bored him and did him no good. Finally, raising his voice in a flash of defiant courage: 'Why should I listen to them. It is all such bosh.'

Still his thoughts stayed with death and the hereafter. He noted, 'Reincarnation is just as likely to be true as other theories of that kind. In a former existence I may have been a bird,' but also, 'Suicide is a legal and a religious offence. It is making the worst of both worlds.' And more than once he quoted Pascal's '*Le silence eternel de ces espaces infinis m'effraie.*'

Yet he knew for two months that he was dying and was not in the least fearful. Among his last visitors was Nye Bevan, a surprising new friend. Both were moved and, though they found distraction in playing with the kitten that jumped onto the bed, both were in tears as he left. Two hours before the end a new doctor arrived from London and Berners said, 'Thank you for coming but I'm afraid I'm rather wasting your time.'

He died on 19 April 1950 aged sixty-six, 'of bad heart and blood pressure,' in Heber Percy's phrase, 'absolutely quietly and no pain just as he always hoped, do you remember', as Diana Mosley reported to Nancy Mitford. To her mother, Diana wrote:

> I am heartbroken, I miss him so dreadfully; but I must say he didn't enjoy his life at all the last few months. I saw him on Sunday and he was very quiet and it has been sad lately because he found talking so difficult; but he always liked to listen to anything one could think of to say –

terribly difficult it had to be almost a monologue. Up till a fortnight ago I used to take him to his farm wrapped in his dressing gown, he loved to see the cats in the cowshed. I am going to the funeral tomorrow. He was very pleased a few days ago because Sir Thomas Beecham has written an article saying he is the greatest English composer, and Sir T is making new recordings of all his work. I am so glad he knew it before he died. He talked a lot about his music on Sunday. I loved him better than anyone else outside the family.

A few days later she wrote:

It was one of those perfect days, Faringdon looking beautiful. I went there and saw the men carry him out, it was so sad William and Fred and all of them in their dark suits . . . William looked absolutely white as though he had been crying (he was the chauffeur). Robert and I and the accountant drove behind the hearse . . . to Oxford crematorium and there were several friends John Betj and Hugh and Georgia and one or two dons . . . One note of pure comedy Gerald would have enjoyed – the new Baroness and her mother were there and nobody knew them . . . They asked someone whether they should go to Faringdon, who replied Better ask Mr Percy. They said Who is Mr Percy?

Berners' will, made a week before his death and witnessed by nurses, left £2,000 each to Frederick Law and William Crack and everything else, including shares in the Berners Estate Company worth £214,306, to Heber Percy. The doctor who had attended him constantly during his last years refused to send a bill, saying that the pleasure of Berners' company had been payment enough. Letters of condolence poured in to Robert, several echoing Frederick Ashton's sentiment: 'His house must live on and all it stood for through you alone now.' And so it did.

In a touching note to Osbert Sitwell, Heber Percy wrote that he was quite lost and had no idea what to do with the rest of his life. In fact he remained at Faringdon until his death in 1987, running the estates with an efficiency that may have surprised some, converting parts of the house into flats whose tenants remained tactfully unnoticeable. Sometimes his gambling seemed a threat, but always he recovered. His alterations and additions were entirely in the manner of the house. Steps now lead to a swimming pool guarded by vast stone wiverns. Many of the same visitors continued to visit: John Sparrow, the Abdys, Michael Duff, the Harrods, even Harold Acton, who had once been so against him. A new generation arrived: Henry and Dominick Harrod, Candida Betjeman, Sarah Quennell, Kit Lambert. The Mad Boy was entirely accepted but not entirely tamed.

Some *habitués* did not return. In 1952, Clarissa Churchill married Anthony Eden, then Foreign Secretary, soon Prime Minister. In June 1972, Cecil Beaton published another volume of his diaries, which included the passage suggesting that Heber Percy had been less than thoughtful in Berners' last years. Not until March 1974 was revenge enacted. Beaton was leaving Peter Quennell's house in Cheyne Walk after a birthday party and greeted Laura, Duchess of Marlborough. Heber Percy was with her and struck Beaton on the jaw, knocking him to the ground. Beaton consulted a doctor and a lawyer but let things drop.

Inevitably some who were essentially Berners' friends and did return felt that the genius of the house had died with him. As early as May 1950, Rowse wrote, 'Though Robert keeps faithful watch over everything and nothing has changed, the spirit has fled.' In December, Waugh wrote to Diana Mosley, 'I went to dinner at Faringdon from the Betjemans. The Mad Boy has installed a Mad Boy of his own. Has there ever been a property in history that has devolved from catamite to catamite for any length of time? It would be interesting to know.' Faringdon was not to be one of them. In 1985, Heber Percy got married again to perhaps the most persistent visitor of all, Lady Dorothy Lygon, but she soon moved back into a house that he had previously organised for her a few hundred yards from the gates of Faringdon. After some indecision, Heber Percy left Faringdon to the daughter of Victoria, Sofka Zinovieff, who has married Vassilis Papadimitriou and now lives there.

Appendix I

Lord Berners' Bibliography

AUTOBIOGRAPHY

First Childhood (Constable, 1934)
A Distant Prospect (Constable, 1945)

NOVELS

The Camel (Constable, 1936)
The Girls of Radcliff Hall (privately published, 1937)
Far from the Madding War (Constable, 1941)
Count Omega (Constable, 1941)
Percy Wallingford and Mr Pidger (Blackwell, 1941)
The Romance of a Nose (Constable, 1942)

Appendix II

Discography

The following (compiled by Philip Lane of the Berners Trust) represents all Berners' works available on CD. Duplicate performances (in whole or in part) for some works were available previously on LP, cassette or 78 disc, but will be found by only the most perseverant of browsers.

'Complete Songs and Piano Solos', Felicity Lott/Roderick Kennedy/Peter Lawson, Albany TROY 290

'Red Roses and Red Noses', Felicity Lott/Graham Johnson, Chandos, CHAN 8722

Les Sirènes, Cupid & Psyche (Suite) and *Caprice Peruvien* (arr. Constant Lambert), RTE Sinfonietta/David Lloyd-Jones, Marco Polo 8.223780

The Triumph of Neptune (Suite), London Philharmonic/Sir Thomas Beecham, EMI, CDM 7634052; Philadelphia Orchestra/Sir Thomas Beecham, Sony, SMK 46683

The Triumph of Neptune (Suite), *Fugue in C Minor*, *Nicholas Nickleby* (incidental music), *Trois Morceaux* and *Fantaisie Espagnole*, Royal Liverpool Philharmonic/Barry Wordsworth, EMI, CDM 650982

The Triumph of Neptune (complete), *L'umo dai baffi*, *Valses Bourgeoises* and *Polka*, English Northern Philharmonic/David Lloyd-Jones/Royal Ballet Sinfonia/Philip Lane, Marco Polo 8.223711

Valses Bourgeoises, *Fantaisie Espagnole* and *Trois Morceaux*, Peter Lawson/Alan MacLean, Albany TROY 142

A Wedding Bouquet, *March* and *Luna Park*, RTE Chamber Choir & Sinfonietta/Kenneth Alwyn

Lord Berners' Desert Island Discs

Berners was never asked to select his Desert Island Discs but sometime after 1942, when the programme began, he amused himself by doing so:

'My taste in music depends to a large extent on moods. I haven't the least idea how I should feel on a desert island and what sort of music would appeal to me in such uncivilized conditions. For that reason I have made my selection as varied as possible. I have purposely excluded music that is noble and solemn. Such music always makes me want to think about my immortal soul and I am certain that that is the last thing I should wish to think about on a desert island. Some of the pieces I have chosen for associations which in my solitude it would give me a sentimental pleasure to evoke.

I have never made a point of explaining to myself why I like certain things. You must remember that I am a Victorian – at least I was born in the last decade of the Victorian era [in fact 1883] – and good Victorians never analyzed their motives. If you were to force me to turn an analytical eye on my musical taste, I'm afraid that it would conclude that my musical taste was capricious, over-catholic and impure (in the sense that it is often mixed up with literary and other associations) and I find myself occasionally put off composers for other then purely musical considerations. My affection for Sibelius, Brahms, Delius and Wagner has weakened a little in face of a too enthusiastic adulation in certain quarters.

The development of my musical taste has had its landmarks of infatuation. Taking them in chronological order these have been Chopin, Bach, Wagner, Richard Strauss, Debussy, Schoenberg and Stravinsky. My greatest infatuation dating from the age of fifteen was perhaps for Wagner. But now I find that I can hardly listen to his music. In spite of the fact that art knows no political boundaries, I think that I definitely stopped liking Wagner when he was taken up by the Nazis. I still like certain things of Richard Strauss. *Till Eulenspiegels*. The incidental music to the *Bourgeois*

Gentilhomme. The Rosenkavalier. But here I think the literary side protrudes.

The violent interest I took, for a time, in Schoenberg was I fancy the interest of an explorer. He had opened up for me the new territory of atonal music, but this territory, that at one time seemed almost a promised land, has proved itself infertile, an enclosed, dry, rocky, academic valley with no issue.

Of the moderns I prefer Stravinsky, Bartok and of the younger English composers Benjamin Britten. At the risk of seeming priggish I say that I like all music that is good of its kind and I am not impressed, like so many of the English music critics, by pretentious emptiness.

In making this selection of gramophone records I have purposely avoided anything that is unduly serious and edifying and have concentrated on what I consider charming or stimulating music that appeals to the senses rather than to the intellect. The excerpt from Bach that I have chosen has of course an intellectual [appeal] but it is so stimulating that I feel it ought to exhilarate even the most lowbrow of listeners.

I have chosen one piece of my own, the polka from *The Triumph of Neptune*, a ballet produced by Diaghileff in 1926. It was, incidentlaly, one of the numbers of the ballet that Diaghileff himself preferred.'

1. Kurt Weill: Querschmitt aus Mahagonny, 1st part, H.M.V. (62–962, Kat no EH736)

2. Bach: Concerto for 3 pianos in C, Third movement (4th side of record)

3. Viennese seven singing sisters: Lizst Hungarian Rhapsody No. 2, Regal Zonophone MR 1755

4. Tchaikovsky: Pizzicato movement of 4th symphony

5. Berners: Triumph of Neptune, Polka (Columbia [added in biro, 13161 or B161])

6. Chabrier: March Joyeuse

7. Stravinsky: Jeu de Cartes (1st part of Third Record)

8. Maurice Ravel: Last movement of piano concerto

Notes

Many quotations are drawn from Berners' autobiographical writing, his notebooks, draft letters, his letters to and from his mother, and from his mother's diary. Apart from his autobiographies, all this material is in the Berners archive, which is not available to the public.

Quotations are also drawn from interviews conducted by Peter Dickinson, Gavin Bryars and myself. Some people have undergone questioning from both Dickinson and Bryars: Sir Harold Acton, Lord David Cecil, William Crack and Robert Heber Percy. Lady Harrod and Lady Mosley have had questions from all three of us, so much so that attribution becomes difficult. Perhaps it is fair to mention that Gavin Bryars spoke at great length to David Cecil, and Peter Dickinson saw Robert Heber Percy several times. Bryars also recorded interviews with Lady Diana Cooper, Derek Jackson and Edward James, Dickinson with Lady Dorothy Lygon, Daphnie Fielding, Michael Ayrton, Sir Frederick Ashton and Lady Betjeman. I also saw Daphne Fielding and Dr Rowse.

Where a chapter draws particularly heavily on any one source, I have mentioned it, as I have with particular books. Diana Mosley's essay in *Loved Ones* has been ransacked and scattered throughout, and the same applies in a more limited way to A. L. Rowse's *Friends and Contemporaries*. I refer the interested reader to the Select Bibliography.

I: Forebears

Unattributed quotations are from *First Childhood* by Berners.
Some Pictures from the Past History of the Berners Family by M. Spencer Warwick,
     privately printed, 1907
Tape of family memories lent by Kevin Pollock

'He was devoted': Aberconway

II: First Childhood

All quotations are from *First Childhood* by Berners, his notebooks, letters from and to his mother, and from his mother's diary.

III: Eton

Changing Eton by Byrne and Churchill
'Memories of Eton' by Sir David Montagu Scott (unpublished)
Unattributed quotations are from *A Distant Prospect* by Lord Berners, and from letters to his mother.

IV: Europe

Unattributed quotations are from 'Résènlieu', 'Dresden' and 'Weimar' by Lord Berners (both unpublished), letters to and from Berners' mother, Berners' notebooks and his mother's diary.

'No, it doesn't: Diana Mosley, *Loved Ones*
'My temperament': undated draft letter to Cyril Connolly
'He courted my mother': Kennard
'He was impeded': obituary of Berners by Harold Nicolson, *Spectator*, 28 April 1950
'He was a funny old chap': William Crack to Gavin Bryars

V: A Diplomat at Last

Harold Nicolson by James Lees-Milne
Unattributed quotations are from letters from Berners' to his mother, and her diary.

'social life was little affected' et seq.: Rennell Rodd
'a prancing satyr': Sermoneta
'very plain and unpretentious': Stravinsky
'Diaghilev's public': Garafola
'He has brought odium': Wellesley
'overjoyed to learn' and passim: Craft
'Ansermet, Bakst, Picasso': Stravinsky
'I remember tin goldfish': Preface by Harold Acton to Berners' *First Childhood*.
   Repeated to Peter Dickinson by Harold Acton.
'Helped by Lord Berners': Casella
'one of the most impudent': reported by Edward James to Gavin Bryars

VI: The Composer Inherits

Unattributed quotations are from letters to relations and Berners' notebooks.

'pleased at having created': Osbert Sitwell, 'The Love-Bird', *Collected Stories*
'Strongly drawn': ibid.
'more like a figure': quoted in Ziegler
'He always seemed': Harold Acton to Gavin Bryars
'He was remarkably ugly': Nichols, *The Sweet and Twenties*
'window-face': Reresby Sitwell to Mark Amory
'It would be an exaggeration': Constant Lambert
'respectful, chatty': Powell, *The Strangers All Are Gone*

'What do you do': Osbert Sitwell, *Laughter in the Next Room*
'Luisa looked: Sermoneta
'During dinner' et seq.: Hart-Davis
'The diversity of our music': Buckland

VII: London's Darkest Drawing-rooms

Diaghilev by Richard Buckle
Diaghilev by Serge Lifar
Diaghilev's Ballets Russes by Lynn Garafola
Emerald and Nancy by Daphne Fielding
A Passion for Friendship by Kirsty McLeod
The Sweet and Twenties by Beverley Nichols
Portrait of Walton by Michael Kennedy
Unattributed quotations are from Berners' notebooks.

'Diaghilev's encounter': Garafola
'canary of prey': Drogheda
'her legs had the fragility'. Beaton, *The Glass of Fashion*
'Maud Cunard is a pest': Cooper
'the first': Lees-Milne, *Prophesying Peace*
'jigging about': Osbert Sitwell, *Laughter in the Next Room*
'When he dined': Diana Mosley, *Loved Ones*
'This Lord': Bell, Vol. 2
'Stockish, resolute': Bell, Vol. 3
'a particularly mad': Holroyd
'in the years' et seq.: Osbert Sitwell, ibid.
'One of his acquaintances': Edith Sitwell
'This afternoon Ottoline': Hart-Davis
'very old': William Crack to Peter Dickinson and Gavin Bryars
'her way of speaking': Buckland

VIII: *The Triumph of Neptune*

Lanhydrock House, National Trust
Ronald Firbank, A Memoir by I. K. Fletcher
Prancing Novelist by Brigid Brophy
Ronald Firbank: Memoirs and Critiques edited by Mervyn Horder
Ronald Firbank by Miriam J. Benkowitz
Diaghilev by Richard Buckle
Diaghilev's Ballets Russes by Lynn Garafola
The Lamberts by Andrew Motion
George Balanchine, Ballet Master by Richard Buckle
Latin Among Lovers by Diana Holman Hunt
Unattributed quotations are from Berners' notebooks.

'a bit of a connoisseur': in a letter to Mark Amory
'Of late, certain tourists': Nichols, *Oxford-London-New York*
'he'd put on a different hat': William Crack to Gavin Bryars

'Those who have no children': Lees-Milne, *Harold Nicolson*
'Very boyish' et seq.: David Cecil to Gavin Bryars
'the rest of us': Cooper
'looking with a hint of mockery': Sokolova

IX: The Painter

Corot in Italy by Peter Galassi
Christopher Wood by Richard Ingleby
'Lord Berners as a painter' by Mark Steyn, *Apollo*, August 1984
Unattributed quotations are from Berners' notebooks.

'Lord Berners': among the winners of a clerihew competition set by Raymond
    Mortimer in the *New Statesman*, 1939
'For what is the difference': Nichols, *Are They the Same at Home?*
'the view': Galassi
'used to come down': Robert Heber Percy to Peter Dickinson
'I think she must have' et seq.: Blume
'Very nice' et seq.: Lawrence
'He was the most': Lees-Milne, *Harold Nicolson*
'Novello worshipped culture': Pryce-Jones
'When the Forum': Anatole France describing a conversation with Giacomo Boni,
    an archaeologist
'A lovely big drawing-room' et seq.: Rex Whistler, in a letter to his mother
    (private papers of Laurence Whistler).
'Tito bred canaries': Diana Mosley, *A Life of Contrasts*
'He seemed rather out of sorts': Penelope Betjeman in a letter to Berners,
    September 1936
'This is the first night': John Betjeman in a letter to Berners, 6 September 1936
'People ran from room to room': Buckle, *Diaghilev*
'It may be': Amory, *Selected Letters of Evelyn Waugh*
'Then he sat down': Nichols, *The Sweet and Twenties*
'All very strange': Beaton, *Ballet*
'Gerald Berners had an exhibition': Amory, ibid.

X: Heber Percy

Us Four by Cyril Heber Percy
Loved Ones by Diana Mosley
Unattributed quotations are from Berners' notebooks.

'It is plain and grey' et seq.: 'Faringdon House' by Nancy Mitford, *House and
    Garden*, 1948, collected in Charlotte Mosley (ed.), *A Talent to Amuse*
'Went to stay': Hassall
'What's for pud?': reported by Frederick Ashton to Peter Dickinson
'He liked a good Beaujolais': Derek Jackson to Gavin Bryars
'They saw the milk-cart' et seq.: Berners, *The Girls of Radcliff Hall*
'Daddy took little part' et seq.: Heber Percy
'Brown corduroys, a yellow polo shirt': Duff

'Shall I leave?': reported by Jonathan Burnham to Mark Amory
'It was the first time': Robert Heber Percy to Mark Amory
'He was not at all nice': Isaiah Berlin to Mark Amory
'I expected at least a crucifix': Diana Heber Percy to Mark Amory
'We must have': Diana Mosley to Mark Amory
'Perhaps worldly people': Diana Mosley, *A Life of Contrasts*
'When one first arrived' et seq.: Diana Mosley, *Loved Ones*
'At first applauded': Taylor, *English History 1914–45*
'The magistrate was': Derek Jackson to Gavin Bryars
'As well send a tramp': Cooper
'Because he asked him': Robert Heber Percy to Peter Dickinson

XI: *The Girls of Radcliff Hall*

The Power of a Parasol by Michael Duff
Unattributed quotations are from Berners' notebooks.

' "No dogs admitted" ': Patrick Leigh Fermor in a letter to Mark Amory
'He considered it the height': Robert Heber Percy to Peter Dickinson
'Odd large-beaked birds': Rose, *Saying Life*
'The process which was done': Constant Lambert
'It was a common sight': Rose, ibid.
'Why am I mixed up': Rose, *Glimpses of the Great*
'Diana looked like an actress': Robert Heber Percy to Ann Fleming, Amory, *The Letters of Ann Fleming*
'Berners was a man': Sykes
'What a good thing': Amory, *Selected Letters of Evelyn Waugh*
'The dullest book': ibid.
'God doesn't pay': Diana Mosley to Mark Amory
Oh, I told the gardener': Robert Heber Percy to Gavin Bryars
'I wouldn't mind': Amory, ibid.
'Oliver has become': quoted in Vickers
'A fashionable health clinic': Middleboe
'Ridiculous character': Robert Heber Percy to Mark Amory
'I absolutely adored': Noël Coward in a letter to Berners
'What in life': Hoare, *Serious Pleasures*
'It would be better': *Oxford Mail*, 12 September 1934
'But you could not see': *Morning Post*, 4 October 1934
'Gerald loved having him there': Penelope Betjeman to Peter Dickinson
'John Sparrow staying here': letter from Penelope to John Betjeman (private papers)

XII: His Finest Year

Dali by Meredith Etherington-Smith
The Shameful Life of Salvador Dali by Edward James
A Surrealist Life by John Lowe
The Final Quest of Edward James by Philip Purser

The Biography of Alice B. Toklas by Linda Simon
Gertrude and Alice by Diana Southami
Unattributed quotations are from Berners' notebooks.

'It's supposed': Penelope Betjeman to Peter Dickinson
'And what is that' et seq.: Edward James to Gavin Bryars
'the great double doors': Middleboe
'Madame de Polignac': Nicolson, 1930–39
'I much fear': ibid.
'the fashionable life': Diana Mosley to Peter Dickinson and Mark Amory
'She answered effectively': David Cecil to Gavin Bryars

XIII: *A Wedding Bouquet*

Saying Life by Francis Rose
Unattributed quotations are from Berners' notebooks.

'He thought it all out': Frederick Ashton to Peter Dickinson
'Anything you want' et seq.: letters from Gertrude Stein to Berners
'Very professional' et seq.: Frederick Ashton to Peter Dickinson
'And then gradually': Stein
'As he came on stage': Edward James to Gavin Bryars
'Berners is taking': Middleboe
'A wicked woman': Billa Harrod to Mark Amory
'Sometimes thought': Diana Mosley, *Loved Ones*
'We worked hard' et seq.: Rose, *Saying Life*
'Cupid and Psyche': Clarke

XIV: War and Collapse

Unattributed quotations are from Berners' notebooks.

'That did not work out': Rowse, *Friends and Contemporaries*
'A delightful whimsical' et seq.: Isaiah Berlin to Mark Amory
'And the next thing': Billa Harrod to Mark Amory, Gavin Bryars and Peter
  Dickinson
'Where he was greeted': Taylor, *A Personal History*
'Very down': Harold Acton to Gavin Bryars
'There was only one thing': Nichols, *The Sweet and Twenties*
'There was this quiet little man' et seq.: Countess of Avon to Mark Amory
'Robert nearly killed a dog': Countess of Avon in a letter to Berners
'A delightful day' et seq.: Diana Mosley, *Loved Ones*
'Couldn't one make a poem': Aberconway

XV: The Novelist

Unattributed quotations are from Berners' notebooks.

'I'm afraid Beethoven's better': reported by David Cecil to Gavin
Bryars

XVI: War and Recovery

Unattributed quotations are from Berners' notebooks.

'In fact I doubt': Scott-James
'He was suddenly': Jennifer Ross to Mark Amory
'a paradise to people' et seq.: Charlotte Mosley, *A Talent to Amuse*
'And a good thing': A. L. Rowse to Mark Amory
'I hate it': Billa Harrod to Mark Amory
'Jennifer Heber Percy': Lees-Milne, *Prophesying Peace*
'after lunch we all went out': Glendinning

XVII: Peace

Unattributed quotations are from Berners' notebooks.

'He looked': David Cecil to Gavin Bryars
'At 5.30 to tea with Emerald': Lees-Milne, *Prophesying Peace*
'Daisy Fellowes is said': Amory, *Selected Letters of Evelyn Waugh*
'Short and bald': Quennell
'Just off to see Gerald': unpublished letter from Nancy Mitford to her mother
'dressed in a gray suit' et seq.: Harris
'While Gerald Berners': Beaton, *The Happy Years*
'Gerald is fading fast': Beaton, *The Strenuous Years*
'He seemed old': Quennell
'Thankyou for coming': Robert Heber Percy to Mark Amory
'Though Robert keeps faithful watch': Rowse, *Friends and Contemporaries*

Select Bibliography

Aberconway, Christobel, *A Wiser Woman?*, Hutchinson, 1966
Acton, Harold, *Memoirs of an Aesthete*, Methuen, 1970
    More Memoirs of an Aesthete, Methuen, 1970
    Nancy Mitford, Hamish Hamilton, 1975
Adair, Gilbert, *The Post Modernist Always Rings Twice*, Fourth Estate, 1992
Agar, Eileen, *A Look at My Life*, Methuen, 1988
Amory, Mark (ed.), *The Selected Letters of Ann Fleming*, Collins, 1985
    The Selected Letters of Evelyn Waugh, Weidenfeld & Nicolson, 1986
Annan, Noël, *Our Age*, Weidenfeld & Nicolson, 1990

Barr, Charles, *Elstree Studios*, Studio Vista, 1993
Beaton, Cecil, *Diaries: The Wandering Years, 1922–39*, Weidenfeld & Nicolson,
    1961
    The Years Between, 1939–44, Weidenfeld & Nicolson, 1965
    The Happy Years, 1944–48, Weidenfeld & Nicolson, 1972
    The Strenuous Years, 1948–55, Weidenfeld & Nicolson, 1973
    The Glass of Fashion, Weidenfeld & Nicolson, 1954
    Ballet, Wingate, 1951
Bell, Anne (ed.), *The Diaries of Virginia Woolf*, Vols 2 and 3, The Hogarth Press,
    1978 and 1980
Benkowtiz, Miriam J., *Ronald Firbank*, Weidenfeld & Nicolson, 1970
Berners, Gerald, *First Childhood*, Constable, 1934
    The Camel, Constable, 1936
    The Girls of Radcliff Hall, privately printed, 1937
    Far from the Madding War, Constable, 1941
    Count Omega, Constable, 1941
    Percy Wallingford and Mr Pidger, Blackwell, 1941
    The Romance of a Nose, Constable, 1942
    A Distant Prospect, Constable, 1945
Bernie, Olivier, *Fireworks at Dusk: Paris in the Thirties*, Little, Brown, 1993
Blume, Mary, *Côte d'Azur*, Thames & Hudson, 1992
Boston, Richard, *Osbert: A Portrait of Osbert Lancaster*, Collins, 1989
Boulton, James (ed.), *The Letters of D. H. Lawrence Vol. 5, 1924–27*, Cambridge
  University Press, 1991

Bradford, Sarah, *Sacheverell Sitwell*, Sinclair-Stevenson, 1993
Bridgeman, Harriet and Elizabeth Drury, *The British Eccentric*, Michael Joseph, 1975
Brophy, Brigid, *Prancing Novelist*, Macmillan, 1973
Buckland, Sidney (trans., ed.); *Selected Correspondence of François Poulenc, 1915–63*, Gollancz, 1991
Buckle, Richard, *Diaghilev*, Hamish Hamilton, 1979
   with John Taras, *George Balanchine, Ballet Master*, Hamish Hamilton, 1988
Butler, Christopher, *Early Modernism*, Clarendon Press, 1994
Byrne and Churchill, *Changing Eton*, Jonathan Cape, 1937

Calloway, Stephen, *Baroque: The Culture of Excess*, Phaidon, 1994
Carpenter, Humphrey, *The Brideshead Generation*, Houghton Mifflin, 1990
Cassella, Alfred, *Music in My Time*, trans. Spencer Norton, University of Oklahoma Press, 1955
Castle, Charles, *Oliver Messel*, Thames & Hudson, 1955
Cecil, David, *Max*, Constable, 1964
Cochran, Charles B., *Showman Looks On*, Dent, 1946
Cooper, Diana, *The Light of Common Day*, Hart-Davis, 1959
Cossart, Michael de, *Princesse Edmond de Polignac (1865–1943) and Her Salon*, Hamish Hamilton, 1978
Craft, Robert (ed.), 'Correspondence with Gerald Tyrwhitt, 1916–39', in *Selected Correspondence of Stravinsky*, Vol. II, Faber & Faber, 1984
Cronin, Vincent, *City of Light 1919–39*, Harper Collins, 1994

Davie, Michael (ed.), *The Diaries of Evelyn Waugh*, Little, Brown, 1976
Dominic, Zoe and John Selwyn, *Gilbert Frederick Ashton: A Choreographer and His Ballets*, Harrap, 1971

Fielding, Daphne, *Emerald and Nancy*, Eyre & Spottiswoode, 1968
Fisher, Clive, *Cyril Connolly*, Macmillan, 1995
Fletcher, I. K., *Ronald Firbank: A Memoir*, Duckworth, 1930
Fonteyn, Margot, *Autobiography*, Star Books, 1976

Galassi, Peter, *Corot in Italy*, Yale University Press, 1991
Garafola, Lynn, *Diaghilev's Ballets Russes*, Oxford University Press, 1989
Gill, Anton, *A Dance Between Flames: Berlin Between the Wars*, Abacus, 1995
Glendinning, Victoria, *Elizabeth Bowen: Portrait of a Writer*, Phoenix, 1993
Golding, John, *Visions of the Modern*, Thames & Hudson, 1994

Harris, Gerald (ed.), *Letters to a Friend, 1940–66*, by K. B. McFarlane, Magdalene College, 1997
Hart-Davis, Rupert (ed.), *Diaries of Siegfried Sassoon, 1920–25*, Faber & Faber, 1981 (2 vols)
Hassall, Christopher, *Edward Marsh*, Longman, 1959
Hastings, Selina, *Evelyn Waugh*, Sinclair-Stevenson, 1994

Heber Percy, Cyril, *Us Four*, Faber & Faber, 1963
Herbert, David, *Second Son*, Peter Owen, 1972
    Engaging Eccentrics, Peter Owen, 1990
    Relations and Revelations, Peter Owen, 1992
Hillier, Bevis, *Young Betjeman*, John Murray, 1988
Hoare, Philip, *Serious Pleasures: The Life of Stephen Tennant*, Hamish Hamilton,
    1990
    Noël Coward, Sinclair-Stevenson, 1995
Holman Hunt, Diana, *Latin Among Lovers: Alvaro Guevara*, Michael Joseph, 1974
Holroyd, Michael, *Lytton Strachey*, Heinemann, 1968
Horder, Mervyn (ed.), *Ronald Firbank: Memoirs and Critiques*, Duckworth, 1977
Huggett, Richard, *Binkie Beaumont*, Hodder & Stoughton, 1989

Ingleby, Richard, *Christopher Wood*, Allison & Busbey, 1995

James, Edward, *The Shameful Life of Salvador Dali*, Faber & Faber, 1997

Kavanagh, Julie, *Secret Muses: The Life of Frederick Ashton*, Faber & Faber, 1990
Kennard, George, *Loopy*, Leo Cooper, 1990
Kennedy, Michael, *Portrait of Walton*, Oxford University Press, 1989

Lambert, Angela, *Unquiet Souls*, Papermac, 1985
Lambert, Constant, *Music Ho!*, Faber & Faber, 1934
Lees-Milne, James, *Diaries: Ancestral Voices*, Faber & Faber, 1975
    Prophesying Peace, Chatto & Windus, 1977
    Harold Nicolson, Hamish Hamilton, 1981
    Caves of Ice 1946–47, Chatto & Windus, 1983
Lewis, Jeremy, *Cyril Connolly*, Cape, 1997
Lifar, Serge, *Diaghilev*, Putnam, 1940
Longford, Elizabeth, *The Pebbled Shore*, Sceptre, 1988
Lowe, John, *Edward James: A Surrealist Life*, Collins, 1991
Lycett Green, Candida (ed.), *Letters of John Betjeman, Vol. 1, 1926–51*, Methuen,
    1994
Lynn, Olga, *Oggie*, Weidenfeld & Nicolson, 1955

Mackenzie, Jean, *The Children of the Souls*, Chatto & Windus, 1986
McCook, Sinead, *A Life of Lady Lavery*, Lilliput Press, 1996
McLeod, Kirsty, *A Passion for Friendship*, Michael Joseph, 1991
Middleboe, Penelope, *Edith Olivier: From Her Journals, 1924–28*, Weidenfeld &
    Nicolson, 1989
Mitford, Nancy, *The Pursuit of Love*, Hamish Hamilton, 1945
    The Water Beetle, Hamish Hamilton, 1962
Moore, George, *Letters to Lady Cunard, 1895–1933*, Hart-Davis, 1957
Mosley, Charlotte (ed.), *The Letters of Nancy Mitford*, Hodder & Stoughton, 1993
    A Talent to Amuse, Hamish Hamilton, 1986
Mosley, Diana, *A Life of Contrasts*, Hamish Hamilton, 1977

Loved Ones, Sidgwick and Jackson, 1935
Motion, Andrew, *The Lamberts*, The Hogarth Press, 1987

National Trust, *Lanhydrock House*, 1991
Nebraka, Simon, *Gertrude Stein Remembered*, University of Nebraska, 1994
Nichols, Beverley, *Are They the Same at Home?*, Cape, 1927
    Oxford-London-New York, Cape, 1934
    The Sweet and Twenties, Weidenfeld & Nicolson, 1958
Nicolson, Nigel (ed.), *Harold Nicolson: Diaries and Letters, 1930–39*, Weidenfeld &
    Nicolson, 1966
    Harold Nicolson: Diaries and Letters, 1945–62, Collins, 1968

Orledge, Robert (ed.), *Satie Remembered*, Faber & Faber, 1995

Palmer, Alan, *The Decline and Fall of the Ottoman Empire*, John Murray, 1992
Pearson, John, *Façades*, Macmillan, 1978
Powell, Anthony, *To Keep the Ball Rolling*
    Infants of the Spring, Heinemann, 1976
    Messengers of Day, Heinemann, 1978
    Faces in My Time, Heinemann, 1980
    The Strangers All Are Gone, Heinemann, 1982
Purser, Philip, *The Final Quest of Edward James*, Quartet, 1991
Pryce-Jones, Alan, *The Bonus of Laughter*, Hamish Hamilton, 1988
Pryce-Jones, David (ed.), *Cyril Connolly: Journals and Memoirs*, Collins, 1983

Quennell, Peter, *The Wanton Chase*, Collins, 1980

Rennell Rodd, Sir J., *Social and Diplomatic Memoirs, 1902–19*, Edward Arnold,
    1925
Rose, Francis, *Saying Life*, Cassell, 1961
Rowse, A. L., *Memories and Glimpses*, Methuen, 1980
    Glimpses of the Great, Methuen, 1985
    Friends and Contemporaries, Methuen, 1989

Scott-James, Anne, *Sketches from a Life*, Michael Joseph, 1993
Sermoneta, Vittoria Colonna, Duchess of, *Things Past*, Hutchinson, 1929
Simon, Linda, *The Biography of Alice B. Toklas*, Bison Books, 1991
Sitwell, Edith, *Taken Care Of*, Hutchinson, 1965
Sitwell, Osbert, *Collected Stories*, Duckworth, 1953
    Laughter in the Next Room, Macmillan, 1949
Sokolova, Lydia, *Dancing with Diaghilev*, John Murray, 1960
Southani, Diana, *Gertrude and Alice*, Pandora Press, 1991
Stein, Gertrude, *Everybody's Autobiography*, Virago, 1985
Stravinsky, Igor, *Chronicle of My Life*, James Barrie, 1952
Sykes, Christopher, *Evelyn Waugh: A Biography*, Penguin, 1977

Taylor, A. J. P., *English History, 1914–45*, Oxford University Press, 1965
 A Personal History, Hamish Hamilton, 1983

Vickers, Hugo, *Cecil Beaton*, Weidenfeld & Nicolson, 1985

Walton, Susanna, *Behind the Facade*, Oxford University Press, 1989
Wellesley, Dorothy, *For I Have Travelled*, James Barrie, 1952
Wheen, Francis, *Tom Driberg: His Life of Indiscretion*, Chatto & Windus, 1990
White, Palmer, *Elsa Schiaparelli*, Allison & Busbey, 1995
Wright, Adrian, *Foreign Country*, André Deutsch, 1996

Young, Kenneth (ed.), *The Diaries of Sir Bruce Lockhart 1915–30*, Macmillan, 1973

Zeldin, Theodore, *An Intimate History of Humanity*, Sinclair-Stevenson, 1994
Ziegler, Philip, *Diana Cooper*, Hamish Hamilton, 1981

Index